democracy.com?

Governance in a Networked World

*Edited by Elaine Ciulla Kamarck
and Joseph S. Nye, Jr.*

HOLLIS
PUBLISHING

Library of Congress Cataloging—in—Publication Data

democracy.com? : governance in a networked world / edited by Elaine
    Ciulla Kamarck and Joseph S. Nye.
            p.   cm.
        Includes bibliographical references and index.
        ISBN 1–884186–10–6 (alk. paper)
            1. Information society —Political aspects—United States.
        2. Information technology —Political aspects—United States.
    I. Kamarck, Elaine Ciulla. II. Nye, Joseph S.
    JK468.A8D45 1999
    025.06'32463'0973—dc21   99–28884
                                                      CIP

Hollis Publishing Company, 95 Runnells Bridge Road, Hollis NH 03049

Printed in the United States of America

∞ The paper used in the book complies with the Permanent Paper Standard
issued by the National Information Standards Organization (Z39.48-1984).

10 9 8 7 6 5 4 3 2

ACKNOWLEDGMENTS

This publication was made possible by generous gifts from

ORACLE

The Pew Charitable Trusts
The Stratford Foundation

∼

The editors would like to thank *Kristin Schneeman* and *Lynn Akin* for their hard work in orchestrating this effort.

∼

We also owe a debt of gratitude to the other faculty who participated in our conference at Bretton Woods in July 1998 and contributed their intellectual capital to this effort: *Nolan Bowie, Richard Cooper, Mickey Edwards, Jeffrey Eisenach, Peter Frumkin, Ed Glaeser, David Hart, Deborah Hurley, Robert Lawrence, Taeku Lee, Mark Moore, Joseph Newhouse, Anthony Oettinger, Robert Stavins, John Thomas, Julie Wilson,* and *Richard Zeckhauser* (with assistance from *Carolyn Gideon* and *Shashi Kant Verma*).

∼

Special thanks as well to those who agreed to read and comment on our work: *Reed Hundt, Kevin Kelly, Larry Lessig, Russ Neuman, Andrew Shapiro,* and *Don Tapscott*.

∼

And finally, many thanks to *Fred Lyford, Mary Maguire,* and *Rebecca Shannon* of Hollis Publishing.

TABLE OF CONTENTS

Introduction

introduction

This volume is the second collection of essays to come out of "Visions of Governance for the Twenty-First Century," a project of the John F. Kennedy School of Government at Harvard University. The project began in 1996 amidst concern that, as the twentieth century came to an end, democratic governance was losing the support of the governed. Declining trust in government, perceived and actual performance deficits in government and a sense that, as President Clinton said in his 1996 State of the Union address, "The era of big government is over," led to a decision by Dean Joseph S. Nye, Jr. to devote several years to the study of the future of governance.

The first volume of the project was titled *Why People Don't Trust Government.* It examined the scope and performance of government and the possible causes of citizens' dissatisfaction with government. Following publication of that study, a group of faculty met for a second time to identify the factors that were forcing major changes in the form and functions of government. They identified three: information technology, globalization, and marketization. Although the three factors are interrelated—information technology, for instance, has been a critical factor in globalization, as it has been in the spread of markets—we decided that for purposes of dividing the study into manageable bits, it made sense to examine each one independently.

In 1998 we asked a group of professors, drawn largely but not exclusively from the Kennedy School faculty, to examine different aspects of governance—representation, community, politics, the bureaucracy, international relations—using the revolution in information technology as an independent variable. In other words, we wanted to know how information technology was or was not affecting traditional, time-honored institutions of governance. To do this we sought out people who were experts in areas of governance and familiar with information technology.

The resulting volume consists of essays originally presented at a retreat held in Bretton Woods, New Hampshire, in the summer of 1998 and comments written in response to those essays. Some of the papers, such as those that dealt with the 1998 election cycle, underwent considerable revision as the result of new data; others are pretty much as delivered that summer. In all they offer a balanced and sometimes skeptical look at the transformations that the information revolution is making in our basic institutions and processes of governance.

In the first essay in this volume, Dean Nye places the information revolution in historical context and in the context of the other major forces that are contributing to significant changes in governments around the world. Then he lays out a series of hypotheses that exist to predict the impact of what some have called the "Third Industrial Revolution" on politics and on government.

This introductory essay is followed by Arthur Applbaum's speculations on the nature of deliberative or Madisonian democracy in the information age. In one of the livelier responses from beyond the grave, James Madison himself (a.k.a. Dennis Thompson) @*founding.gov* ruminates on the ability of the new technologies to mitigate the effects of faction.

William Galston's essay takes a skeptical look at the concept of "community" on the Internet and sets up a series of provocative research questions about the development of affective ties and mutual obligation—two characteristics of traditional communities—and whether or not they appear in online communities. In a different vein, L. Jean Camp writes that the Internet can match real-world communities in many ways, including emotional support.

Moving from theory to practice, studies by Pippa Norris and Elaine Kamarck use empirical research to explore the use of the Internet in the political process. Norris employs Pew Research Center data to investigate the nature of citizen activism on the Internet and to explore online political activism. She asks whether the Internet will expand political participation and whether it will serve to mobilize new activists or simply reinforce the participation of traditional activists. Anna Greenberg's comment moves beyond the question of individual participation to suggest that "perhaps the political promise of the Internet rests not so much on its effect on individuals but rather in how groups are using the Internet to facilitate political mobilization."

Elaine Kamarck's essay is the first comprehensive description of campaigning on the Internet. She looks at all the Internet campaigns for Congress and for governor in the 1998 midterm elections and analyzes what the candidates were doing on the Web in 1998, with some speculation as to how this new technology will change elections in the future. While Kamarck concludes that the Internet in the 1998 elections was largely the site of "electronic brochures," David King's essay takes the next step and shows how David Hart, a mythical future candidate, might use the Web.

The section on politics is followed by a section on bureaucracy. Jane Fountain's essay argues that one can find a useful starting point for a theory of information-based bureaucracy by examining the core concepts of traditional bureaucracy—capacity and control. She shows how changes in the information processing capacity of the bureaucracy will cause evolution and transformation during the next several decades. Sheila Burke's response reminds us that "Information technology will never replace the wink"—shorthand for the substantial barriers that exist between the promise and the reality of information technology use in government. In a similar vein, Richard Darman suggests that perhaps what we need at this point in time is a theory of bureaucracy that explains the *lack* of rapid change.

In this same section, Jerry Mechling's essay offers some examples of how information technology is changing government from what we know to what he calls "networked government." For instance, in one set of examples he shows how information technology is improving service delivery, allowing for greater accessibility, customization and integration. John Donahue's comment distinguishes between those public functions that have relatively clearcut goals and those that do not, and predicts that the major effect of information technology will be to increase the rate at which the former functions are contracted out or privatized. In addition, Donahue provides us with a real-life example of the limits of a wired policymaking process.

In the final chapter, Joseph S. Nye, Jr. and Robert Keohane discuss the implications of the information revolution for world politics, in particular the notion that "the information revolution creates a new politics of credibility in which transparency will increasingly be a power asset."

These essays are meant to provoke thought and further research about the ways in which the information revolution is transforming our institutions of governance. As such they offer an important window on the challenges and the promises of twenty-first century government.

Elaine C. Kamarck

technology.gov

INFORMATION TECHNOLOGY AND DEMOCRATIC GOVERNANCE

\<Joseph S. Nye, Jr.\>

Public confidence in government has declined over the past few decades in a large number of democratic countries.[1] The causes are complex. Some see the decline, at least in the United States, as a return to a deeply ingrained American suspicion of concentrated power after expectations about government rose to unrealistic heights in the aftermath of success in World War II.[2] Others see it as a result of a long term shift toward post-industrial values that emphasize the individual over the community and diminish respect for authority and institutions.[3] Still others see it as a reaction against the centralization of government in the twentieth century that saw the federal budget grow from 3 percent of GNP in 1929 to 20 percent in the past two decades.

Joseph S. Nye, Jr., *is Dean of Harvard University's John F. Kennedy School of Government and Don K. Price Professor of Public Policy. He has a special interest in the causes of and potential solutions to public disaffection with government. As Dean of the School, Nye launched Visions of Governance for the Twenty-First Century, a major project to examine and debate the role of government in the next century. Nye returned to Harvard in December of 1995 after serving as Assistant Secretary of Defense for International Security Affairs, where he won two distinguished service medals, and as Chairman of the National Intelligence Council. His most recent books are* Why People Don't Trust Government, Understanding International Conflicts, *and* Bound to Lead: The Changing Nature of American Power.

Some analysts argue that centralized government, unlike private enterprise, has not yet adapted to the changes being wrought by the "Third Industrial Revolution."[4]

Historical Analogies

In the first industrial revolution around the turn of the 19th century, the application of steam to mills and transportation had a powerful effect on the economy, society, and eventually, government. Patterns of production, work, living conditions, social class and political power were transformed. Public education arose as literate trained workers were needed for increasingly complex and potentially dangerous factories. Police forces such as London's "bobbies" were created to deal with urbanization. Subsidies were provided for the necessary infrastructure of canals and railroads.[5] In what is sometimes called the second industrial revolution, around the turn of the twentieth century, electricity, synthetics, and the internal combustion engine brought similar economic and social changes. The United States, for example, went from a predominantly agrarian to a primarily industrial and urban nation. In the 1890s, most Americans still worked on farms or as servants. A few decades later, the majority lived in cities and worked in factories.[6] Social class and political cleavages were altered. And again, with lags, the role of government changed. The bipartisan progressive movement ushered in antitrust legislation; early consumer protection regulation by the forerunner of the Food and Drug Administration; economic stabilization by the Federal Reserve Board.[7] In what some have called the third industrial revolution, at the turn of the twenty-first century, the impact of computers and communications technology on the economy and society should eventually produce analogous major changes in the functions of government.

One can raise a number of criticisms of such grand analogies. At a semantic level, the words "industrial revolution" are not totally appropriate for what is sometimes called a postindustrial phenomenon. Daniel Bell, for example, argues that the term "industrial revolution" conflates both the introduction of steam power as a form of energy and the creation of factories, which are social organizations. He prefers to refer to three great technological revolutions with the current one marked by electronics, miniaturization by transistors, digitalization, and software.[8] And "revolution," defined as a disjunction of power, is often difficult to discern except in retrospect. Moreover, historians differ on the dating and duration of earlier industrial revolutions. The term was not coined until 1886, a century after it began.[9] And while there may have been discontinuities in technological progress, with new leading sectors in each era, it has been difficult to prove the existence of long waves or cycles of economic growth. Efforts to specify the exact timing of Kondratieff's or Schumpeter's cycles of technological change have not been successful.[10] And finally, one must be wary of technological determinism.[11] Technology affects society and government, but the causal arrows work in both directions. Technological change creates new challenges and opportunities for social and political organization, but the response to those challenges depends on history, culture, institutions, and paths already taken or foregone.

Nonetheless, with appropriate caveats and caution, the historical analogies can help suggest hypotheses and avenues for exploration. Abrupt changes often occur after long build-ups, and one can look for punctuation points. Analysts need not fall into the fallacy of technological determinism to see that technology is one of the significant causes of social and political change. As Bell argues, "since the techno-economic changes pose 'control' problems for the political order, we find that the older social structures are cracking because political scales of sovereignty and authority do not match the economic scale. In many areas we have more and more economic integration and political fragmentation. . . . If there is a single overriding sociological problem in post-industrial society—particularly in the management of transition—it is the management of scale."[12]

Centralization or Diffusion?

Six decades ago, the eminent sociologist William Ogburn cited technology as he predicted greater political centralization. In 1937, he argued that "government in the United States will probably tend toward greater centralization because of the airplane, the bus, the truck, the Diesel engine, the radio, the telephone, and the various uses to which the wire and wireless may be placed. The same inventions operate to influence industries to spread across state lines. . . . The centralizing tendency of government seems to be world-wide, wherever modern transportation and communication exist.[13]

By and large, Ogburn was right about his next half century, but will this continue to be true in the twenty-first century? President Clinton and other politicians have proclaimed that the era of big government is over, but they have said little about what will take its place. Is the basic premise correct? And if so, for all dimensions of democratic government? If this is the case, what are the causes and how reversible are they?

Questions of appropriate degrees of centralization of government are not new. As Kindleberger points out, "how the line should be altered at a given time—toward or away from the center—can stay unresolved for long periods, typically fraught with tension."[14] If Bell and others are correct that the nation state has "become too small for the big problems of life and too big for the small problems,"[15] we may find not centralization or decentralization, but a diffusion of governance activities in several directions at the same time. Some functions may migrate to a supragovernmental or transnational level. Some may devolve to local units. Other aspects of governance may migrate to the private sector. The following matrix lays out the possible diffusion of activities away from central governments—vertically to other levels of government and horizontally to market and private nonmarket actors—the so-called third sector. The matrix is simply a map of the possible dimensions of the locus of collective activities. It can be combined with a hypothesis that the twentieth century saw a predominance of centripetal forces and that the next period may see a greater role of centrifugal forces.

The Diffusion of Governance			
	Private	Public	Third Sector
Supranational	Transnational Corporations	Intergovernmental Organizations	Nongovernmental Organizations
National	National Corporations	↖ ↑ ↗ ← 20th Century Model → ↙ ↓ ↘	National Nonprofits
Subnational	Local Businesses	State/Local Government	Local Groups

There is some evidence of diffusion. For example, in the U.S., federal civilian employment saw a net growth of 15 percent between 1962 and 1995, while state and local employment grew by 150 percent during the same period.[16] As a share of GNP, federal expenditures (excluding transfers) have fallen while state and local expenditures have increased.[17] In the last two decades, privatization has transferred a number of functions out of the public sector in a large number of countries.[18] Nonprofit organizations are playing an increasingly large role in the U.S., where after two decades of proliferation they represent almost 7 percent of all paid employment.[19] International nongovernmental organizations have increased tenfold over the past two decades, and have increased their influence on a number of issues.[20] Transgovernmental networks of bureaucrats and judicial officials have increased in autonomy and quantity, with the effect of disaggregating the state for certain policy issues.[21] The transnational domains of international production set limits on national welfare measures, and many functions such as credit ratings and arbitration of disputes are handled largely in the private transnational sector.[22] International security, the ultimate function of the state, now involves defense against transnational actors as a primary threat.

On the other hand, the overall trends are far from clear. Some issues show centralization, some decentralization, and some show both at the same time. For example, in the area of personal security, there has been an enormous increase in privatization of security forces. In 1970, there were one-and-a-half times as many private as public security personnel. By 1996, there were three times as many private as public.[23] Nonetheless, the early 1990s witnessed a demand for federalization at the same time, suggesting a rise in the demand for several types of governance in response to a perception of rising crime. And even after the privatizations of state-owned enterprises in the 1980s, the share of national income spent by the state in the wealthy democratic countries averaged 46 percent.[24] Moreover, countries vary. In contrast to Europe, total government spending has held steady at around a third of the economy in the United States and Japan, and declined in New Zealand.[25] Some states are weaker than the private forces within them; others not. Panama, Sierra Leone, or Haiti are different from Brazil, South Africa, or Singapore. The trends from external forces feel stronger for European states than they do for the American superpower. In short, the jury is still out, and it is not clear how strong the trends toward decentralization will be

in an information age. More work needs to be done in refining the
dependent variable and understanding the implications for democratic
governance, as well as analyzing the strength of the causes that could be
leading to diffusion.

Three Trends

Three independent but interrelated current trends give credence to the
prospect that the next century may see a shift in the locus of collective
activities away from central governments: globalization, marketization,
and the information revolution.

Globalization refers to the increase in the scale and speed of flows
of goods, people, and ideas across borders with the effect of decreas-
ing the effects of distance. It is not new.[26] Globalization increased
rapidly in the nineteenth century and during the first decades of the
twentieth, but was curtailed at least in its economic dimensions from
the early 1930s through the end of World War II. Globalization preceded the information revolution, but has been greatly enhanced by it.
In its recent incarnation, globalization can be traced in part back to
American strategy after World War II and the desire to create an open
international economy to forestall another depression and to balance
Soviet power and contain Communism. The institutional framework
and political pressures for opening markets were a product of American power and policy, but they were reinforced by developments in
the technology of transportation and communications which made it
increasingly costly for states to turn away from global market forces.
Raymond Vernon argues that nearly half of all industrial output is
produced by multinational enterprises whose strategic decisions on
the location of production now have a powerful effect on domestic
economies and wage structures even in the absence of international
trade.[27] At the same time, as Dani Rodrik points out, globalization still
has a long way to go, and its post-World War II progress in democratic countries has been concomitant with the development of the welfare state in what John Ruggie calls "embedded liberalism."[28] A failure
of that social contract in the democracies or a deepening of the Asian
financial crisis into a world depression might revive protectionism,
but predictions to that effect have proven wrong for the past three
decades. Meanwhile, globalization constrains states' ability to levy
taxes and maintain lavish benefits, and it opens opportunities for

private transnational actors to establish standards and strategies that strongly affect public policies that were once the domain of central governments.

Marketization is part of globalization, and like it has been enhanced by the information revolution, but it also has an independent domestic aspect and origins. Susan Strange argues that the balance between states and markets has shifted since the 1970s in a way that makes the state just one source of authority among several and that leaves "a yawning hole of non-authority or ungovernance."[29] She argues that power has diffused from governments to markets in such critical functions as maintaining the value of the currency; choosing the form of the economy, taxation, providing infrastructure, counter-cyclical policy, and protection from crime. This can be debated, as we have seen, by citing the fact that government as a percent of GNP remains above 40 percent in a number of major European countries. But even in such states as Sweden and France, not to mention Eastern Europe and the less economically developed countries, there have been significant privatizations and expansion of market forces in the past two decades. The causes of marketization are complex. They include the failure of planned economies to adapt to the information revolution, the inflation that followed the oil crises of the 1970s, the early success of the East Asian economies, and changes in political and ideological coalitions inside wealthy democracies. The net effect, however, is to accelerate the diffusion of power away from governments to private actors.

The *information revolution* refers to the dramatic decrease in the costs of computers and communications and the effects that has on the economy and society. According to Jeremy Greenwood, the price of a new computer has dropped by 19 per cent per year since 1954, and information technologies have risen from 7 percent to about 50 percent of new investment.[30] Information technology has been responsible for a quarter of U.S. growth over the past five boom years, and makes up 8 percent of GDP.[31] Microprocessors have doubled computing power every 18 months to two years, and computing power now costs less than one percent of what it did in 1970.[32] As late as 1980, phone calls over copper wire could carry one page of information per second; today a thin strand of optical fiber can transmit 90,000 volumes in a second.[33] The growth in the Internet has been extraordinary, with traffic increasing by 100 percent every year, versus under ten percent for the voice network.[34] The effect has been the virtual erasing of costs of communicating over distance.

As with steam in the late eighteenth century and electricity in the late nineteenth, there have been lags in productivity growth as society learns to fully utilize the new technologies.[35] Social organization changes more slowly than technology. For example, the electric motor was invented in 1881, but it was over three decades before Henry Ford pioneered the reorganization of factories to take full advantage of electric power. Computers today account for 2 per cent of America's total capital stock, but "add in all the equipment used for gathering, processing and transmitting information, and the total accounts for 12 percent of America's capital stock, exactly the same as the railways at the peak of their development in the late nineteenth century. . . . Three-quarters of all computers are used in the parts of the service sector such as finance and health where output is notoriously hard to measure."[36] Whether in reorganization or measurement, it is generally agreed that we are still in the early stages in the current information revolution.

Political Effects of the Information Revolution

Critics correctly point out that the current period is not the first to be strongly affected by changes in the technology and flows of information. Gutenberg's invention of movable type, which allowed printing of the Bible and its accessibility to large portions of the European population, is often credited with playing a major role in the onset of the Reformation. The advent of truly mass communications and broadcasting a century ago, which was facilitated by newly cheap electricity, might be considered a second information revolution. It ushered in the age of mass popular culture.[37] The effects of mass communication and broadcasting, though not the telephone, tended to have a number of centralizing political effects. While information was more widespread, it was more centrally influenced even in democratic countries than in the age of the local press. Roosevelt's use of radio in the 1930s is a case in point. These effects were particularly pronounced in countries where they were combined with the rise of totalitarian governments which were able to suppress competing sources of information. Indeed, some theorists believe that totalitarianism could not have been possible without the mass communications that accompanied the second industrial revolution.[38] On the other hand, as the use of films, cassettes, and faxes spread, the later technologies of the second information revolution helped to undermine governmental efforts at information autarky.[39] The overall effects were not always democratizing. In some cases, such as Iran, the technologies of the second information revolution merely changed the nature of the autocracy.

At one stage, it was believed that the computers and communications of the third information revolution would also have the effect of further enhancing central governmental control. George Orwell's vision of 1984 was widely feared. Mainframe computers seemed set to enhance central planning and increase the surveillance powers of those at the top of a pyramid of control. State controlled television would dominate information flows. Even today, through central data bases and removing the gray areas of noncompliance, computers can enhance some central government functions, and privacy issues remain an important concern. Some aspects of surveillance have become cheaper and easier. Nonetheless, on balance the prevalent current view is closer to de Sola Pool's description of "technologies of freedom."[40]

As computing power has decreased in cost and computers shrunk in size and become more widely distributed, their decentralizing effects have outweighed their centralizing effects. Moreover, the marriage of computers and communications technology that has evolved into the Internet, creates a system with few central nodal points and with a robust capacity in case of a central failure. Power over information is much more widely distributed. Central surveillance is possible, but governments that aspire to control information flows through control of the Internet face high costs and ultimate frustration. Rather than reinforcing centralization and bureaucracy, the new information technologies have tended to foster network organizations, new types of community, and demands for different roles for government. By changing how we work, they change our social attitudes and political behavior.

Morley Winograd and Dudley Buffa argue that the extensive corporate work pyramid, dominated by centralized commands, divided management and working class, white-collar and unionized blue-collar workers.[41] This pyramid dominated the political process and strongly influenced the evolution of government in the second industrial revolution that shaped the twentieth century. Now, they argue, new information technologies are again reorganizing work. Speed, agility, and customization are the best ways to produce value in the consumer marketplace. Large bureaucratic pyramids turn out to be a less effective way to organize such work than are networks within and between firms. The knowledge workers who staff network organizations see themselves neither as labor nor capital. To earn their loyalties, both companies and governments must appeal to them in new ways. They want government to have the convenience and flexibility of the marketplace. The result may be a transformation of politics, and, more slowly, of government.

There are a number of other hypotheses about how information technology may affect politics and collective action. First, information technology reinforces global production strategies and markets with the constraining effects on governmental action that have been discussed above. Second, it decreases the relative importance of commodities and territory, which makes geographical distance less important. This in turn has an effect on the communities that underlie political action. Third, the Internet makes borders more porous and jurisdiction less important. Fourth, information technology is changing the nature of banks and money in a way that will make both taxation and central control of monetary policy more difficult. The exponential rates of technological change and shortening of product cycles make it difficult for governmental institutions and regulations to keep up. More information and shorter news cycles mean less time for deliberation before response. Fifth, some virtual communities may develop interests and power independent of geography. In some countries the Internet may enhance both local and transnational communities more than national community. Sixth, the demise of broadcasting and the rise of narrowcasting may fragment the sense of community and legitimacy that underpins central governments. Seventh, educational patterns will change, and the greater agility of younger generations with the new technologies may further erode deference to age, authority, and existing institutions.

Obviously, these information revolution hypotheses are not the only possible causes of change in the locus and quality of governance activities in the next century. We have already shown that globalization and marketization, while closely related to and enhanced by the information revolution, have autonomous causes. Moreover, there are strong cultural institutional and political forces that are particular to each country. Race, for example, has had a strong effect in American history: decentralizing before 1865; centralizing during Reconstruction; decentralizing before World War II; centralizing shortly after the war; perhaps decentralizing since the defection of the South from the Democratic coalition after 1970. Immigration and ethnic diversity may have a decentralizing effect, though that has been a recurrent and sometimes exaggerated concern in American history. The current demographic trends towards older populations with their entitlements may have a centralizing effect. While there may be changes at the margin, the entitlement philosophy of the welfare state remains strong. A variety of forces tug the locus of collective activity in different directions, and in different ways on different issues and in different countries. Nonetheless, it seems plausible to look closely at the hypothesis that the three new interrelated trends, and particularly the information revolution (or whatever other label), will have a stronger net effect of diffusion.

Even though there is evidence to support the effects of these three trends, it would be a mistake to believe that such effects are irreversible. Technology is only one factor in a complex set of social causes. We should also ask what conditions these trends depend upon, and what it would take to slow, derail, or reverse them. For example, would a strong and prolonged economic downturn lead to demands for government response that would alter marketization and globalization? Would "grand terrorism" or the equivalent of a domestic Pearl Harbor lead to a demand for intrusive government even at the cost of civil liberties?[42] Would the increasing power of states such as China, India, or a revived Russia—particularly if accompanied with an expansionist ideology—transform the international system so that the defense functions of government would return to the Cold War model? Could ecological trends such as global warming become so clear and alarming that the public would demand much stronger governmental action? Such scenarios are worth exploring both as contingencies as well as counterfactual thought experiments to check our reasoning about the strength of the new causes. On the other hand, barring such low-probability but high-impact events, a trend toward diffusion of governance activities seems plausible.

The effects on central governments of the third information revolution are still in their early stages. The dispersal of information means that power is more distributed and networks tend to undercut the monopoly of traditional bureaucracy. The speed or instantaneity of Internet time means that all governments, whether central or local, have less control of their agendas. This may make all government more difficult, as there will be fewer degrees of freedom for political leaders to enjoy before they must respond to events. Changes in the nature of money, the disintermediation of banks, and diminished ability to identify and collect taxes may particularly reduce central governmental capacity. More privatization and public-private partnerships may be a response. Horizontal shifts on the matrix outlined above may outweigh vertical changes. All government bureaucracy may become flatter and more service-oriented. Moreover, while government may become flatter, governance may nonetheless become more complex. But at this stage, all of the foregoing is speculation.

Similar changes may occur in the political processes of democracy—what might be considered the "input" rather than the "output" side of government. One can imagine both a better and a worse political world resulting from the impact of the third information revolution. In a bleak vision of the future, one can imagine a thin democracy in which deliberation has greatly diminished. Citizens will use the set-top boxes on their Internet TVs to engage in frequent plebiscites that will be poorly understood and easily manipulated behind the scenes. The growth of thin direct democracy will lead to a further weakening of institutions. In addition, political community will be fragmented by the replacement of broadcasting by narrowcasting. While broadcasting may have often produced a lowest common denominator, at least something was common. In the new world, each community will "know" only its own perspective. The prospects for deliberative democracy as outlined in the *Federalist Papers* will look dim.

Alternatively, one can envisage a better political process in the future. New virtual communities will crosscut geographical communities, both supplementing and reinforcing local community. In Madisonian terms the extensive republic of balancing factions will be enhanced. Access to information will be plentiful and cheap for all citizens. Political participation, including voting, can be made easier. The low costs of contact and contract will reduce the costs of participation. The Internet may end the hegemony of broadcast television that has undercut political parties and made the process of politics extremely costly in terms of the funds that must be raised. Just as television came to dominate campaigns some four decades ago, the Internet may come to dominate the political process in the decades to come. Access to the political process will be easier and cheaper. Again, both of these futures are highly speculative at this point. Technology alone will not produce one or the other outcome. Much will depend on other political choices.

Political Choices

"This is the second age of democracy," argues British Prime Minister Tony Blair. "The first was the vote, getting the basic decent standard delivered and pensions, housing and all the rest of it, but people want choice today, and people want freedom to do things differently at [the] local level, to have better and more innovative ways of deciding their own priorities."[43] Information technology has the capacity to make such a world possible, but it will not happen automatically. As collective activities diffuse across the space described by the matrix outlined above, there will be important implications for democratic governance. The European Union extolls the principle of "subsidiarity," or deciding issues at the lowest possible level as a means of bringing government closer to the people. And in the American federal system, public opinion polls show that local and state governments enjoy somewhat higher levels of public trust than does the central government.[44]

In principle, devolution and subsidiarity seem to enhance democratic governance, but as James Madison pointed out two centuries ago, local communities with dominant factions are more likely to suffer from a tyranny of the majority. In American history, for example, central government interventions in the states were essential for the democratic enfranchisement of Black citizens. Moreover, as some actors became more mobile across state and national jurisdictions, local government tax bases erode and burdens are shifted onto the shoulders of those who are relatively immobile, which often means those who are poor.[45] The unstructured development of information technology may increase inequality and accentuate gaps between haves and have-nots. Information technology may enhance life choices for some people while diminishing them for others.

Among many enthusiasts of information technology, there is a strong libertarian tendency which assumes that the growing perfection of markets through the Internet will solve the problems of democratic governance. They believe that as more and more activities shift horizontally on the matrix described above, the role of government will diminish. Micro-contracting will allow people to make their own choices on an ever-increasing range of issues. It is true that markets enhance choice, but they provide more choices for those who can enter the game with a large pile of chips than for those who cannot.

Aside from the question of inequality of opportunity, there is also a question of public spaces and public goods.[46] Public goods are nonexclusive and nonrivalrous. Once produced, no one can be excluded from their consumption, and one person's consumption does not diminish that of others. Lighthouses have been a classic example in economics textbooks. Today's technology makes it possible to construct a lighthouse (or a navigational satellite) whose signal can be made available to some users and not to others. This ability to exclude lays the basis for a private market relationship and diminishes one of government's traditional roles, the provision of public goods. Highways, including the information highway, can be turned into toll roads. Indeed, one can imagine a situation where information technology could produce automated pricing systems that could privatize all public spaces such as roads and parks. Alternatively, one can imagine deliberate government actions to preserve public spaces and to widen the access to information technology across social and organizational barriers. Such policies could encourage the use of the Internet as an adjunct rather than a substitute for face-to-face relations in reinforcing civic involvement. Similarly, one can imagine alternative choices in the governance of cyberspace. As Lawrence Lessig argues, software and hardware codes and architecture constitute cyberspace. They imbed political values that have constitutional importance. Yet "they are private and therefore outside the scope of constitutional review."[47]

In short, we are only in the early stages of the information revolution. As in earlier periods of "industrial revolution," public responses to technology are lagging behind private ones. Some aspects of that lag are fortuitous, but some are not. The future of democratic governance depends upon improving our ability to make the relevant distinctions.

Endnotes

1. Joseph Nye, "Introduction: The Decline of Confidence in Government," in Nye, Philip Zelikow, David King, eds., *Why People Don't Trust Government* (Cambridge, MA: Harvard University Press, 1997), pp. 1–2; Pippa Norris, ed., *Critical Citizens: Global Support for Democratic Government* (New York: Oxford University Press, 1999).

2. See for example Robert Samuelson, *The Good Life and Its Discontents: The American Dream in the Age of Entitlement, 1945–1995* (New York: Vintage, 1995, 1997).

3. Ronald Inglehart, "Postmaterialist Values and the Erosion of Institutional Authority," in Nye et al., eds.

4. See for example Peter Drucker, "The Next Information Revolution," *Forbes*, 8/24/98, pp. 46–58; Alvin and Heidi Toffler, *The Politics of the Third Wave* (Kansas City, MO: Andrews and McMeel, 1995); Morley Winograd and Dudley Buffa, *Taking Control: Politics in the Information Age* (New York: Henry Holt, 1996); Don Tapscott, *The Digital Economy: Promise and Peril in the Age of Networked Intelligence* (New York: McGraw-Hill, 1996).

5. David S. Landes, *The Unbound Prometheus: Technological Change and Industrial Development in Western Europe from 1750 to the Present* (Cambridge, UK: Cambridge University Press, 1969), chaps. 2–3; David Thomson, *England in the Nineteenth Century, 1815–1914* (New York: Viking Penguin, 1950, 1978), pp. 63–68; Alfred Chandler, Jr., *The Visible Hand: The Managerial Revolution in American Business* (Cambridge, MA: Belknap Harvard, 1977), pp. 90–91.

6. Zane L. Miller, *The Urbanization of Modern America: A Brief History*, 2nd ed. (San Diego: Harcourt Brace Jovanovich, 1987), passim.

7. Stuart W. Bruchey, *Growth of the Modern American Economy* (New York: Dodd Mead, 1975); Thomas McCraw, *Prophets of Regulation: Charles Francis Adams, Louis D. Brandeis, James M. Landis, Alfred E. Kahn* (Cambridge, MA: Belknap Harvard, 1984), chaps. 1–5.

8. Daniel Bell, "Foreword: 1998" (author's draft) to the forthcoming edition of *The Coming of Post-Industrial Society: A Venture in Social Forecasting* (New York: Basic Books, 1976), p. 8.

9. Bell, p. 5.

10. Nathan Rosenberg, *Exploring the Black Box: Technology, Economics, and History* (New York: Cambridge University Press, 1994), chap. 4 .

11. See Anthony G. Oettinger's presentation at the 1998 Visions Conference— Bretton Woods, "Information Technologies, Governance and Government: Some Insights from History," available online at the Kennedy School's Web site *(www.ksg.edu/visions)*.

12. Bell, pp. 94, 97.

13. William Fielding Ogburn, "The Influence of Inventions on American Social Institutions in the Future," *American Journal of Sociology*, v. 43 n. 3 (11/37), p. 370.

14. Charles P. Kindleberger, *Centralization Versus Pluralism* (Copenhagen: Copenhagen Business School Press, 1996), p. 13.

15. Bell, p. 94.

16. John D. Donahue, *Disunited States* (New York: Basic Books, 1997), p. 11.

17. Donahue, pp. 9–11.

18. Daniel Yergin and Joseph Stanislaw, *The Commanding Heights: The Battle Between Government and the Marketplace That is Remaking the Modern World* (New York: Simon and Schuster, 1998); Susan Strange, *States and Markets*, 2nd ed., (New York: Pinter, 1994), pp. 14, 73.

19. *Nonprofit Almanac, 1996–97* (San Francisco : Jossey-Bass, 1996), p. 29.

20. Jessica T. Mathews, "Power Shift," *Foreign Affairs,* Jan./Feb. 1997; Marc Lindenberg, presentation on "Declining State Capacity, Voluntarism, and the Globalization of the Not-For-Profit Sector," Harvard University Center for International Affairs, 6/22–24 1995.

21. Anne-Marie Slaughter, "The Real New World Order," *Foreign Affairs,* Sept./Oct. 1997; see also Robert Keohane and Joseph S. Nye, Jr., "Transgovernmental Relations and World Politics," *World Politics* XXVII, Oct. 1974.

22. Deborah Spar and Jeffrey J. Bussgang, "Ruling the Net," *Harvard Business Review,* May/June 1996; Saskia Sassen, *Globalization and Its Discontents* (New York: New Press, 1998), p. 16.

23. "Policing for Profit: Welcome to the New World of Private Security," *Economist,* 4/19/97, pp. 21–24.

24. "The Visible Hand," *Economist,* 9/20/97, pp. 17–18.

25. Organization for Economic Co-operation and Development, "The Presence of Government in National Economies," table 1, "General Government Total Outlays" *(www.oecd.org/puma/stats/window/index.htm#).*

26. David Held et al., *Global Transformations: Politics, Economics and Culture* (Cambridge, UK: Polity Press, 1999).

27. Raymond Vernon, *In the Hurricane's Eye: The Troubled Prospects of Multinational Enterprises* (Cambridge, MA: Harvard University Press, 1998), chaps. 1–2.

28. Dani Rodrik, *Has Globalization Gone Too Far?* (Washington, DC: Institute for International Economics, 1997), p. 65.

29. Susan Strange, *The Retreat of the State* (Cambridge, UK: Cambridge University Press, 1996), p. 14.

30. Jeremy Greenwood, *The Third Industrial Revolution: Technology, Productivity, and Income Inequality* (Washington, D.C.: AEI Press, 1997), pp. 20–23.

31. "Electronic Commerce Helps to Fuel US Growth," *Financial Times* (London), 4/16/98, p. 5.

32. Intel co-founder Gordon Moore formulated his now-famous "Moore's Law" of microprocessing power and cost in 1965. As Intel's Web site essay on Moore's Law notes, "The average price of a transistor has fallen by six orders of magnitude due to microprocessor development. This is unprecedented in world history; no other manufactured item has decreased in cost so far, so fast." *(http://developer.intel.com/solutions/archive/issue2/focus .htm#OVER)*.

33. U.S. Department of Commerce, *The Emerging Digital Economy,* chap. 1, "The Digital Revolution" *(www.doc.gov/ecommerce/danc1.htm)*.

34. K.G. Coffman and Andrew Odlyzko, "The Size and Growth of the Internet," *First Monday: Peer-Reviewed Journal on the Internet (www.firstmonday .dk/isues/issue3_10/coffman/index.html)*.

35. Douglass North, *Structure and Change in Economic History* (New York: W. W. Norton), pp. 163–64.

36. "Productivity: Lost in Cyberspace," *Economist*, 9/13/97, p. 72.

37. See for example Marshall McLuhan, *The Gutenberg Galaxy: The Making of Typographic Man* (Toronto: University of Toronto Press, 1962). Drucker, "The Next Information Revolution"; Neal M. Rosendorf, "El Caudillo and American Pop Culture: How Postwar Franco Spain Attempted to Use Hollywood, US Tourism, and Madison Avenue for Its Own Political and Economic Ends" (Harvard University Ph.D. Dissertation, forthcoming), chap 1.

38. Carl F. Friedrich and Zbigniew Brzezinski, *Totalitarian Dictatorship and Autocracy*, 2nd ed. (Cambridge, MA: Harvard University Press, 1965).

39. Rosendorf, chap. 1.

40. Ithiel de Sola Pool, *Technologies of Freedom* (Cambridge, MA: Belknap Harvard, 1983).

41. Morley Winograd and Dudley Buffa, *Taking Control: Politics in the Information Age* (New York: Henry Holt, 1996).

42. Ashton Carter, John Deutch, Philip Zelikow, "Catastrophic Terrorism: Tackling the New Danger," *Foreign Affairs,* Nov./Dec. 1998.

43. "Undivided Loyalties: FT Interview Tony Blair," *Financial Times* (London), 1/14/99.

44. Nye, Zelikow, and King, "Introduction" and passim; David W. Moore, "Public Trust in Federal Government Remains High," Gallup News Service, 1/8/99 (available online at *www.gallup.com/POLL_ARCHIVES/latest.htm*).

45. Donahue, cited above.

46. Deborah L. Spar, "The Public Face of Cyberspace: The Internet as a Public Good," unpublished manuscript, 1999.

47. Lawrence Lessig, "Cyber-Governance," *CPSR Newsletter,* v. 16 n. 4, (Fall 1998), p. 4.

representation.gov

FAILURE IN THE CYBERMARKETPLACE OF IDEAS

<Arthur Isak Applbaum>

The Year Two Thousand Bug has struck hard already. I don't mean the dreaded glitch in the date function of computers. I mean the phenomenon of otherwise perfectly sober commentators getting giddy in the face of a very, very round number. We have a great need to make history tidy by naming and dating epochs, and the temptation in the next year or two to prognosticate revolutionary, indeed, millenary change is great. So when asked to write about the effects of the Information Revolution on the ideal of Madisonian democracy, my first reaction was skeptical and contrarian. But that very day I got the following unsolicited e-mail:

<This 'telephone' has too many shortcomings to be seriously considered as a means of communication. The device is inherently of no value to us.>

—*Western Union internal memo, 1876*

<Heavier-than-air flying machines are impossible.>
—*Lord Kelvin, president, Royal Society, 1895*

<Everything that can be invented has been invented.>
—*Charles H. Duell, Commissioner, U.S. Office of Patents, 1899*

Arthur Isak Applbaum *is Associate Professor of Public Policy at Harvard University's John F. Kennedy School of Government, where he developed and teaches the School's core course in political ethics.*

<Who the hell wants to hear actors talk?>
—*H. M. Warner, Warner Brothers, 1927*

<Stocks have reached what looks like a permanently high plateau.>
—*Irving Fisher, Professor of Economics, Yale University, 1929*

<I think there is a world market for maybe five computers.>
—*Thomas Watson, chairman of IBM, 1943*

<I have traveled the length and breadth of this country and talked with the best people, and I can assure you that data processing is a fad that won't last out the year.>
—*The editor in charge of business books for Prentice Hall, 1957*

<We don't like their sound, and guitar music is on the way out.>
—*Decca Recording Co. rejecting the Beatles, 1962*

<There is no reason anyone would want a computer in their home.>
—*Ken Olson, president, chairman, and founder of Digital Equipment Corp., 1977*

<640K ought to be enough for anybody.>

—*Bill Gates, 1981*

Now, we've all chuckled over such lists before. The fortuitous arrival of this one cured me right away of my smugness. It also started me thinking about how new the new information technologies really are. Though uninvited, the joke got my attention. I knew who passed it along, but not where it originated, or how many thousands saw it before, or how many mutations it underwent before turning up in my mailbox. I don't and can't know if the lines are accurate or libelous. But I can, with a quick cut and paste, pass them along to you, and so I do, with the meagerest of disclaimers. Lord Kelvin can't help looking foolish, but Bill Gates can, whether or not his quote is accurate. He can make himself out to be as visionary as he wants to be, and praise himself quickly, cheaply, and anonymously to millions. Or he can attack his enemies. And soon enough he will be able to send a customized message that has been tested to be effective in influencing the opinions of someone who matches your demographic characteristics, surfs your favorite Web sites, subscribes to your favorite magazines, rents your favorite videos, and takes your favorite medications. There are smallish companies that own more mainframes than Tom Watson thought would ever be built, and in their databases are details about all your credit-card transactions, for starters.

If you are a financial analyst or large investor who follows such companies, you are invited to participate in quarterly interactive tele-conference calls with the CEO. The company gets to decide who's a member of this club, and small shareholders are not. If you are listening, the company knows who you are, because you signed up for the call. But unless you ask a question, no one else on the call knows that you are listening. Sometimes the first question is a slow pitch down the middle from a bullish, friendly analyst. If companies are screening tougher questioners, no one would know. The particular rules of this game could have been very different, because the technology allows many variants. Some options have been physically ruled out by the particular path along which teleconferencing technology has developed—two callers probably cannot, through this system, easily connect with each other for a private conversation while the main call is going on. But if there were enough demand for such a variant, someone would design it. The identities of callers could be known to all, to none, or to a select few; all could hear the same message or different messages; control over who can say what when to whom can be allocated in many ways. The Securities and Exchange Commission might have a say in this, but the basic technological capability exists.

The only prognostication about the new cyberdemocracy technologies that I will engage in is to sketch out what is possible given the existing basic technological capabilities. Possible doesn't mean likely, and much of what I will sketch will never come to pass, either because there won't be enough demand, or industry standards will close some options, or paths will be blocked by regulation or social custom. The most visible capability is the vastly expanded possibilities for interactive communication: fast, cheap, and round-the-clock access to thousands of news sources, political chat rooms, electronic town halls, and millions of individualized pitches from politician to citizen and back again. Much of this will be junk, of course, and new technical and institutional ways to search, filter, verify, and identify will emerge. The dominant gatekeepers could be centralized, vesting a lot of power in either existing or new media organizations and content providers; or they could be "intelligent agents" that automatically search and filter, identify and block identification, under the direction of users. Predictably, there also will be new ways to grab your attention despite the filtering mechanisms. Some interactive communication will be shallow, and some deep. James Fishkin has pioneered the deliberative poll, in which a representative sample of Americans are brought together for a weekend to discuss issues and then render their opinions. The new technologies will greatly lower the cost and increase the frequency of such encounters.

This is the face of cyberdemocracy that we are now starting to see, but there are three other background capabilities of great, perhaps greater importance: vastly expanded capacities for data collection, for computation, and for automation. The "record" of politicians and public officials could explode with detail, with every word and move, promise and vote, tracked over many years. So could the record of citizens: their every purchase, membership, donation, plane ticket, speeding ticket, and account balance. Much of this already exists in far-flung commercial databases, and insofar as there are barriers to consolidation and access, they are not technical. Politicians will have greatly improved profiles of citizens by district, neighborhood, block, or individual. And when a private citizen enters the public arena, her individual file will be in great demand by reporters and opponents. But we shouldn't forget that alongside all this rapidly expanding political intelligence will be rapidly expanding policy intelligence: data-intensive policy areas such as the economy, healthcare, social policy, and the environment will be awash in information.

The capacity to crunch all this data will mushroom. The policy wonks will know more and be able to say more with more confidence . . . and so will the political junkies. Fed by nonstop, real-time opinion polling, endless market-testing of messages and images, instant and cheap online focus groups, no social scientist need go hungry again. More complex simulations with better and better models will be run on alternate political strategies. Look for mid-course corrections on the teleprompter. Better political analysis will generate greater refinements in narrowcast political communications. Your buttons will be found and pushed.

Voters will not only be able to follow in great detail what their elected representatives are doing, but they will be able to exert more direct influence. There are no technical barriers to establishing online auctions trading campaign contributions for legislative action, perhaps mediated by advocacy groups, perhaps made up of thousands and thousands of small contingent bids, settled automatically upon performance. Before each roll call, the senator sees on screen the opportunity cost of independence. What can be done with money in the coffer can also be done with votes at the poll. If voting online is possible, so is advance voting. Advocacy groups could deliver the votes of their members midterm in exchange for important legislation. Just about any market that one can imagine can be implemented online, and anything implemented online can be automated, like stock market program trading, to take action on your behalf in response to a precipitating event. And, of course, no physical constraint will prevent citizens from making law and policy directly in electronic assemblies that could always be in session.

These possible technology-driven innovations, some more fantastic than others, can be sorted along two dimensions: one, call it *directness*, measures the effect of the innovation on the power of constituents relative to their elected representatives; the other, call it *deliberativeness*, measures the effect of the innovation on the quality of public discussion. Information-based innovations fit in all four quadrants. Some favor the professional politicians by giving them more refined ways to manage and manipulate public opinion and voter behavior at the polls, and some deliver to citizens a greatly expanded capacity to monitor public officials, register views, contribute funds, extract commitments, or govern themselves. Some promote demagogic pander and others promote know-nothing populism; some lead to enlightened statesmanship and others to reasoned and responsible citizen participation. All in all, a move to any quadrant is possible, and to say much more about what in fact will happen over the coming decades is to engage in pure speculation.

Much can be said, however, about what we should want to happen, and insofar as we can influence what happens, what we should aim at. We can evaluate moves toward more or less direct and more or less deliberative democracy. But to do so, we need to take (and defend) a stand on one of the central questions of political philosophy: how can we rule each other legitimately? I will argue for an unpopular view of democratic legitimacy—but it is part of this view that its correctness does not depend on how many people hold it. If you think I'm mistaken, offer (and defend) another view. But no serious assessment of cyberdemocracy can proceed without doing some political philosophy first.

Legitimacy

The argument goes something like this: among the highest values is the freedom to rule oneself. But living in society requires mutual limitations on our freedom—law is coercive. The puzzle of collective self-rule is how to justify to each other this mutual coercion. The unjustified exercise of political coercion is simply tyrannical, so we must explain why we are not to each other tyrants. We are not if, when we exercise collective rule over one another, we treat each other as moral equals. Treatment as a moral equal in this context requires, among other things, that we recognize that we each have a valid claim to a fair share of control over how we collectively rule ourselves. To secure that claim, we are each entitled to a fully adequate scheme of political liberties consistent with equally adequate political liberties for everyone else. If we deprive others of the equal political liberties, we deprive them of their fair share of collective self-rule, and so, we tyrannize them. Simply put, what justifies mutual political coercion is the realization and protection of the equal political liberties.

To treat each other as moral equals does not require equal treatment. There are morally relevant reasons for treating persons in different circumstances differently. In the distribution of resources, differences in need or in merit might be morally relevant reasons. In the restriction of freedoms, differences in past violation of or future threat to the liberty of others, or differences in our obligations to others, might be morally relevant reasons. But for some to exercise political coercion over others for a morally irrelevant reason is to act illegitimately. Here are some reasons for coercing others that are always illegitimate: because I am being paid to do so; because it will enrich my sister-in-law; because it will benefit my tribe; because I hate them; because God wills it. When questions of justice are in the balance, legitimacy requires that proposals for legislation appeal to a conception of justice, to what we owe one another, and not to self-interest or to the interests of the many.

If reasons for depriving others of liberty can be illegitimate, then the test of legitimate collective self-rule is in part substantive, and not purely formal or procedural. Legislative majorities elected properly under fair procedures can still act illegitimately and thus tyrannically. They do this most clearly when they deprive a minority of the equal political liberties for irrelevant reasons, thereby failing to treat all citizens as moral equals.

The guarantee of at least some political liberties is a conceptual or practical precondition of legitimate democratic rule. No regime that disenfranchises, silences, or enslaves a minority counts as a legitimate democracy. This is why the constraints on majoritarian lawmaking that a bill of rights imposes makes a constitutional democracy more, not less, legitimate than a regime with no constraints on majority rule. For the same reason, a representative democracy is more, not less, legitimate than a direct democracy if it does a better job of protecting political freedom.

Where does the political participation of citizens fit in this view? The equal political liberties include the right to an equal vote in free and fair elections, equal protection under law, freedom of thought and discussion, the right to petition, assemble, and organize, the right to be informed about government activities, and—to give these liberties fair value—the right to a decent education, among other things. In short, we treat each other as moral equals when we provide for each other the freedom to exercise a fair share of political control without fear or favor, as long as doing so does not deprive others of their liberties. But a reasonably informed voter who freely chooses not to participate more actively in politics is not for that reason less free, nor is the government for that reason more tyrannical and less legitimate. There are reasons to be a passive citizen that are consistent with collective self-rule: an informed voter may have confidence in her elected representatives to advance her interests in ways consistent with justice and legitimacy, she may be satisfied with how things are, and she may have other valuable projects and commitments that demand her time and attention. There might be circumstances under which a passive citizen wrongly free-rides on active citizens, and so fails in her obligations to the rest of us; but she does not fail to be free. And the circumstances of wrongful free-riding must be carefully specified. Hiring someone to do a job for you ordinarily does not involve free-riding.

The claim that the greater participation of all entails the greater freedom of all suffers from a fallacy of composition. True, if coercive government were more responsive to *my* will, I would be more free. I cannot tyrannize myself. But it does not follow that if the government were more responsive to the *majority* will, we *all* would be more free, because we can—and do—tyrannize each other. There is nothing to the view that direct democracy is intrinsically more legitimate than representative and constitutional democracy.

It is often claimed that checks on the will of the majority, such as representative government and judicial review, are paternalistic, and so disrespectful to a competent and mature people. It is paternalistic to restrict your liberty to keep you from harming yourself; it is not paternalistic to restrict your liberty to keep you from harming others. Constitutional constraints on majoritarianism aim at the second, not the first, and it is a dangerous romanticism to suppose, in the United States today, that "we the people" need more protection from "them the government" than we need from each other. Unjustly treated minorities can be forgiven if they reject a reified account of "we" under which their injuries are self-inflicted.

Where does deliberation fit in this view? First, we have to say something about what is meant by the term. Just about every form and venue of political communication has, at one time or another, been claimed as a part of a deliberative process, from New England town meetings to election campaign smear tactics and everything in between. If we take the widest definition, democratic deliberation is any practice of interactive communication in which actors in a democracy seek to affect the decisions of one another by influencing beliefs about politically relevant facts, values, concepts, or interests. Note that this does not rule out deceptive and manipulative political communication. An actor need only seek to affect another's politically relevant belief, not necessarily in the direction of beliefs that are true or believed by the actor to be true. Broad as it is, this preliminary definition is incompatible with views of politics that take interests and values to be known and fixed, as some models of interest-group pluralism have done. Also, broad as this is, it does not cover all political activity. Not all political acts seek to influence belief: some acts aim at affecting the decisions of others through the provision of incentives and disincentives, and some acts aim at forcing or coercing others. Many political activities are complex in that they contain both deliberative and nondeliberative aspects. A negotiator, for example, might seek to affect another's decisions in all three ways: by influencing beliefs, by offering incentives, and by coercively worsening or threatening to worsen the other party's alternative to agreement. Some political activities are efficacious precisely because of an ambiguity in whether or not they operate deliberatively: most politicians do not want to view campaign contributions as legalized bribery.

Of course, the sort of deliberation advocated by proponents of deliberative democracy is much more noble than this. They mean something like a reflective process of honestly giving and listening to reasons and arguments among persons who are open to changing their views about facts, interests, and values for the right reasons, and who have the capacity and the motivation to imaginatively occupy the perspectives of others. As have most academics, I have committed my life to *that* sort of deliberation, and of course I wish there were more of it in democratic politics.

But if the concept of deliberation is to be useful in assessing the design of political institutions, rather than simply as a pious exhortation, it cannot be defined by the quality of the motivations of participants any more than it can be defined by the quality of the outcomes. We can dictate neither. A usable definition of deliberative democracy refers to processes and institutions that aim at changing motivations, and consequently outcomes, for the better. So, as I am going to use the term, what makes the Supreme Court a deliberative institution is not that its members are fair, impartial, and honest. We hope that they are, but we cannot make them so. Rather, the court is deliberative in that its practices include hearing arguments, discussing cases, taking its time, and giving reasons in opinions; the institution attempts to screen out improper motives by granting justices lifetime tenure and by having rules about ex parte contact and conflict of interest.

For any actual deliberative process, we want to know how good it is at drawing out from participants better motives and more reasoned changes in view. And since no process will wholly succeed, we want to know how robust the process is to cheaters and incompetents. Good, just, and legitimate political outcomes might better be served by avoiding a deliberative process that is not sufficiently strategy-proof or foolproof. This is not to say that one should not offer reasons. Treating our fellow citizens as moral equals worthy of respect requires both that we have good reasons before we restrict their liberty or set back their interests, and that, generally, we give them those reasons and consider their objections in return. But if we have the formal legal authority to unilaterally decide a matter, we surely are not required to defer to the outcome of a deliberation conducted in bad faith. One must resist, here and elsewhere, the temptation to compare the ideal form of one's favored institutional arrangement with realized instantiations of the disfavored alternatives.

When it comes to deliberation, this temptation is especially great because it is easy to confuse the enterprise of designing actual legitimate institutions with the enterprise of modeling the principles of morality or of justice as the outcome of a hypothetical deliberation conducted by idealized persons under idealized conditions. I think some version of the contractualist moral theories of Kant, Rawls, Scanlon, and Habermas is correct. But it does not follow that we should try to mimic in our real institutions the devices they employ to model unanimous agreement under the conditions of freedom, equality, and reasonableness. No real deliberative process can succeed in eliminating background inequalities in bargaining power or in motivating participants not to exploit the advantages that such inequalities confer; no real deliberative process will leave participants equally and fully informed; no real deliberative process can assure that all are moved to seek agreement on terms that all can reasonably accept. If any real deliberative process of any size resulted in unanimity, we would first turn for an explanation to duress or fraud, rather than sweet reason; and when real deliberations are not unanimous, we do not suppose that the dissenters are being unreasonable. Surely we should encourage deliberative processes to shape the views of citizens if the alternative is for their opinions to be formed by superficial sound-bites, uniformed prejudice, and unreflective self-interest. But there is no reason to suppose that the unconstrained rule of deliberating majorities is a more legitimate solution to the puzzle of collective self-rule than a system with constitutional constraints on majoritarianism. Think of all the provisions and interpretations of the U.S. Constitution that, in your view, properly protect basic liberties, along with those provisions that you believe are mistakes. Now suppose you have a choice: you can either keep the Constitution as it is or substitute representative samples of the American people who will periodically meet for a month or more and deliberate about what our basic liberties are and how they should be protected. Under which scheme are you more secure against tyranny? Deliberation is a fine thing, but when it comes to preventing tyranny, one doesn't remove the belt when one adds the suspenders.

Madison

And so we come to Madison. It is a bit misleading to speak of the ideal of Madisonian democracy, since James Madison is the great theorist of the nonideal. He framed institutions, to borrow a phrase from

Rousseau, for men as they are. This doesn't mean that we cannot construct normative principles that Madison could endorse—that is what I have been doing—but that for Madison, facts about the nature of politics require us to be pessimistic about realizing a normative *ideal*. Madison's world is always second-best.

Madison understood that normative principles of political philosophy and pragmatic prescriptions for the design of political institutions were connected by enduring facts about human nature: men are not angels, one cannot judge one's own cause without bias, passions and interests give rise to faction, and factions are prone to tyrannize. Since the causes of faction cannot be removed without also destroying liberty—a prescient observation—his institutional prescription is to control the effects of faction. Representation, separation of powers, and an extended republic of large enough size will diminish the chances that any one faction will gain a majority or be able to act in unison. In short, the great evil is tyranny, the cause is faction, and the solution is an institutional design that deters the formation of majority factions by making ambition counteract ambition, and that mediates passion through representation.

Does the arrival of the new information technologies call for a revision in the Madisonian account? Surely it does not change the normative principle. Liberty is no less important, tyranny is no less wrong. Do the information technologies change the facts about the nature of politics that cause factional interests and passions? One might object that Madison's view is too dismal (though I do not). But if we grant, *arguendo*, that he was right about the deep causes of faction before the advent of the Internet, the new technologies do not mitigate the causes, which are self-love and passion. Note that Madison does not argue that faction is caused by lack of information or expertise, which the vast resources of the Information Revolution could cure. Neither partisan interests nor collective passions are brought on by ignorance. "Had every Athenian citizen been a Socrates; every Athenian assembly would still have been a mob" (*Federalist* no. 55). So the problem to which representative democracy is the solution is not bad information—lack of expertise, narrow bandwidth, informational complexity or overload. The problem is bad will—factional interests or inflamed passions, the defect of the better motive. Representation as a remedy for deficiencies in information or expertise is Mill's argument, not Madison's.

Do the new technologies change the effects of faction? If Madison is right about the importance of the extended republic as a check against the mischiefs of faction, then there is cause to worry. The extended republic provides two safeguards: greater numbers multiply interests, making it less likely that a majority will have a common interest in oppressing a minority, and geographic spread makes it harder for factions to recognize their strength and organize for action. The Internet doesn't shrink the number of interests, but precisely those aspects of interactive communication that thrill the direct democrats make the identification and organization of factious majorities more likely.

It is by now obvious that, for Madison, the logistical difficulties of direct democracy and mass political participation are not at all a regrettable circumstance that necessitate representation as a poorer substitute. It is Burke who offers the logistical circumstance as a justification for legislative independence: "But government and legislation are matters of reason and judgment, and not of inclination; and what sort of reason is that, in which the determination precedes the discussion; in which one set of men deliberate, and another decide; and where those who form the conclusion are perhaps three hundred miles distant from those who hear the arguments?" ("Speech to the Electors of Bristol"). If presented with the electronic remedies that covered the three hundred miles and allowed his constituents to instruct him after parliamentary deliberation, Burke no doubt would fall back on his other reasons for legislative independence. But Madison has no need to retreat. For him, distance and difficulty of communication are to be celebrated as checks on majorities in their own right, and he can only lament the electronic contraction of the extended republic.

The upshot of information technology on the effectiveness of representation in deterring faction is harder to assess: innovations in all of the basic capabilities—communication, data collection, computation, and automation—make representatives more accountable to politically active citizens. Voters and contributors will have a greatly expanded capability to follow the legislator's record, to gain access, and to make credible threats and promises about support. Legislative independence is self-defeating if independent legislators are swiftly replaced by more deferential ones. Cyberdemocrats welcome the prospect of mimicking direct democracy by tightening control on representatives. Whether direct democracy or direct oligarchy is mimicked depends on the numbers and distribution of active citizens. And whether this is good or bad for the protection of liberty depends on the interests and passions of the electronically active.

The elected official looking for elbow room will also have new tools to employ. Market-tested, narrowcast political communication could be very effective at attracting and keeping the more passive voters. If the Internet brings more manipulatory politics, the advantage is likely to go to the professionals. If we suppose instead that the deliberationists succeed in getting a rich and thoughtful conversation going, it is unclear whether this will result, on balance, in more legislators being reeducated by the majority of their constituents, or in more legislators successfully explaining their positions or winning room for discretionary judgment. The rise of deliberation might just select for a different kind of candidate with different oratorical skills . . . but we should all keep our day jobs.

Equilibrium

Why has the possibility of direct electronic democracy generated more enthusiasm than dread? The prospect of large numbers, speed, iteration, and complexity that information technology offers triggers appealing images of equilibrating mechanisms. We of course know that not all equilibria are good. Natural equilibria can be catastrophic—ask the dinosaurs—and social equilibria unjust—look at segregated housing. But the temptation to analogize from the favorable equilibria of prosperous economic markets and beautiful old growth forests to any complex system is strong. So, the director of the Aspen Institute's Internet Policy Project can believe this:

> Drawing on recent research at the Santa Fe Institute and elsewhere that holds that any complex system, whether technological or biological, will spontaneously order itself, Mr. Johnson predicts that the Internet will produce its own social order—one that, because it arises from the network itself, will have its own legitimacy (*New York Times*, 29 June 1998).

David Johnson no doubt has more to say on this than the *Times* reports, but surely more must be said before we accept the Panglossian claim that spontaneous ordering is good, just, or legitimate. Remember *Lord of the Flies*?

An appeal to the good consequences of an equilibrating process assumes a *mechanism*, and *conditions* under which the mechanism will lead to a favorable equilibrium. The mechanism must be described and the conditions under which good results obtain must be specified. For example, general equilibrium theory in economics describes a pricing mechanism in which producers and consumers bid, and states the conditions of perfect competition that must hold for the price system to yield efficient allocations in the production and consumption of goods: a large number of firms free to enter and exit, frictionless market transactions, costlessly enforceable contracts, markets for capital, risk and information, etc. This obviously is an idealization that will never be met by an actual economy, and economic theory goes on to describe the equilibria that can be expected when these conditions are only partly satisfied. For example, in the well-known lemons problem, George Akerlof shows how, under certain conditions, information asymmetries can lead to the unraveling of a used-car market, so that no buyer is willing to buy any car that a seller is willing to sell, even though there are gains to trade.*

Similarly, if factual claims for the good effects on the democratic process of the new information technologies are to be taken seriously, the conditions that must hold for the good results to occur must be specified, along with an account of how robust good results are to the relaxation of some of these conditions. This has never been done for the suggestively named but poorly specified marketplace of ideas, so we do not know if the hyperactivity of an electronic marketplace of ideas will be better or worse.

Consider Oliver Wendell Holmes's much-quoted celebration of the marketplace of ideas in his *Abrams v. United States* dissent:

> But when men have realized that time has upset many fighting faiths, they may come to believe even more than they believe the very foundations of their own conduct that the ultimate good desired is better reached by free trade in ideas—that the best test of truth is the power of the thought to get itself accepted in the competition of the market, and that truth is the only ground upon which their wishes safely can be carried out. That at any rate is the theory of our Constitution. It is an experiment, as all life is an experiment (250 U.S. 616, 630 [1919]).

---

* See "The Market for 'Lemons': Quality Uncertainty and the Market Mechanism," *The Quarterly Journal of Economics*, 84 (August 1970), pp. 488–500.

Now, this is false in two ways. If the Constitution has a theorist, it is James Madison, and Madison would never endorse Holmes's test of truth. He needed no procedural test to pick out injustice and illegitimacy. Nor should he have endorsed the test, because Holmes is either making the false empirical claim that even deceptive and manipulative political communication leads to a convergence of belief on the truth, or the false philosophical claim that truth is whatever we think it is after we are all talked out.

Now, Madison invokes his own equilibrium mechanism, but a more modest and so a more plausible one. Under a separation of powers, opposite and rival interests are to supply the defect of better motives, and check each other's tyrannical tendencies. It is more modest because Madison does not predict confidently that great good, such as truth, will come from defective motives; rather, his aim is to prevent a great bad, tyranny, and he is not entirely confident that he will succeed. It is a serious misreading of Madison to attribute to him the view that, with divided and representative institutions in place, better motives are unnecessary, let alone counterproductive.

I have argued that democratic legitimacy is in part a substantive notion: to be legitimate, a government must protect its minorities from majority tyranny, and what counts as tyranny is not up to the majority. No democratic procedure alone can solve the puzzle of legitimate political coercion. Therefore, in evaluating various changes to the directness of the democratic process and the levels of political participation that information technology might bring about, we cannot simply deduce the answer from our view of some procedural ideal: direct democracy is more legitimate, the Internet is direct, therefore the Internet increases legitimacy. Rather, we must look to the effects these technological innovations will have on realizing, protecting, or violating the equal political liberties.

American government now fails at realizing political freedom in some serious ways: the current system of campaign financing amounts to legalized corruption; equality before the law is out of the reach of most Americans because lawyers are; millions of children fail in school to develop the most basic capacities for self-rule. Information technology is not going to remedy these faults, even if every poor kid were to be given a laptop, as Newt Gingrich once proposed. The Internet might make campaign financing worse.

What information technology will do, in ways that are difficult to predict, is create new powerful gatekeepers, increase the ease of political organization and participation for some (but not all) citizens, and give politicians much more sophisticated tools for political analysis and communication. How this will alter the balance between passion and reason, factional interest and the public interest, majorities and minorities, constituents and representatives, is at this point simply guesswork. If I had to, I'd bet on the professional pols, and I'm enough of a Madisonian to root for them too.

JAMES MADISON ON CYBERDEMOCRACY

\<Dennis Thompson\>

```
Date: Tue, 04 Jul 1998 12:01:00 -0400
To: "Arthur Applbaum"
<arthur_applbaum/FS/KSG@ksg.harvard.edu>
From: "James Madison" <jmadison@founding.gov>
bcc: "Thomas Jefferson"
<tjeff@monticello.org>, "Publius"
<dennis_thompson@harvard.edu>
Subject: cyberdemocracy
```

Message Text

Your recent paper on the implications of information technologies for Madisonian democracy has come to my attention. I do not usually deign to respond to the surfeit of messages I receive each week purporting to determine "what Madison would have said." Indeed, I receive so much spam that I have installed a filter utility that blocks, inter alia, all messages containing "Hamilton" "anti-Federalist," and "the War of 1812."

Nevertheless, I am compelled to respond to your paper because of its extraordinary combination of truth and error. You come closer than any writer I have read to representing accurately my views about the new technologies, but for that reason your errors more urgently stand in need of correction.

Dennis Thompson *is the Alfred North Whitehead Professor of Political Philosophy at Harvard and Director of the University's Program in Ethics and the Professions. His most recent book is* Democracy and Disagreement *(with Amy Gutmann).*

You are certainly correct in perceiving that the new technologies are not a panacea for the ills of American democracy, and that they may even exacerbate its already perilous condition. (I have abandoned all hope of persuading anyone to employ the proper term, "republic," especially now that I have seen the uses to which the so-called Republicans have put its cognates.) The Internet undoubtedly provides more information to more people than ever before, and by means of this service certainly effects a positive contribution. Who could dispute that it is better that citizens and their representatives be more rather than less informed?

But as you perspicaciously observe, the most severe source of troubles lies not in the dearth of information but in the lack of good will—in (one might say) "the defect of the better motive." The motive of tyranny—the desire to rule over others without regard to their liberty—is deleterious in any democracy, and by diminishing the effects of geographical dispersion, the Internet removes one of the chief impediments to the formation of tyrannical factions.

I wish to acknowledge that in my previous writings I dwelt excessively on the danger of *majority* factions. (I regret to observe that you follow me in this error.) Tyranny, I would still affirm, is a serious problem, but its threat, I now see more clearly, derives less from any well-organized majority than from temporary and shifting combinations of minorities. In support of this proposition, I appeal to the authority of a distinguished political scientist, Robert Dahl, who though laboring in a less reputable institution than yours redeemed himself by devoting nearly a whole book to discussing the Madisonian theory of democracy. Professor Dahl concluded his insightful work thusly: "The making of governmental decisions is not a majestic march of great majorities . . . it is the steady appeasement of relatively small groups. . . ."

Professor Dahl also remarked that this consequence would please me "enormously." But I should concur only if the "minorities rule" he so aptly describes is not itself tyrannical. At the risk of sounding like my friend Mr. Jefferson, I should say that as I observe the practice of American democracy today, I detect more than a few instances in which privileged minorities combine (be they corporations or professions) to thwart the will of the people.

The inference to which we are brought is that any faction, whether majority or minority, may seek to rule tyrannically, and when it does it will find the new technologies a useful means to further its baneful ends. The Internet offers potent means to overcome the geographical barriers that I had hoped would help keep factious combinations from executing their schemes of oppression.

If you are correct in emphasizing this danger, you are mistaken in neglecting the possibilities that the Internet offers to check its effects. First of all, you should recall that to prevent factious combinations from endangering republics I rely not only on the "extent of territory" but also on "the greater variety of parties and interests." Under these circumstances the agreement required to sustain robust combinations is to be less often expected. "Communication is always checked by distrust in proportion to the number whose concurrence is necessary." In the chat rooms and the bulletin boards across America, diversity of opinion is great but the frequency of concurrence is small. The more regularly that citizens have a chance to express themselves, the less reliably they will be able to forge agreement and form stable coalitions.

The second attribute of the new technologies that may help constrain the political effects of factions is somewhat paradoxical. The ease of communication itself assists citizens all too well in finding compatriots who share their interests, however particular and even eccentric these interests may be. In my leisure (which I now possess in greater quantities than previously), I confess that I have from time to time found myself surfing the Net. In this new world, I have observed that the political interest groups are remarkable not only for their variety but also for their specialization. I here record a random list of several that came to my attention in one recent session: the California Federation of Republican Women, Hikers to Free our Parks, National Whistleblower Union, Citizens against Daylight Saving Time, Citizens for Finnish-American Power, the U.S. Committee to Support the Revolution in Peru, and the Anarchists Anti-Defamation League. If citizens communicate with the like-minded more than before, what their minds like is also more circumscribed than before.

In my own experience on the Net, I found that nearly half of the chat rooms and newsgroups reached through the most common gateways declare a preference for a particular point of view. The chat group designated as the second most popular on Lycos is "dedicated to discussion of politics from a right wing perspective." Other sites, while eschewing commitment to partisans of left and right, nevertheless reinforce political cynicism: among those with the greatest "hits" is the home page of "Voters for None of the Above," a nonpartisan organization devoted to "giving voters the ballot option to reject all the candidates for an office. . . ."

I recognize that citizens may post on multiple sites and may take part in multiple organizations, just as they now join different, cross-cutting interest groups (at least according to pluralist theories of contemporary politics). I also acknowledge that some users may occasionally log on to sites more out of curiosity than out of commitment. But in general, it must be recognized, that in the routine of surfing and posting on the Internet, citizens have both less need and less incentive to seek out sites and groups that embrace a broad range of interests and bring together a wide range of perspectives.

Furthermore, one should keep in mind that most of the activity on the Internet is not political at all. (This is the third factor which may impede factious combinations.) At the most popular gateways the categories that attract the most "hits" are "Entertainment," "Shopping," "Travel," "People," and "Relationships."

These checks on the political potential of majorities perhaps should cause me, as Professor Dahl suggests, to be "enormously pleased." In some moods I confess I am. :-) The capacity of the Internet and its kindred technologies to reinforce the apolitical tendencies of citizens can help prevent politics from becoming excessively intense, and politicians from suffering undue pressure. The less politically interested (and therefore less politically competent) devote their attention to other activities and leave government to those who know best.

Yet in a more reflective mood, I find that I am not so pleased. :-(Nothing is more important for good government than "fidelity to the object of government, which is the happiness of the people." To pursue this object, I would still rely on the people's representatives, who have at least more experience and perhaps more public spirit than ordinary citizens. However, these representatives are accountable to the electors—and more directly now than in my time. Representatives are likely in the future to be still more directly accountable as citizens take advantage of the populist potential of information technology. If most electors care little about politics, and those few who do care frequent chat rooms and newsgroups that cater only to their special interests, then representatives will stand at the mercy of electoral power that is at best indifferent and at worst inimical toward the public weal.

There are two ways of curing these mischiefs of the Internet: the one, by improving the citizenry; the other, by enlightening its representatives.

The new technologies could assist in effecting both. Some Internet sites welcome diverse opinions from all citizens, and set a tone that encourages participants to respect the views of others, and to regard politics as an activity that promotes not only factional but also public interests. An exemplar is "The Democracy Network," which promises interactive debates in which participants communicate with candidates for offices as well as one another, drawing on the site's archives, which contain previous statements by the candidate and other information relevant to the campaign. The deliberative polls initiated by Fishkin, whom you cite, could also be made more effective by exploiting the virtues of the Internet.

Yet it is in vain to expect the new technologies alone to create sufficient public spirit on the part of citizens. In the first place, the Internet mostly reinforces the tendencies already present in the wider civil society. Left to their own devices, the providers will offer more advice on "relationships" than counsel on public policy. In the second place, even when citizens engage in political discussion in the proper deliberative spirit on the Internet, they may not become more public spirited. In Fishkin's deliberative polls, the participants usually changed their minds when they learned they were mistaken about facts but rarely when they confronted views that challenged their own values. In the third place, most citizens spend most of their time attending to their private affairs. While familiarity with the business of private life may be of some assistance in governing, there is no substitute for the experience of carrying out the duties of public office itself.

It must be acknowledged that enlightened statesmen will not always be at the helm of the ship of state. But we have no choice but to rely on representatives, especially on the men (and women, I would now say) who are prepared to devote themselves to public service. It is this political class to which we should turn our attention, and it is this class for whom the new technologies may prove more effectual. I do not presume, as you evidently do, that our political leaders will use these new instruments to manipulate more than to instruct citizens in the pursuit of the public good.

Is there any reason to suppose that the new technologies can further this object? You mention their capability of providing plentiful quantities of information, which may be used for good or for ill. (I must say that I am thankful that the Anti-Federalists did not have access to so potent a medium during the ratification debates.)

But like other commentators you ignore an important probable consequence of this superabundance of information. The greater the quantity and more variable the quality of information, the greater the demand for authorities who can assess its reliability and relevance. The fabrications and falsehoods to which the Internet gives voice may admittedly serve some useful purposes. As Matt Drudge has said: "All truths begin as hearsay." But even while half-believing the rumors they find on the Net, most citizens, I trust, will seek guidance about which they may fully believe, which stand some chance of becoming the political truths of tomorrow. The authority of the *New York Times* or *Wall Street Journal* is no less, and indeed may be greater, in an era when its readers have access to the *Drudge Report*.

As in the good government I commend, so in the good technology I recommend, there will be a need "to refine and enlarge the public views by passing them through the medium of a chosen body of citizens, whose wisdom may best discern the true interest of the country." Although your paper neglects this need as a force in cyberdemocracy's marketplace of ideas, may I presume that you would agree that some leadership—some refinement and enlargement of public opinion—is not only desirable but also possible through the instruments of the new technologies. I am encouraged—by the declaration at the end of your paper in which you "root" for the "professional pols"—to believe that you yourself would look, not to the media barons, but to the political classes to provide this species of leadership in cyberdemocracy.

You and I also seem to concur on the nature of deliberative democracy. Certainly, I would aver that representative democracy is no less legitimate than direct democracy. Indeed, one of the great dangers of cyberdemocracy is that it can increase directness at the expense of deliberation, exacerbating the imbalance from which our system already suffers. However, it is possible to agree with this conclusion, but for reasons quite different from those which you and I affirm. You assess the balance between directness and deliberativeness according to how well it protects and promotes liberty. Democracy for its own sake, deliberative or otherwise, is not the chief goal. In this, I concur.

But you know, perhaps better than I, that some deliberative democrats—indeed, some who are your friends and colleagues—take a rather different view. You have courageously resisted their efforts to induce you to trade eighteenth century tradition for twentieth-century innovation. ;-) The most dangerous theorists of this school, Professors Gutmann and Thompson in their recent book, *Democracy and Disagreement*, concede (or I suppose they would say, insist upon) the value of representative democracy. They also make a point of defending liberty, which they believe a constitution should guarantee.

Yet while paying this apparent deference to liberty, they pose an insidious question: because citizens disagree about the meaning and implications of liberty, how can any individual or group justify imposing through the coercive power of the state his understanding of liberty on everyone else? Even the most thoughtful citizens and their representatives disagree about liberty: Mr. Jefferson and I did not always see eye to eye on such fundamental questions.

In my time, we were quite prepared to appeal to the authority of natural rights, but I doubt that you are, and certainly few of your fellow citizens would follow anyone who invoked such traditional notions. On what basis then should democrats decide what liberty means in practice? Professors Gutmann and Thompson, along with some other deliberative democrats, are thus led to say that citizens or their representatives should decide in a process of mutual justification that recognizes the equal moral standing of all citizens.

While I would not go so far as to permit the meaning of liberty to be contingent on deliberation, I am more sympathetic to the aims of the deliberative democrats than to those of most of the other varieties of democrats who populate the intellectual landscape these days—the interest-group pluralists, the game theorists, the postmodernists, the strict conservatives and their ilk. Democracy should rest on more than voting, even votes for liberty, and should encompass more than bargaining, even bargains for the public good. All good democrats should welcome the deliberationists' call for sustained exposure to diverse opinions; recognition of the difference between reasonable and unreasonable disagreement; and openness to change in one's fundamental political views through interaction with one's fellow citizens.

It must be confessed that these worthy aims place a greater burden on the new technologies. If the Internet were asked to facilitate only voting, it would not need to be interactive. If it were expected to provide for merely bargaining, it would need to be interactive only to the extent necessary for conducting negotiations. Democracy, properly understood, requires technologies that support forums accessible to citizens of diverse perspectives and opportunities for active and regular interchange, all governed by norms of mutual respect and openness.

In the spirit of those aspects of deliberative democracy that I can accept, and in the terms of those elements of cyberdiscourse I can apprehend, I propose five criteria for assessing the extent to which new technologies may promote the aims of democracy, properly understood. I shall not scruple to object if you conceive of them as the first five amendments to the constitution of cyberdemocracy (a Bill of Cyberrights).

  I. Forums shall be open to all (*no bozo filters*).

 II. Surfing shall be participatory (*no lurking*).

III. Interactions shall be sustained (*no churning*).

 IV. Posting shall be civil (*no flame bait*).

  V. Downloading shall be transparent (*no cookies*).

These amendments will no doubt require interpretation, which will give some of your friends cause to reaffirm the need for more deliberation. Yet you and I know that, like all worthy liberties, these are best protected by statesmen who are able to discern the true interest of the nation. May these statesmen join, with more than deliberate speed, the ranks of the digerati.

MR. THOMPSON'S INSIDIOUS QUESTION

Arthur Isak Applbaum

Dennis Thompson's cyberséance with Mr. Madison is a treat. I have some very small quibbles with his reading of Madison and his Madison's reading of me, and I'll get to them, but we should not forget that the important question before us is not what James Madison's view of democracy is, but what the correct view of democracy is. On this, it may appear that Thompson and I disagree, in that I am a constitutional democrat and he is a deliberative democrat. But I think that the real disagreement is that he is no less of a constitutionalist than I am, and he hasn't owned up to it yet. Thompson and I have been deliberating in good faith about this for a long time and still have not settled the matter, which might say something about how much hope one should put in deliberation.

First, the quibbles. Thompson surely is right to point out that we should fear the tyranny of temporary and shifting combinations of minorities as well, but I don't think that Madison overlooks this. The threat of such combinations in a majoritarian institution comes from their becoming, temporarily, majorities, so when Madison speaks of majority faction, it is not to the exclusion of minority factions that combine to form a majority. Why else refer repeatedly to majorities combining, rather than simply existing? Perhaps Madison sees the factions that arise from interests as fairly stable, but not those that arise from passions, which can decree "the hemlock on one day, and statues on the next" (*Fed.* 63).

Madison would not obviously share Thompson's optimism about the check provided by the diversity of opinions on the Internet. The distrust in proportion to number that Thompson cites arises, according to Madison, "where there is a consciousness of unjust or dishonorable purposes" (*Fed.* 10). I detect no such consciousness in the impassioned groups of the day that might combine to do mischief.

Thompson says I ignore the demand for authorities to assess the quality of the superabundance of electronic information. Not so: I mention filters and gatekeepers. What I can't do is predict with any confidence whether, on balance, influential political information in the coming decades will be more or less mediated by authorities than it is today.

Enough quibbling. How are we to answer Thompson's "insidious" question: "because citizens disagree about the meaning and implications of liberty, how can any individual or group justify imposing, through the coercive power of the state, his understanding of liberty on everyone else?" My answer is that justice and legitimacy are not wholly determined by procedure, so one cannot avoid making substantive judgments about the content of concepts such as liberty, and one cannot avoid making substantive judgments about one's legitimate authority to impose such judgments on others. If a lawmaker has deliberated with constituents and still disagrees with them about matters of basic liberty, her understanding of liberty, not theirs, should determine her vote. Though Thompson in some moods suggests otherwise, when push comes to shove his answer is the same: "Deliberative democracy recognizes constitutional liberties and opportunities as constraints on majority will, and authorizes representatives to resist majority will if it threatens to violate these liberties and opportunities. Accountability does not require representatives to defer to constituents under these circumstances" (Gutmann & Thompson, *Democracy and Disagreement*, pp. 139f.). Deliberative democracy, in Gutmann and Thompson's view, requires that officials give reasons that citizens *can* accept, not reasons that they *do* accept. Now, this gets it exactly right. It is also fully compatible with Madisonian checks on majoritarianism. So I don't see why Madison would find Thompson's question insidious. My conclusions still stand: direct democracy is not more legitimate than representative democracy, and what counts as tyranny is not up to the majority. So to assess the new information technologies we will need to look at both their effects on legislative independence and the effects of legislative independence on the equal political liberties.

community.org

(HOW) DOES THE INTERNET
AFFECT COMMUNITY?

SOME SPECULATION IN SEARCH OF EVIDENCE

<William A. Galston>

Introduction: Problems and Analogies

Suppose that in the summer of 1952, someone had convened a conference on the topic, "Visions of Governance in the Age of Television." The symposiasts would have faced two crucial problems. First, social reality was moving faster than empirical scholarship. Television was diffusing at an explosive rate, from a relative rarity in the late 1940s to near-ubiquity only a decade later. Scholars in 1952 studying (say) the social effects of television might have noted how neighbors crowded into a living room to watch the only set on the block, and they might have drawn conclusions about the medium's community-reinforcing tendencies that would have seemed antique only a few years later.

The second difficulty would have been even harder to cope with. Reasoning by analogy from (say) the automobile's effects on sexual

William A. Galston *is Professor at the University of Maryland's School of Public Affairs and Director of the University's Institute for Philosophy and Public Policy. He is currently serving as Executive Director of the National Commission on Civic Renewal.*

morality in the 1920s, these scholars might have suspected that television's unintended consequences would turn out to be at least as significant as its directly contemplated purposes. But they would have been hard-pressed to move much beyond this general insight to hypotheses with predictive power. The insertion of a powerful new communications medium into a complex social system was bound to reconfigure everything from intimate relations to the distribution of public power. But how, exactly?

According to Alan Ehrenhalt, the front stoop was one of the centers of social life in Chicago's blue-collar neighborhoods of the early 1950s. But during that decade, the penetration of television into nearly every home affected not only the dissemination of news and entertainment, but also patterns of social interaction. Families spent more time clustered around the television set, and less talking with their neighbors on the street. In turn, the increased atomization of social life had important ripple-effects. Spontaneous neighborhood oversight and discipline of children became harder to maintain, and less densely populated streets opened the door for increased criminal activities.[1]

I don't mean to suggest (nor does Ehrenhalt) that television was solely responsible for these changes; the advent of air-conditioning also helped depopulate streets by making the indoors far more habitable during summer's dog-days. I do want to suggest that it's roughly 1952 for the Internet and that the methodological problems I just sketched are the ones we face today.

In the face of such challenges, it is natural, perhaps inevitable, that our thought will prove less flexible and our imagination less capacious than the future we seek to capture. In our mind's eye, we may hold constant what will prove to be most mutable. One of my favorite examples of this (there are many) comes from an article published in the *St. Louis Globe-Democrat* in 1888:

> The time is not far distant when we will have wagons driving around with casks and jars of stored electricity, just as we have milk and bread wagons at present. . . . The arrangements will be of such a character that houses can be supplied with enough stored electricity to last twenty-four hours. All that the man in the cask will have to do will be to drive up to the back door, detach the cask left the day before, replace it with a new one, and then go to the next house and do likewise.[2]

As Carolyn Marvin points out, this vision of the future reflects the assumption of, and hope for, the continuation of the economically and morally self-sufficient household, unbeholden to outside forces, productively and privately going about its own business—a way of life undermined by the very patterns of distribution and concentration that electrical power helped foster.

I draw two lessons from this cautionary example. First, in speculating about the impact of the Internet on community life, we should be sensitive to the often surprising ways in which market forces can shape emerging technologies to upset entrenched social patterns. (This maxim is particularly important for an era such as ours in which the market is practically and ideologically ascendent.) And, second, we should be as self-conscious as possible about the cultural assumptions and trends that will shape the way we use, and respond to, new technologies such as the Internet. In this connection, I want to suggest that contemporary American society is structured by two principal cultural forces: the high value attached to individual choice and the longing for community.

Choice and Community

Scholars in a range of disciplines have traced the rise during the past generation of choice as a core value. Daniel Yankelovich suggests that what he calls the "affluence effect"—the psychology of prosperity that emerged as memories of the Depression faded—weakened traditional restraints:

> People came to feel that questions of how to live and with whom to live were a matter of individual choice not to be governed by restrictive norms. As a nation, we came to experience the bonds to marriage, family, children, job, community, and country as constraints that were no longer necessary.[3]

In Alan Ehrenhalt's analysis, the new centrality of choice is a key explanation for the transformation of Chicago's neighborhoods since the 1950s.[4] Lawrence Friedman argues that individual choice is the central norm around which the modern American legal system has been restructured.[5] Alan Wolfe sees individual choice at the heart of the nonjudgmental tolerance that characterizes middle-class morality in contemporary America.[6]

The problem (emphasized by all these authors) is that as individual choice expands, the bonds linking us to others tend to weaken.[7] To the extent that the desire for satisfying human connections is a permanent feature of the human condition, the expansion of choice was bound to trigger an acute sense of loss, now expressed as a longing for community.[8] (The remarkable public response to Robert Putnam's "Bowling Alone" (in *Journal of Democracy* (January, 1995) 6:65–78.) can in part be attributed to this sentiment.) But few Americans are willing to surrender the expansive individual liberty they now enjoy, even in the name of stronger marriages, neighborhoods, or citizenship. This tension constitutes what many Americans experience as the central dilemma of our age: as Wolfe puts it, "how to be an autonomous person and tied together with others at the same time."[9]

I do not believe that this problem can ever be fully solved; to some extent, strong ties are bound to require compromises of autonomy, and vice versa. (This exemplifies Isaiah Berlin's pluralist account of our moral condition: the genuine goods of life are diverse and in tension with one another, so that no single good can be given pride of place without sacrificing others.) Still, there is an obvious motivation for reducing this tension as far as possible—that is, for finding ways of living that combine individual autonomy and strong social bonds.

This desire gives rise to a concept that I will call "voluntary community." This conception of social ties compatible with autonomy has three defining conditions: low barriers to entry; low barriers to exit; and interpersonal relations shaped by mutual adjustment rather than hierarchical authority or coercion. Part of the excitement surrounding the Internet is what some see as the possibility it offers of facilitating the formation of voluntary communities, so understood. Others doubt that the kinds of social ties likely to develop on the Internet can be adequate substitutes—practically or emotionally—for the traditional ties they purport to replace.

Are Online Groups "Communities"?

Writing thirty years ago, Licklider and Taylor suggested that "life will be happier for the online individual because the people with whom one interacts most strongly will be selected more by commonality of interests and goals than by accidents of proximity."[10] Whether Internet users are in fact happier and, if so, because they are users, remains to be seen and may never be known (the problems of research design for that issue

boggle the mind). The underlying hypothesis—that "accidents of proximity" are on balance a source of unhappiness—seems incomplete at
best. But Licklider and Taylor were certainly right to predict that online
communication would facilitate the growth of groups with shared interests. Indeed, participation in such groups is now the second most frequently interactive activity (behind e-mail) among online users.[11]

Anecdotal evidence suggests that these groups fill a range of significant needs for their participants. For some, the exchange of information and opinions about shared enthusiasms—e.g., rock groups, sports
teams—is satisfying as an end in itself. For others, this exchange serves
important personal or professional goals. Those suffering from specific
diseases can share information about promising doctors, therapies, and
treatment centers more widely and rapidly than ever before. A friend of
mine who works as the lone archivist in a city library system tells me
that participating in the online group of archivists from around the
country mitigates the otherwise intense sense of personal and professional isolation. In this sense, computer-mediated communication can
be understood as raising to a higher power the kinds of non place-
based relationships and associations that have existed for centuries in
industrialized societies.

But are these shared activities "communities"? What is at stake in
this question? One commentator skeptical of the claims of technocom-
munitarian enthusiasm argues:

> A community is more than a bunch of people distributed in all 24 time
> zones, sitting in their dens and pounding away on keyboards about the
> latest news in alt.music.indigo-girls. That's not a community; it's a fan
> club. Newsgroups, mailing lists, chat rooms—call them what you will—
> the Internet's virtual communities are not communities in almost any
> sense of the word. A community is people who have greater things in
> common than a fascination with a narrowly defined topic.[12]

Note that this objection revolves around the substance of what members of groups have in common, not the nature of the communication
among them. By this standard, stamp clubs meeting face to face would
not qualify as communities. Conversely, Jews in the diaspora would
constitute a community, even if the majority never meet one another
face to face, because what they have in common is a sacred text and its
competing interpretations as authoritative guides to the totality of tem-
poral and spiritual existence.

To assess these claims, we may begin with Thomas Bender's classic definition of community:

> A community involves a limited number of people in a somewhat restricted social space or network held together by shared understandings and a sense of obligation. Relationships are close, often intimate, and usually face to face. Individuals are bound together by affective or emotional ties rather than by a perception of individual self-interest. There is a "we-ness" in a community; one is a member.[13]

Upper-middle-class American professionals tend to dismiss this picture of community as the idealization of a past that never was. But Bender insists that it offers a tolerably accurate picture of town life in America prior to the twentieth century:

> [T]he town was the most important container for the social lives of men and women, and community was found within it. . . . The geographic place seems to have provided a supportive human surround that can be visualized in the image of concentric circles. . . . The innermost ring encompassed kin, while the second represented friends who were treated as kin. Here was the core experience of community. Beyond these rings were two others: those with whom one dealt regularly and thus knew, and, finally, those people who were recognized as members of the town but who were not necessarily known.[14]

A recent personal experience has convinced me that community, so understood, is not only a part of a vanished past. On a recent trip to Portugal, my family stopped for the night at the small town of Condeixa, about ten miles south of the medieval university of Coimbra. After dinner I went to the village square, where I spent one of the most remarkable evenings of my life. Children frolicked on playground equipment set up in the square. Parents occupied some of the benches positioned under symmetrical rows of trees; on others, old men sat and talked animatedly. At one point a group of middle-aged men, some carrying portfolios of papers, converged on the square and discussed what seemed to be some business or local matter. The square was ringed by modest cafés and restaurants, some catering to teenagers and young adults, others to parents and families. From time to time a squabble would break out among the children playing in the square; a parent would leave a café table, smooth over the conflict, and return to the adult conversation. As I was walking around the perimeter of the square, I heard some singing. Following the sound, I peered into the small Catholic church on the corner and discovered a young people's choir rehearsing for what a poster on the next block informed me was a forthcoming town festival in honor of St. Peter.

Many aspects of this experience struck me forcibly, particularly the sense of order, tranquility, and human connection based on years of mutual familiarity, stable social patterns, and shared experience. I was not surprised to learn subsequently that about half of all young people born in Portuguese small towns choose to remain there throughout their adult lives—a far higher percentage than for small-town youth in any other nation of western Europe.

Bender's examples of community (and my own) are place-based. But it is important not to build place, or face-to-face relationships, into the definition of community. To do this would be to resolve by fiat, in the negative, the relationship between community and the Internet. Instead, I suggest that we focus on the four key structural features of community implied by Bender's account—limited membership, shared norms, affective ties, and a sense of mutual obligation—and investigate, as empirical questions, their relationship to computer-mediated communication.

Limited membership

While technical restrictions do exist and are sometimes employed, a typical feature of online groups is weak control over the admission of new participants. Anecdotal evidence suggests that many founding members of online groups experience the rapid influx of newer members as a loss of intimacy and dilution of the qualities that initially made their corner of cyberspace attractive. Some break away and start new groups in an effort to recapture the original experience.

Weak control over membership is not confined to electronic groups, of course. Up to the early 1840s, for example, Boston was conspicuous among American cities for the relative stability and homogeneity of its population, which contributed to what outside observers saw as the communitarian intimacy and solidarity of Boston society. And then, in the single year of 1847, more than 37,000 immigrants arrived in a city of less than 115,000. By the mid-1850s, more than one third of its population was Irish. Boston was riven, with consequences that were to persist for more than a century.[15]

While many kinds of groups can undergo rapid changes of membership, they may respond differently. In a famous discussion, Albert Hirschman distinguishes between two kinds of responses—exit and voice—to discontent within organizations. "Exit" is the act of shifting membership to new organizations that better meet our needs, while "voice" is the effort to alter the character of the organizations to which we already belong. Exit is, broadly speaking, marketlike behavior, while voice is political.

An hypothesis: when barriers to leaving old groups and joining new ones are relatively low, exit will tend to be the preferred option; as these costs rise, the exercise of voice becomes more likely. Because it is a structural feature of most online groups that border-crossings are cheap, exit will be the predominant response to dissatisfaction. If so, it is unlikely that online groups will serve as significant training grounds for the exercise of voice—a traditional function of Tocquevillian associations. In Boston, by contrast, because the perceived cost of exit was high, the Brahmins stayed put and struggled with the Irish for a hundred years, a tension that helped develop one of this country's richest political traditions.

In a diverse democratic society, politics requires the ability to deliberate, and compromise, with individuals unlike oneself. When we find ourselves living cheek by jowl with neighbors with whom we differ but from whose propinquity we cannot easily escape, we have powerful incentives to develop modes of accommodation. On the other hand, the ready availability of exit tends to produce internally homogeneous groups that may not even talk with one another and that lack incentives to develop shared understandings across their differences. One of the great problems of contemporary American society and politics is the proliferation of narrow groups and the weakening of structures that create incentives for accommodation. It is hard to see how the multiplication of online groups will improve this situation.

Shared norms

A different picture emerges when we turn our attention from intergroup communication to the internal life of online groups. Some case-studies suggest that online groups can develop complex systems of internalized norms. These norms arise in response to three kinds of imperatives: promoting shared purposes; safeguarding the quality of group discussion; and managing scarce resources in what can be conceptualized as a virtual commons.[16]

As Elinor Ostrom has argued, the problem of regulating a commons for collective advantage can be solved through a wide range of institutional arrangements other than private property rights or coercive central authority.[17] Internet groups rely to an unusual degree on norms that evolve through iteration over time and are enforced through moral suasion and group disapproval of conspicuous violators. This suggests that despite the anarcho-libertarianism frequently attributed to Internet users, the medium is capable of promoting a kind of socialization and moral learning through mutual adjustment.

I know of no systematic research exploring these moral effects of group online activities and their consequences (if any) for offline social and political behavior. One obvious hypothesis is that to the extent that young online users come to regard the internal structure of their groups as models for offline social and political groups, they would be drawn to (or demand) more participatory organizations whose norms are enforced consensually and informally. If so, it would be important to determine the extent to which this structure reflects the special imperatives of organizations where barriers to entrance and exit are low. The ideal of voluntary community reinforced by the Internet is likely to run up against the coercive requisites of majoritarian politics.

Affective ties

Proponents of computer-mediated communication as the source of new communities focus on the development of affective ties among online group members. One of the gurus of virtual community, Howard Rheingold, asks whether telecommunication culture is "capable of becoming more than . . . 'pseudocommunity,' where people lack the genuine personal commitments to one another that form the bedrock of genuine community?"[18] He defines virtual communities as "social aggregations that emerge from the Net when enough people carry on . . . public discussions long enough, with sufficient human feeling, to form webs of personal relationships."[19]

In this connection, the crucial empirical question is the relationship between face-to-face communication (or its absence) and the development of affective ties. How important are visual and tonal cues? How important is it to have some way of comparing words and deeds? Here's one hypothesis: it is impossible to create ties of depth and significance between A and B without each being able to assess the purposes and dispositions that underlie the other's verbal communications. Is the interlocutor sincere or duplicitous? Does he really care about me, or is he merely manipulating my desire for connection to achieve (unstated) purposes of his own? Does the overall persona an interlocutor presents to me seem genuine or constructed? We all rely on a range of nonverbal evidence to reduce (if never quite eliminate) our qualms about others' motivations and identities.

Internet enthusiasts respond to these questions by deconstructing the ideal of face-to-face communication. They point out (correctly) that duplicity and manipulation have been enduring facts of human history and the advent of computer-mediated communication raises at most questions of degree rather than kind.[20] I must confess that I come away unconvinced. Considerable evidence suggests that the Internet facilitates the invention of online personalities at odds with offline realities and that the ability to simulate identities is one of its most attractive features for many users (gender-bending is said to be especially popular). But the playful exercise of the imagination, whatever its intrinsic merits and charms, is not readily compatible with the development of meaningful affective ties. (Devotees of what might be called postmodern psychology, with its emphasis on social construction and *bricolage* and rejection of the distinction between surface and depth, might want to quarrel with this. So be it. I see no way of discussing affective ties without invoking some distinction between genuine and spurious emotions and identities.)

Another hotly debated issue is the relationship between computer-mediated communication and the tendency to express strong sentiments in antisocial ways. Some researchers have argued that because the absence of visual and tonal cues makes it more difficult to see the pain words can inflict, the Internet reduces restraints on verbal behavior and invites individuals to communicate in impulsive ways. (An analogy would be the asserted desensitizing effects of high-altitude bombing.) Other researchers argue that it is precisely the absence of traditional cues that promotes the formation of social norms for Internet speech and that there is no evidence that this speech is more antisocial on average than is face-to-face communication.[21]

Given the fragmentary evidence, I see no way of resolving this debate right now. But speaking anecdotally, the controversy and bitterness stirred up by comments on my synagogue's recently established ListServ suggests to me that the pessimists may have the stronger case. Once an initial provocation occurs, the nature of the medium makes it easy to escalate the dispute in ways that might be muted in a face-to-face group. (Full disclosure: on the basis of past controversies, some members of my synagogue believe that face-to-face exchanges on the disputed topics would have been equally uncivil.)

Mutual obligation

The final dimension of community to be considered is the development of a sense of mutual obligation among members. Recall John Winthrop's famous depiction of the communal ideal aboard the *Arbella*:

> We must entertain each other in brotherly affection, we must be willing to abridge ourselves of our superfluities, for the supply of others' necessities. . . . We must delight in each other, make others' conditions our own, rejoice together, mourn together, labor and suffer together.

While this may seem too demanding, at the very least community requires some heightened identification with other members that engenders a willingness to sacrifice on their behalf.

The technology critic Neil Postman argues that whatever may be the case with norms and emotions, there's no evidence that participants in online groups develop a meaningful sense of reciprocal responsibility or mutual obligation. Groups formed out of common interests need not develop obligations because by definition the interest of each individual is served by participating in the group. (If that ceases to be the case, it is almost costless to leave the group.) The problem is that bonds created by "interests" (in either sense of the term) provide no basis for the surrender of interests—that is, for sacrifice.[22]

I find it intriguing that many defenders of online groups concede Postman's factual premise but deny its normative relevance. Nessim Watson, for example, argues that communities characterized by a strong sense of mutual obligation have virtually disappeared in contemporary America; to single out online groups for criticism on this score is both unfair and an exercise in nostalgia. Efforts to resuscitate the obsolescent idea of mutual obligation are likely to prove counterproductive:

> Those who champion Postman's noble metaphor of community as common obligation are most often faced with the task of dragging other community members kicking and screaming into their part of the obligation. Attempts to construct community usually result in the increased frustration of organizers and the increased cynicism of participants toward the entire idea of community.

In late twentieth-century America, Watson concludes, there is no alternative to voluntary community based on perceptions of individual interest; we will have to get along as best we can without antique norms and practices of sacrifice and mutual obligation.[23]

I very much doubt that our society—or any society—can indefinitely do without these civic virtues.[24] The question of whether emerging forms of group activity help foster these virtues or reinforce their absence is likely to prove significant for the future. The magnitude of the impact will depend in part on the consequences of online activities for more traditional forms of group activity. I now turn to that question.

Online Groups and Traditional Communities

In a 1996 Survey of Civic Involvement with 1500 respondents, the AARP explored current community understandings and practices. One of the survey questions reads:

> We often hear people talking about some community, or about things going on in their communities. If I were to ask you about "your community," what community would come to mind?

Up to three separate responses were permitted and recorded. Only 15 percent of respondents failed to offer any example of what they considered to be a community.

The AARP results make it clear that for most people, community is still a territorial concept: 35 percent cited village, town, city, or county; 30 percent mentioned neighborhood, subdivision, or street. Overall, 59 percent of the entire sample offered one or more territorial examples of community.

Formal organizations and voluntary associations (Tocquevillian America or, if you like, Putnamville) were cited by 34 percent of all respondents. Twenty-nine percent mentioned churches or faith-based organizations; no other type of association was mentioned by as many as 4 percent of respondents.

Informal and "abstract" groupings and collectivities also came up frequently, with at least one example cited by 39 percent of all respondents.

Table 1. Defining Community	
Communities	Percent
Professional/occupational groups	20
Friends/social relations	11
School communities	7
Faith communities	4
Recreational/sports groups	3
Racial/ethnic groups	3
Lifestyle/sexual preference groups	2

Source: AARP Survey of Civic Involvement

The authors of the survey note that although percentages of respondents mentioned non-place-based examples of community, electronic information groups were conspicuous by their absence:

> Although the majority of respondents say they have used a computer in the past year, computer groups or people with whom they connect by computer were almost never mentioned directly by our respondents. Surely many respondents are starting to use their computers and the Internet to communicate with some of the others in their communities, whether geographically or socially defined; but they have not come to think of the computer network itself as a significant form of community in its own right.[25]

Young adults are significantly less likely to cite place-based and formal organizations than are other adults, and significantly more likely to cite informal organizations. (They are also somewhat more likely to feel distant from all forms of community.) (See Table 2.)

Among the computer users in the sample, those who participated in computer-mediated communication (e-mail or chat groups) were significantly lower in community attachment than those who have not done so. This would appear to suggest that for some users, computer-mediated communication serves as a replacement for more traditional,

Table 2. Communities Cited by Different Age Groups				
	Age			
Type of community	18–30	31–49	50–70	71+
Place	47.6%	63.6%	65.0%	56.1%
Formal organizations	24.5%	35.9%	39.2%	41.1%
Informal organizations	54.3%	36.2%	34.3%	23.9%
None	18.4%	14.3%	12.8%	17.1%

Source: AARP Survey of Civic Involvement

local forms of attachment. On closer inspection, this result is entirely a function of the fact that young adults are more frequent online users and less attached to localities.[26] The question for the future is whether this pattern will persist as today's cohort of young adults, who have postponed marriage and permanent employment far longer than did their parents and grandparents, enter into the kinds of personal and economic relationships that historically have been correlated with place-based ties.[27]

The AARP survey defined an Index of Social Involvement based on level of self-reported activity in ten key activities. With an index range of 0 to 19, the average American scored 6.3. Sixty-three percent of respondents had used a computer during the past year; they had an average score of 6.7, versus 5.6 for nonusers. (There was no significant difference between those who used computers for some mode of computer-mediated communication and those who used them for noncommunicative activities such as wordprocessing or solitary games.) After taking age, education, and income into account, computer usage had a "[statistically] significant but small effect" on social involvement.[28]

In sum, the AARP survey suggests that online groups have not had a strong generalized effect on either the theory or practice of community in America. There is evidence, however, of shifts among young adults. If this proves to be a generational effect and not merely a life-cycle effect (the jury is still out), then some of the characteristics of online groups discussed earlier in this paper could over time have a significant impact on American society.

Conclusion

I conclude by restating what appears to me to be the central question. Many Americans today are looking for ways of reconciling powerful but often conflicting desires for autonomy and connection. The idea of voluntary community draws its appeal from that quest: if we are linked to others by choice rather than accident, if our interaction with them is shaped by mutual adjustment rather than hierarchical authority, and if we can set aside these bonds whenever they clash with our individual interests, then the lamb of connection can lie down with the lion of autonomy. Online groups are paradigmatic examples of voluntary community—whence the enthusiasm they have aroused in many quarters.

It is far too early to know what kinds of effects they will have over time on the relations between individuals and communities in America. But three kinds of structural doubts can be raised about the civic consequences of voluntary communities. Because they give pride of place to exit, they do not promote the development of voice; because they emphasize mutual adjustment, they do not acknowledge the need for authority; because they are brought together and held together by converging individual interests, they neither foster mutual obligation nor lay the basis for sacrifice.

In today's cultural climate, the response to these doubts is obvious: anything less than voluntary community will trap individuals in webs of oppressive relations. And what could be worse than that? My answer: learning to make the best of circumstances one has not chosen is part of what it means to be a good citizen and mature human being. We should not organize our lives around the fantasy that entrance and exit can always be cost-free. Online groups can fulfill important emotional and utilitarian needs. But they must not be taken as comprehensive models of a future society.

Endnotes

1. Alan Ehrenhalt, *The Lost City: Discovering the Forgotten Virtues of Community in the Chicago of the 1950s* (New York: Basic, 1995), chaps. 4 and 12.

2. Carolyn Marvin, *When Old Technologies Were New: Thinking About Communications in the Late Nineteenth Century* (New York: Oxford, 1988), p. 77.

3. Daniel Yankelovich, "How Changes in the Economy Are Reshaping American Values," in Henry J. Aaron, Thomas E. Mann, and Timothy Taylor, eds., *Values and Public Policy* (Washington, DC: Brookings, 1994).

4. *The Lost City,* chaps. 12 and 13.

5. Lawrence Friedman, *The Republic of Choice: Law, Authority, and Culture* (Cambridge, MA: Harvard University Press, 1990).

6. Alan Wolfe, One Nation, After All (New York: Viking, 1998).

7. An influential formulation of this tension is found in Ralf Dahrendorf's *Life Chances: Approaches to Social and Political Theory* (London: Weidenfeld and Nicolson, 1979). Yankelovich summarizes his argument as follows:

   > Dahrendorf sees all historic shifts in Western culture as efforts to balance *choices* and *bonds*. Choices enhance individualism and personal freedom; bonds strengthen social cohesiveness and stability. In societies where the bonds that link people to one another and to institutions are rigid, the individual's freedom of choice is limited. As people struggle to enlarge their sphere of choice, the bonds that bind them together slacken. ("How Changes in the Economy Are Reshaping American Values," p. 20)

8. A sign of this: A recent survey asked Americans which decade in they past half century they would most prefer to live in if they could. In every age cohort, the 1950s proved to be the most popular choice.

9. *One Nation, After All*, p. 132.

10. Quoted in Steven G. Jones, ed., *Virtual Culture: Identity & Communication in Cybersociety*, (Thousand Oaks, CA: Sage, 1977) p. 10.

11. "Technology and On-line Use Survey," The Pew Center for the People and the Press," 1996; cited in Pippa Norris, "Who Surfs? New Technology, Old Voters, and Virtual Democracy in America," p. 71, this volume.

12. J. Snyder, "Get Real," *Internet World* 7, 2 (1996): 92–94.

13. Thomas Bender, *Community and Social Change in America* (Baltimore: Johns Hopkins, 1982), pp. 7–8; emphasis added.

14. Bender, p. 99.

15. See Doris Kearns Goodwin, *The Fitzgeralds and the Kennedys: An American Saga* (New York: St. Martin's, 1987), chapter 3.

16. Margaret McLaughlin, Kerry K. Osborne, and Christine B. Smith, "Standards of Conduct on Usenet" and Nancy K. Baym, "The Emergence of Community in Computer-Mediated Community," both in Steven G. Jones, ed., *Cybersociety: Computer-Mediated Communication and Community* (Thousand Oaks, CA: Sage, 1995); and Nessim Watson, "Why We

Argue about Virtual Community: A Case Study of the Phish.Net Fan Community," Jones, ed., *Virtual Culture: Identity & Communication in Cybersociety.*

17. Elinor Ostrom, *Governing the Commons: The Evolution of Institutions for Collective Action* (New York: Cambridge University Press, 1990).

18. Quoted in Jones, *Cybersociety*, p. 24.

19. Quoted in Jones, *Virtual Culture*, p. 121.

20. For a discussion along these lines, see Jones, *Cybersociety*, pp. 27–30.

21. For a summary and discussion, see Guiseppe Mantovani, *New Communication Environments: From Everyday to Virtual* (London: Taylor & Francis, 1996), pp. 98–101.

22. See especially Neil Postman, *Technopoly: The Surrender of Culture to Technology* (New York: Vintage, 1993).

23. Nessim Watson, "Why We Argue about Virtual Community."

24. For the reasons why, see Galston, *Liberal Purposes: Goods, Virtues, and Diversity in the Liberal State* (New York: Cambridge University Press, 1991), chap. 10.

25. Thomas M. Guterbock and John C. Fries, "Maintaining America's Social Fabric: The AARP Survey of Civic Involvement," (University of Virginia: Center for Survey Research, 1997).

26. AARP Survey, pp. 44–45.

27. The AARP Survey also finds that computer usage is positively correlated with organizational membership and that among computer users, those who participate in computer-mediated communication on average join more groups than those who do not. In addition, computer users are more likely to engage in informal volunteer activities than are nonusers (pp. 63–64, 81). These results remain statistically significant after correcting for background variable such as income and education.

28. AARP Survey, p. 24.

COMMUNITY CONSIDERED

<L. Jean Camp>

W hat is a community? What purposes have communities served and failed to serve? How can electronic communities serve or fail to serve these needs?

I am not a scholar of communities. However, it appears that the accompanying evaluation implies several functions of communities: companionship, logistical support, trust evaluations, and prevention of ideological isolation. I argue that only in logistical support do Internet communities fail to match or exceed geographical communities.

First a point: there are different types of communities on the Internet. There are chat areas, often with Web-based interfaces. There are d-lists, both open and closed. There are Usenet forums, technical, political, and social, and within each category examples which are moderated or riotous. These all have different characteristics.

Companionship

In terms of emotional support the Internet can match the real-world community. In fact, because of limits of membership, costs of entry, and costs of exit the Internet is superior to real-world communities in terms of emotional support.

Obtaining the emotional support offered by a community usually requires conforming to a community norm. Consider those who deviate from the sometimes arbitrary community norm, either by choice or

Jean Camp *is an Assistant Professor of Public Policy at Harvard University's John F. Kennedy School of Government, where her core research interest is electronic civil liberties, primarily speech and privacy. She is the author of* Risk and Trust in Internet Commerce *forthcoming from MIT Press.*

by inherent characteristic. Such people must pay the high price of exit from one geographical community, leave home completely, and find another community at some risk of never achieving unity. The feminist of the twenties, the gay man of the fifties, the person with AIDS today all may find themselves isolated in their physical homes of choice. The offer of supportive companionship is conditional in a traditional community. Yet the different, the ill, the radical, and passionate lovers of the obscure can all find companionship on the Net.

In many cases, there are people who simply cannot conform to the entry requirements for a community. In the ideal community of Portugal, would a poor refugee from Africa be accepted? In this case geographical community is elusive; the membership is not expensive but impossible.

There are three advantages for electronic communities. First, many of the demographic characteristics that have been the basis for exclusion in physical communities are not easy to detect in electronic communities. Second, once excluded, a person can change identities and return with some ease on the Internet. Thus exclusion is difficult, since cost of entry is low. Third, sudden life changes need not require physical changes to obtain support. For example, having children, getting a promotion, contracting a disease, or losing a family member all create new requirements for emotional support. Communities to support people as their lives change exist on the Internet. For example, there is a mailing list for women based on month/year of infant due date. This is an instant cohort, who will go through the travails of parenting together.

Electronic communities can also exclude. Subgroups of Usenet subscribers form private (closed) lists. People get unsubscribed even from open d-lists. Specific domains (most notably cmu.edu or mit.edu) get excluded from some Internet chats (because of the combination of technical skills and less lofty manners). Individuals get excluded from Usenet groups from the sheer force of group loathing, or by every regular contributor putting the person in his or her kill file. (A kill file filters incoming mail so that mail with certain attributes, e.g., the name of the sender, is transferred automatically and unseen to trash. On LotusNotes this would be an "agent.") Yet on the Internet even the strangest one can always find a community that will accept the odd one as part of the norm. If you are one in a million there were at least 33 of you on the Internet last year.

The essay on which I comment, "Community Considered," notes that the difficulty of exit is what makes communities valuable. This argument suggests that difficulty of exit creates constraints on behaviors, and makes communities stable. It is not the difficulty of exit but also the difficulty of entry that defines traditional communities. The difficulty of exit also allows the community to enforce arbitrary or unjust standards.

In stable geographical communities there can be very high entry costs. In these communities people are often judged by their families. Thus changing communities can be impossible, with the new immigrant hoping that the children are then accepted. The cost of exit in an on-line community is equal to the loss of that community. That is, when you leave you lose exactly what you got from that community, nothing more or less.

Logistical Support

In this one area the Internet fails most grievously. However, advances in the service industry have made some level of distance logistical support possible.

Let me take one example—my own long term Internet community. It is admittedly a fairly wired group of people. The focus of this group is on balancing work and family. This group provides much companionship. We share information about jobs, dates, marriages, divorces, pregnancy, and, of course, child care. We share family fights. One friend spent her first stage labor on line, and we shared her excitement asynchronously.

We have provided for each other during difficulties. In Boston, Phoenix, and the Bay Area there are subgroups which also have geographical community. These formed from the electronic community. However there are many lone midwestern and western subscribers. These people have found support not only in the form of email. There is also 1-800-FLOWERS and phone calls. It is possible to fix dinner for a person across the country with the aid of a phone and a credit card. New York Cheesecakes can be shipped anywhere in America, even to Phoenix at 101°F.

Certainly there is more to logistical support than dropping by with dinner or sharing an opinion of that awful or awesome purchase. I can share recipes and shopping, but I have never held the children of my distant co-subscribers, nor can I get glass of water in Kansas at 5 A.M.

On this one dimension electronic communities do not excel. Yet this inability to provide logistic support is mitigated by the growth in the service industry. I cannot be there to hold a hand at 5 A.M. but I can have the house cleaned at 9 A.M. from three time zones away using a phone and a credit card.

Trust

One of the other issues argued in the original essay on community is that communities enable trust relationships. Yet I would argue that trust has traditionally been ill-served by community. Trust itself is now being transformed from a community-based social evaluation to an explicit evaluation. This is not a loss. In an informal evaluation people take cues which are meaningless in themselves, and discriminatory in the whole. People evaluate each other based on how similar they are to themselves: race, region of origin, physical attractiveness, charisma, and other completely meaningless information.

Trust will become more formal as communities become more electronic. Even if public key cryptography does not becomes ubiquitous, the mechanisms for determining trust now being developed will require explicit decision making. Person A must be approved by entity B for action Z before being trusted. Extending trust for action Z does not imply trust for action Y. This is a rational manner for distributing trust that will not be arbitrarily or consistently biased against one region or demographic group.

Fraud works not because of the Internet, but because we as humans extend trust for simply silly reasons. "Of course I trusted the neighbor with my child. I had borrowed his mower. He lives next door." Trust was distributed in an irrational manner far before the Internet was a gleam in the DOD's electronic eye. Ponzi did not require an Internet to prosper with his scheme. On the Internet, trust can be based on a formal evaluation of other's claims. The questions on the Internet are: What do you know; are your credentials in order; and what exactly are you trusted to do? The questions in community are: Who are you; what are your demographics; what is your personal and family history?

The transformation of trust has happened before. In an agrarian society economic trust is embodied as credit at the local store. Credit might be denied on the basis of race and gender, as these are community norms. Denial of credit in a community makes economic survival difficult. Now credit is provided through formal and quantitative risk evaluations. This makes credit easier to regulate, although I would by no means suggest that the biases of the people involved no longer play a role. Yet since the Fair Credit Reporting Act, gossip, claims against your family, or localized norms of behavior should not play a role.

Tolerance

The Internet has often been identified as a threat to diversity, in that it will create balkanized groups who cannot function together as a citizenry. That there is too much information does not mean that there will be less cohesion. First, the vision of cohesion is sometimes false. Second, increased information will mean more contact with abhorrent ideas.

Is balkanization truly a problem? Or is it only that with the Internet the many communities which previously consist of previously isolated and ignored individuals can come together? In the vision of the public square in Portugal it is important, and impossible, to see who is missing. All those voices together on the Internet can create babel, true, but to my mind this is preferable to silencing dissent.

In the past the ability to select information provided a few powerful media outlets and opinion makers the power to distribute such a powerful signal that all else was drowned out as noise. Thus, in matters economic and political, there has been some ability to create the future by predicting it. (This is an oft-noted difference between economic and weather models—the weather doesn't look at the forecast before deciding to go short on water.) This was a false cohesion and it exists no longer. The Internet is distribution. The same diversity of opinion existed before the Internet, yet a smaller group of individuals controlled the distribution process. The single town paper and the three television stations decided on appropriate headlines and content. In last November's elections the Republican's losses were small compared to the losses of the pundits. The opinion makers lost in 1998 more so than before.

Similarly, people disagree with opinion makers on the importance of apolitical matters. Without the Internet, and the ability to provide citizen feedback, the coverage of the Roswell anniversary* would likely

---

*Refers to the AAF's alleged recovery of remains of a UFO in Roswell, New Mexico, July 1947.

have dwarfed the coverage of *Sojourner* roving Mars. We would all be watching together, but who would be better for it?

There is some threat of separateness emerging but I argue that this threat will be undermined by the availability of those with whom you disagree, both because of the difficulty of censoring the Internet and because of the support the Internet provides marginal viewpoints.

Recall the isolated individual in the geographic community. The Internet offers that person the ability to find intellectual and spiritual community without leaving a geographical community (which may have strong family and/or economic ties). Such a lessening of isolation may mitigate the need to flee for a more supportive place, and thereby provide to geographical communities a diversity the communities might otherwise not tolerate.

There is also the annoying tendency of adolescents to investigate anything prohibited. Thus for the first time any thirteen year old is certain to be able to explore ideas which are abhorrent by community and parental standards. Young people can evaluate outcast groups as these groups represent themselves; and as the groups are represented by those who loathe them. To object to this reality is to assume that the all current moral standards are correct, that there is nothing to learn from open evaluation of the coming generations. It is also to undervalue that cherished marketplace of ideas.

Finally, Usenet forums do predispose individuals to flame wars yet they also allow those who would never interact to meet as previously discussed. A meeting between Act Up! and the Christian Coalition would be as fiery in real life as online, except that it would not happen. And when people talk some will, over time, acknowledge the humanity of the other. It is less difficult to advocate the extermination of a creature who is unknown than one with whom you have corresponded. Of course such a hope for world peace was extended at the dawn of the radio age, and proved ill-founded. I am not claiming such drastic powers for the Internet, that it can overcome greed and end conflict. But I believe that greater electronic connectivity will lead to greater human connectivity.

Summary

The normalization of trust and the formation of voluntary communities will drive social, governmental and business changes. Those changes won't be all bad. The previous chapter noted that a high percentage of Americans would like to live in America in the fifties. I would not. North Carolina was racially segregated, sexist, and un-air conditioned in the fifties. I look forward to changes in public morality and human comfort of the same order in the next four decades.

politics.com

WHO SURFS?

NEW TECHNOLOGY, OLD VOTERS & VIRTUAL DEMOCRACY

<Pippa Norris>

T
he more that Internet use explodes, the more hyperbole and hot air arises concerning its possible consequences for public life. Similar hopes and fears about the power of technology to transform democracy accompanied the rise of other media like the wireless, talkies, and television (see, for example, Douglas 1987). Systematic research has started to explore the impact of politics on the net for parties, candidates, and election campaigns; for new social movements, interest groups, and organizational activism; and for the policymaking process and governing in an information age (see, for example, McLean 1989; Budge 1996; Rash 1997; Bellamy and Taylor 1998; Hill and Hughes 1998; Davis and Owen 1998; Neuman 1998; Kamarck this volume).

This study considers the potential consequences of the Internet for civic engagement, in particular whether new technology will widen the pool of those who participate in politics, or whether it will *reinforce* the existing participation gap between the engaged and the apathetic? The

Pippa Norris *is the Associate Director for Research of the Joan Shorenstein Center on the Press, Politics and Public Policy and a lecturer at Harvard University's Kennedy School of Government. Her most recent book is* Critical Citizens: Global Support for Democratic Governance.

first section outlines the debate between mobilization and reinforcement theories of Internet activism. The second section goes on to analyze the social background and civic attitudes of activists in the 1996 and 1998 American elections. The political use of the Internet has grown sharply since it first became available in the early 1990s. This process has changed the typical profile of users. To monitor developments, evidence is drawn from a series of surveys conducted by The Pew Research Center for the People and the Press from 1995 to November 1998 (*). The conclusion considers the implications of the findings for the future of politics on the net and whether this new medium has the capacity to transform whose voices are heard in American democracy.

Mobilization and Reinforcement Theories

Interpretations about the potential for expanding political participation through the Internet differ sharply. On the one hand *mobilization* theories claim that use of the net will facilitate and encourage new forms of political activism. Enthusiasts such as Nicholas Negroponte (1995) and Michael Dertouzos (1997) believe virtual democracy promises a cornucopia of empowerment in a digital world. Schwartz (1996) emphasizes the potential for a virtual community. Rheingold (1993) argues that bulletin board systems are democratizing technologies, and are used to exchange ideas, mobilize the public, and strengthen social capital. Grossman (1995) anticipates the opportunities for shrinking the distance between governed and government using the new communication technology. Budge (1996) argues that the Web will facilitate direct democracy. The strongest claims of mobilization theories are that net activism represents a distinctive type of political participation which differs, in significant ways, from conventional activities like working for political parties, organizing grass-roots social movements, or lobbying elected officials. By sharply reducing the barriers to civic engagement, leveling some of the financial hurdles, and widening the opportunities for political debate, the dissemination of information, and group interaction, it is thought that more people will become involved in public life. For enthusiasts, the net promises to provide new forms of horizontal and vertical communication, which facilitate and enrich deliberation in the public sphere.

Yet in contrast *reinforcement* theories suggest use of the net will strengthen, but not radically transform, existing patterns of political participation. From this more skeptical perspective, this medium will serve to reinforce, and perhaps even widen, the participation gap between the have and have-nots. Owen and Davis (1998) concluded that the Internet does provide new sources of information for the politically interested, but given uneven levels of access there are good grounds to be skeptical about its transformative potential for democratic participation(Owen and Davis 1998:185). Murdock and Golding (1989) warn that the familiar socioeconomic biases which exist in nearly all conventional forms of political participation seem unlikely to disappear on the net, even if access gradually widens to the electronically disadvantaged. If so, the new medium may merely reproduce or even exacerbate the gap between the information-rich and information-poor. Hill and Hughes (1998:44) argue that Internet activists are self-selecting so that the Internet does not change people, it simply allows them to do the same things in a different way.

One reason why the Internet may reinforce existing patterns of participation is provided by the "uses and gratifications" perspective in political communications (Blumler and Katz 1974; Rubin 1994; McQuail 1997). This account stresses that, given varied media choices, the audience has certain predispositions and needs which motivates them to seek different programs and sources: people going out for the evening, for example, may turn to *Movielink.com*, those interested in socializing can go to an AOL chat room, while those wanting international news may listen to the online BBC *World Service*. The primary functions served by the media are those such as information-seeking, social companionship, and entertainment. This account may be particularly suitable for the Internet where, far more than with television or newspapers, users actively exercise choice (clicking to another Web site, joining a different user group, e-mailing colleagues), thereby controlling the communication process. This assumes that the choice of media sources is essentially purposive, fulfilling certain needs in the audience, rather than simply habitual (if we usually return to a few bookmarked sites), or incidental (if we surf at random).

There are therefore good reasons why both the mobilization and reinforcement theories may be plausible. In the midst of the rhetoric and conjecture it is difficult to find systematic evidence which can throw light on this debate. Given the pace of change in communications, with use of the Web growing by leaps and bounds, we cannot hope to have conclusive answers about future developments. Much depends upon the political and economic conditions, for example how far the public sector intervenes to level the playing field for access. Political activism on the net can also be expected to vary according to the electoral context, for example levels of participation may be different in low-key mid-term elections or in presidential contests. For all these reasons, we need to compare whether patterns of use in the 1996 election are maintained or changed in the 1998 contest.

Analyzing Net Activism

This study analyzes patterns of net activism in the United States from 1995 to November 1998, using evidence from the Pew Research Center for the People and the Press, which has carried out some of the richest surveys of Internet users based on oversampling the user community.[1] The June 1995 survey contained 997 online users, drawn from a representative telephone survey of the general population of 3,603. The October 1996 survey covered 1,003 online users. The November 1998 survey contained 1,993 Internet users drawn from a representative telephone survey of 3,184 adults. We also use the May 1998 Pew survey of Media Consumption (N.3002) and the November 1998 postelection Pew survey (N.1005) to understand Net activism in the midterm elections. People were questioned in these surveys about a wide range of media habits including use of old and new media, as well as about their political knowledge, partisanship, and political trust. The comparison of the 1996 and 1998 campaigns also allow us to compare patterns in the different environments created by presidential and midterm elections. These surveys allow us to explore four related issues:

- The first issue concerns *access and use*. Is the Internet in the process of becoming a new mass medium? In particular, how rapid has been the expansion from 1995–98 in Internet access and in political activism on the Net? If mobilization theories are correct then political use on the Net needs to spread beyond an elite minority into the general population.

- The second issue concerns whether the Net provides *alternative sources* of political information. If claims that the net will transform democracy are correct then online information should displace, not merely supplement, use of traditional news media.

- The third issue concerns the *social profile* of Net activists. Early studies commonly found that, compared with the general population,

Net users were overrepresented among those with higher education and income, among men, and among the younger generation (Davies and Owen 1998:156). Support for mobilization theories could be found if the social differentials evident in the mid-1990s have gradually closed as the user community has expanded.

- The last issue concerns the *political profile* of Net activists. In particular, compared with the electorate, are these users distinctive in their civic attitudes, such as their levels of political trust, knowledge, and interest? And are they different in their party preferences and policy attitudes?

Answers to these questions help us to understand whether Internet activism involves a distinctively new form of political participation, as mobilization theories suggest, or whether it represents "new wine in old bottles," as skeptics argue.

Has the Internet Become a New Mass Medium?

Mobilization theories assume that use of the Internet will expand so much within the next decade that it will eventually rival, and perhaps even overtake, the size of the audience for television and the printed press. The overall rate of growth online has been phenomenal: the number of Americans using online and Internet services has been doubling every twelve months for the past two years.[2] Pew surveys found that the proportion of Americans who ever went online to access the internet surged from 14 percent in 1995, to 23 percent in July 1996, 36 percent in November 1997, and 41 percent in November 1998. By November 1998, Pew estimated that over half of all Americans (57 percent) used a computer at home or at work, while 43 percent owned a computer, 35 percent used e-mail, and 13 percent had bought something online.[3]

Many believe that Internet use has been exploding worldwide but today access varies considerably across advanced industrialized societies, let alone among developing countries. In the 15-country European Union, the EuroBarometer estimates that about 12 percent of citizens had access to the Internet in spring 1998. But there are marked cross-national differences since the proportion was lowest in Greece (3 percent) and Portugal (6 percent) while in contrast about a third or more of all citizens has access in the more affluent countries of Denmark, Sweden, and Finland.[4] Therefore in the EU, at present only Scandinavia seems to reflect levels of access in the United States.[5]

Table 1. Regular Use of News Media by the General Public, May 1998.	Regular Users (%)
Read daily newspaper.	68
Watch local evening TV news.	64
Listen to radio news.	52
Watch network TV news (CBS, ABC, or NBC).	38
Watch TV news magazines (e.g. *60 Minutes, Dateline*).	37
Watch Weather Channel.	33
Go online at least once a week. (*)	→25
Morning TV news (e.g. Today Show, CBS This Morning).	23
Watch Cable News Network (CNN).	23
Go online to get news at least once a week.	→20
Go online to use discussion lists/chat groups. (*)	→20
News magazines (e.g. *Time, U.S. News, Newsweek*).	15
Listen to National Public Radio (NPR).	15
Watch TV tabloids (e.g. *Hard Copy, Inside Edition*).	14
Go online to get information about entertainment. (*)	→14
Watch daytime TV talk shows (e.g. *Jerry Springer*).	13
Listen to talk radio.	13
Watch CNBC.	12
Daytime TV talk shows.	10
Go online to get financial information. (*)	→10
Watch MSNBC.	8
Watch *Court TV*.	6
Watch MTV.	6
Listen to Rush Limbaugh's radio show.	5
Read business magazines (e.g. *Forbes, Fortune*).	5
Watch PBS *Newshour* with Jim Lehrer.	4
Listen to Howard Stern's radio show.	4
Watch C-SPAN.	4
Read print tabloids (e.g. *National Inquirer, The Sun*).	3

Note: Q: "Now I'd like to know how often you watch (or listen to or read) . . . Regularly, Sometimes, Hardly ever, Never." For online sources (*) the question was "Please tell me how often, if ever, you engage in each of the following online activities . . ." *Regular* use is defined as at least once a week.

Source: The Pew Research Center for the People and the Press Media Consumption survey using a nationwide sample of 3,002 adults f/w 24 April–11 May 1998.

The extent of the news revolution caused by this growth in the United States becomes apparent if we compare regular use of conventional and online media. Precise estimates about use of Internet news vary over time, as both news events and the way people think about Internet "news" continues to change. Nevertheless Pew surveys suggest that the percentage of Americans regularly getting news from the Internet (where "regularly" is defined as at least once a week) more than tripled over two years, rising from 11 million users in June 1995 to 36 million in May 1998, or *20 percent of all Americans*. As shown in Table 1, similar levels of use are evident among those who regularly go online to communicate with others via discussion lists and chat groups, while slightly fewer go online for entertainment news (14 percent) or financial information (10 percent). Within the space of just a few years, the regular audience for online news has become larger than for traditional media such as mainstream news magazines like *Time* and *Newsweek* (15 percent), listeners to talk radio (13 percent), let alone viewers of minority outlets like PBS *Newshour* or C-Span (4 percent).

The growth of the Net provides a major rival to traditional news media outlets. The most common activities which engage about two-thirds of all Americans continue to be reading a daily printed newspaper and watching the local evening TV news. The majority also regularly catch radio news sometime during the day and listenership has expanded during the last decade. In contrast network news has suffered a dramatic hemorrhage of viewers due to the fragmentation of cable and satellite stations, and the balkanization of the television audience: today just over a third (38 percent) regularly tune into Jennings, Brokaw, and Rather. The drop has been precipitate: according to Roper polls almost half of all households (48 percent) watched network news *every evening* in 1975, compared with one quarter in 1997 (Davis and Owen 1998:136). To some extent this merely reflects the dispersion of the network audience to cable and satellite, as people may now find MSNBC or CNBC more convenient for their schedules than NBC News at 6.30 P.M. But this phenomenon, combined with the growth of the Net, has clearly caused greater competition for the major networks.

Why Do People Go Online?

Therefore in America, in terms of the *size* of its total audience, the Internet can increasingly claim to be a mass medium. This supports the transformative potential of this means of communication. But is there a common experience of the Net, so that we can talk about the effects of exposure to being online, much as we might discuss the influence of network news, violent movies, or talk radio? If so, then it is legitimate to generalize, as both sides of the debate often do, about the experience and attitudes of "online users." Yet the fragmentation and segmentation of the Web, and the myriad of uses which the Internet can serve, means that perhaps we need a more cautious approach. Given the choices about where to go and what to do in the digital world, the question arises whether we have a shared experience of the Web at all and therefore whether it is part of a mass media in the conventional sense.

The need to refine our concepts of Net users may be particularly important for types of Net political activism. It is generally agreed that political participation is not a single and uniform activity, but rather a multidimensional phenomenon (Verba and Nie 1972; Verba, Nie, and Kim 1978; Verba, Schlozman, and Brady 1996). That is, people who regularly donate money to campaigns, or contact their congressional representative, are not necessarily involved in other dimensions like party work or community activism. There are different costs and benefits associated with different types of participation. The main categories distinguished by Verba and his colleagues concern voting, campaign work, communal activity, and contact specialists. In addition a few citizens are active across all dimensions, while some are involved in none.

Following this approach, participation in virtual democracy on the Internet can be understood to involve many different types of activity. Someone checking the Web pages of the Christian Coalition, or reading Time/CNN's *AllPolitics*, for example, may be engaged in a different sort of activity to someone discussing l'affaire Lewinsky in user groups or e-mailing colleagues about the time of a community meeting. To explore the dimensions of Net use the Pew surveys asked users about how often, if at all, they engage in a wide variety of activities, such as getting information about movies, travel, or the Dow Jones, chatting with people in online forums, and engaging in political discussion. People were questioned about ten types of activity (see Appendix A for details) and we can map the overall pattern using factor analysis.

As shown in Table 2, in 1998 factor analysis revealed two distinct dimensions or types of activity on the Net. On the one hand *general users* were most interested in using the Net for news about current

Table 2. General and Political Online Users, 1998		
	Online Users	
Type of Activity	General Users	Political Activists
Go online for news/information on current events, public issues or politics.	.77	
Go online for news.	.76	
Get entertainment-related information e.g. movies, hobbies.	.59	
Get financial information such as stock quotes.	.57	
Send or receive e-mail.	.52	
Purchased goods or services online.	.49	
Get health or medical information.	.46	
Communicate with others through on-line forums, discussion lists.	.39	
Engage in online discussions about politics.		.85
Contact or e-mail groups or officials about political issues.		.82
Go online for information about the 1998 elections.		.55
% Variance	26	17

Note: The model uses Principal Component Factor Analysis with varimax rotation with Kaiser normalization suppressing coefficients below .35. See Appendix A for questions.

Source: The Pew Center for the People and the Press: Technology and Online Use Survey 1998 Oversample of online users N. 1993. F/w November 1998.

events, entertainment-related information about movies and hobbies, as well as financial information, using e-mail, buying goods online, practical guidance about health, and communicating via online discussion groups. Just as many people turn mainly to the sports results or television listings or stock market results in traditional newspapers, so people seek a wide range of "news," usually apolitical, on the Web.

While some of this activity may bring people in touch with public affairs, as people click from one topic to another, this process is more accidental than purposive. In contrast, *political activists* more often went online to engage in political discussions, to contact officials or groups about an issue, or to get specific information about the 1998 campaign. Therefore Net political activists who sought political information or communication can be categorized as a distinct group within the online user community, as in society.

Were the Internet political activists a small minority? We can compare the most common general types of Net activity, defined as those which occurred "at least one a week" among online users during the 1998 campaign. The pattern in Table 3 shows that the most popular general uses included e-mail (regularly used by almost three-quarters of online users) and work-related research (regularly used by almost half). Searching for information about politics and current events was the next most popular activity, used by 38 percent at least once a week. Yet more active forms of civic engagement were used by far fewer of those online in the 1998 campaign, including political discussion (used by 4 percent) and contacting officials or groups about politics (4 percent). The comparison of the 1996 and 1998 campaigns shows that the greatest increase in use has been in e-mailing, and there has also been some increase in the use of the Net to get entertainment-related and financial information. In contrast the proportions engaged in the more political types of activity hardly changed. Wider access to the Web seems to have expanded the audience for general interest subjects, such as information about the weather or movies, much more than the audience for political or international news.

What do we know about the minority (15 percent of all online users) who went online specifically to get information about the 1996 and 1998 elections? If we look more closely at the type of activities among this select group, we find that the most popular activities included getting information about a candidate's voting record, participating in an online poll, sending e-mail supporting or opposing candidates, downloading election information, and providing information such as e-mail or mailing addresses (see Table 4). But in all cases this activity involved less than 5 percent of the total online community, and therefore an even smaller proportion of the general electorate.

Clearly use of the Net will evolve further in subsequent elections. Like the early years of radio or television, access will gradually widen in

Table 3. Frequency of Activities, All Online Users, 1996–98

Type of Online Activity	At least once every week 1996 %	At least once every week 1998 %
Send e-mail.	64	72
Do research for work.	48	47
Get news on current events, public issues and politics.	39	38
Get entertainment-related information, e.g. movies, hobbies.	30	35
Get financial information.	23	28
Communicate via online forums, discussion lists, chat groups.	23	22
Do research for school.	22	14
Go online for information about the 1996 elections.	12	10
Get travel information.	10	12
Engage in online political discussions.	4	4
Contact groups and officials about political issues.	2	4

Source: The Pew Center for the People and the Press: Technology and Online Use Survey 1996. Oversample of on-line users N. 1003. F/w October 1996. Technology and Online Use Survey 1998 survey N. 1993 F/w November 1998.

the next decade. Different types of election—such as a more exciting and open presidential race in 2000—has the potential to stimulate greater public engagement. Candidates may also develop new ways to communicate interactively via the Web. The passive Web page, where people get vertical access to "top-down" information, much as they would from conventional political leaflets, is gradually being superseded by more active designs allowing horizontal communication among networks of citizens, and "bottom-up" feedback into the political process (Kamarck this volume). Nevertheless such interactivity seems likely to continue to appeal most to the small group of mobilized and interested

Table 4. Online Election Activities, 1996-98 (*)		
	1996	1998
Get information about a candidate's voting record.		30
Participate in an online poll.	34	26
Get or send e-mail supporting or opposing a candidate for office.		22
Download election information.	56	20
Provide information such as your e-mail/mailing address.	31	18
Participate in online discussions.	31	13
Get information about where and when to vote.		12

Note: (*)As a proportion of those who went online to get news or information about the 1998 elections (15 percent of the online user community). Q80. When you went online to get information about the elections, do/did you do any of the following . . .

Source: The Pew Center for the People and the Press: Technology and Online Use Survey 1996. Oversample of online users N. 1003. F/w October 1996. Technology and Online Use Survey 1998 survey N. 1993 F/w November 1998.

activists, rather than reaching citizens with lower levels of political efficacy and confidence. The proportion of Americans currently involved in any form of online election activity suggests the need for caution about the transformative capacity of the Web for democracy, at least in the short term. Online access and use has certainly expanded sharply in the last few years but the proportion of net political activists remains far smaller.

Does Online Information Displace Traditional News Media?

The most common political use of the Internet is to seek out information from a myriad of sources. But the question remains whether this represents a distinctive activity, as proponents of cyberdemocracy suggest. If people commonly browse the Web to consult political sources not available elsewhere, such as the candidate Web pages, nonpartisan organizations like Project Vote Smart, and official sites like the White House web page, then this could encourage more active citizenship. The unmediated quality of candidate and party information, and some attempts at interactivity, are also potentially different to the messages which have been filtered by the press. Just, Crigler, and Kern (1998) concluded that people typically browse several related sites on the Internet so that the Internet has real potential for making a broader range of topics and more diverse sources of information available to citizens. On the other hand, skeptics argue that many people are using the Net to access conventional media sources, like the *New York Times*, *USA Today*, or *Newsweek*, via the Internet not the newsstand. Previous studies have found that people who gravitate towards the online media were also likely to monitor the traditional media, so that there was considerable overlap (David and Owen 1988: 142; Hill and Hughes 1998:35). In this regard news is flowing through new channels, but it remains recognizably traditional journalism. This pattern alters *when* but not necessarily *what* we watch or read.

To examine whether online news sources displace, or supplement, traditional journalism, we can use the Pew 1998 survey to compare those who regularly use online and conventional news media. The correlation confirms that use of online news was weakly but significantly associated with use of newspaper (r=.08 p.>01) and radio news (r=.07 p.>01), but there was no significant association with use of television news. This pattern was even more evident among the smaller group of Net activists, who proved most interested in learning about the campaign from any available news media. There is also some direct evidence about this issue. Among people who regularly get news online, a few (11 percent) said they were using other media sources less often but this was more or less balanced by others (16 percent) who reported using other sources more often.

Additional evidence is available in Table 5, which looks at where people seeking political news went on the Web during the 1996 and 1998 campaigns. The most commonly visited sites were those for the old media: national newspapers and network TV. Cable TV sites were also popular. In contrast, candidate and official government sites proved slightly less popular, as did some of the nonprofit organization sites like Project Vote Smart or Policy.com. This pattern suggests that news is not necessarily a zero sum game: hearing an item about Viagra or Lewinsky on CNN can spark interest in going online to learn more about these stories, and vice versa.[6] In the short term the use of online news seems to supplement, rather than replace, conventional channels. In the long term, however, given the attractions of the Net for the younger generation, it remains unclear whether this pattern will be

Table 5. Web Sites Used for Political News, 1996–98		
	% Ever Visited Site 1996	% Ever Visited Site 1998
Network TV (CBS, NBC, ABC)	27	26
National newspaper sites (*Washington Post, New York Times, LA Times*)	38	23
CNN/Time AllPolitics	42	23
MSNBC	23	23
Local community Web site	20	22
Candidate Web site (*)		17
House of Representatives, Senate or White House (*)		13
C-SPAN	25	12
PBS Online		9
CQ American Voter '96	7	5
The Drudge Report (*)		4
Project Vote Smart or Web, White & Blue (**)		3
Policy.com (**)		3
Online only magazines like *Salon* or *Slate* (**)		2

Note: Only asked of those who got political news online. ** Not asked in a comparable way in 1996.

Source: The Pew Center for the People and the Press: Technology and Online Use Survey 1996. Oversample of online users N. 1003. F/w October 1996. The Pew Center for the People and the Press: Technology and Online Use Survey 1998. Oversample of online users N. 1993. F/w November 1998.

maintained in future decades or whether online sources will gradually come to replace older types of media production and distribution.

What Is the Social Profile of Online News Users?

For advocates of cyberdemocracy the opportunities provided by the Net will eventually lower the barriers to participation and widen access to those currently excluded from the policymaking process. The low costs of setting up a Web page, for example, and free e-mail, means that even a small organization with an imaginative and effective design can appear as professional on the Net as much larger rivals. Unlike costly TV ads, with Web pages smaller parties like the Libertarians or Greens can compete on a more or less level playing field with the Democrats or Republicans. Yet skeptics argue that the familiar socio-economic disparities in political participation, evident throughout public life, are unlikely to disappear on the Net (Murdock and Golding 1989). In the 1996 election online users displayed a clear pattern in their education, income, gender, and age. Online users in general, and online political activists in particular, were more likely than average to be well-educated, affluent, younger, and male (Davis and Owen 1998: 156; Hill and Hughes 1998: 29). Yet have these social differentials gradually closed over time as the audience has widened?

Table 6 shows the social profile of those who went online for news about politics during the 1998 campaign compared with the general electorate. The general trend has been for gradual closure of gender differences in online use in recent years, as women are found in greater numbers among new users. Nevertheless if we focus just on use of the Net for political news the results confirm a marked gender gap persists in 1998, a pattern which reflects the broader gender gap in conventional forms of civic engagement such as party membership and interest group activism (Flammang 1997). The online gender gap is most marked among the older generation, but it also persists among the under-thirties where young men are the most frequent online users.

There is also a significant generation gap among online news users, with the disparities particularly evident among the under-thirties and the over-sixties. One remarkable feature of the results is the predominance of young people seeking news online when this group is least likely to turn to traditional sources like newspapers. The May 1998 Pew survey found that among those in their twenties, more went online the previous day (38 percent) than read a newspaper (28 percent) or magazine (35 percent). In contrast this pattern was reversed among the older groups. If this represents a generational shift in news habits, as seems plausible, then the gradual process of cohort change may eventually produce a major change in how people get their news, whether inky linotype or wired. This provides some of the most important evidence in support of the mobilization thesis, if online information is now reaching the younger generation who are currently least engaged in the political process and least attentive to conventional news media.

Table 6. Social Profile of Online Elections News Users, 1998

Percent of Persons Receiving Election News or Information from Online Sources	None	Some	Significant
ALL	90	10	
GENDER			
Men	44	60	
Women	56	40	.31**
RACE			
White	85	88	
Nonwhite	9	10	
AGE			
20s	14	25	
30s	22	24	
40s	18	33	
50s	15	12	
60+	31	7	.37**
INCOME			
$75,000+	10	25	
$50,000–$74,999	14	17	
$40,000–$49,000	11	11	
$30,000–$39,999	11	8	
$20,000–$29,000	14	11	
<$20,000	15	5	.22**
EDUCATION			
College grad	25	39	
Some college	27	28	
High school or less	48	32	.24**
N.	1378	144	

Note: The coefficient of the association was measured by gamma. **=.01 *=.05

Source: The Pew Research Center Post-Election Survey November 1998

The disparities in terms of class and educational background confirm that online users remain atypical of the general public. In 1998 the most affluent (with a household income over $75,000) were more than twice as likely to seek news online as their proportion in the total electorate. In contrast the poorest groups, and those with high school education or less, remain strongly underrepresented among online news users. If we compare the background of online users in the 1996 and 1998 elections, the trends show income and educational disparities continue although they have closed slightly with the widening size of the online community. The familiar socioeconomic biases found in conventional forms of political participation like voting are therefore currently replicated in cyberdemocracy. The one exception to this usual pattern is found in terms of race, where the evidence shows that minorities are represented proportionally in the news online community.

What Are the Political Attitudes of Net Activists?

The mobilization thesis suggests that the new media will attract groups who might otherwise be uninvolved in conventional forms of activism, especially the younger generation who have low levels of voting turnout and civic engagement, and those who feel alienated from mainstream society. In contrast, skeptics argue that "to them that hath shall be given": the people most likely to prove motivated to communicate and organize via the Web are also those who probably would become most engaged in traditional forms of political activism in parties, groups, and lobbying (Hill and Hughes 1998: 43).

Table 7 compares the political attitudes of all online users and of Net political activists in the 1998 election.[7] The results confirm that Net activists tended to be higher-than-average consumers of all types of media news, including television and radio. Net activists also displayed particularly high levels of reported turnout: not surprisingly, those who were most motivated to seek out news about the election were far more willing to vote than the average online user. This pattern is clearly reflected also in levels of political knowledge: when asked which party had control of the House of Representatives Net political activists were more likely than the average online user to get the answer right. There were no significant differences between Net activists and general online users in levels of political and social trust.

Does use of online news have any impact on the outcome in terms of votes and, in particular, what are the characteristics of Net activists

Table 7: The Political Profile of Net Political Activists			
	All Online Users 1998	Net Political Activists	Sig.
Read paper yesterday.	70	76	.15**
Watched TV yesterday.	63	68	.11**
Listened to radio news yesterday.	47	51	.09**
Voted in 1998.	56	78	.46**
Voted Republican 1998.	42	44	
Voted Democrat 1998.	41	40	.04
Know GOP hold House.	62	80	.41**
Social trust: high	42	45	.04
Political trust: high	28	26	.02

Note: "Net Political Activists" are defined as those who engage in online discussions about politics, write, call, or e-mail groups or officials about political issues, or go online for information about the 1998 elections. The coefficient of the association was measured by (gamma. **=.01 *=.05)

Source: The Pew Research Center Online Technology Survey November 1998

in terms of their partisanship? The pattern in 1996 and 1998 shows that the group of Net activists proved similar to the online community as a whole in terms of their 1998 House vote. Nevertheless there was a significant difference between the online community and the general electorate in terms of approval of House Republicans where online users proved more positive (see Table 8). Moreover the pro-Republican partisanship of online users was not simply the product of the gender, income, and educational biases among the user community, since approval of congressional Republicans remained a significant factor in predicting online news use even after controlling for the social background of voters.

Conclusions and Discussion

For democracy, voices can be heard claiming that the Internet may produce the best of times, or perhaps the worst of times. The evidence serves to confirm an overall pattern of *reinforcement* rather than *mobilization*: Net political activists were already among the most motivated,

Table 8. Political Predictors of Online Election News Users, Nov. 1998

	Coefficient	S.E.	R	Sig
Gender	.90	.22	.14	.01
Age	.04	.00	.23	.01
Education	.15	.06	.07	.02
Income	.19	.05	.14	.01
Vote 1998	.27	.22	.00	.24
Approval of Congressional Republicans	.18	.08	.06	.02
Approval of President Clinton	.01	.10	.00	.97
Constant	.55	.70		
-2 log likelihood	843.59			
Goodness of fit	1316.07			
Nagelkerke R^2	.15			

Note: Logistic regression model with use of online news in the 1998 election as the dependent variable.

Source: The Pew Research Center Technology Online Surveys 6–10 November 1998.

informed, and interested in the electorate. In this sense, during recent campaigns the Net was essentially preaching to the converted. It still provided a valuable service in widening the range of information which was easily available during the campaign. But the Web seems to have been used more often as a means to access traditional news rather than as a radical new source of unmediated information and communication between citizens and their elected leaders. Whether the Internet has the capacity to reach beyond this group, and beyond these news sources, as access gradually ripples out to broader groups in the electorate, remains an open question.

Sweeping generalizations about the positive or negative effects of the digital age are common without distinguishing whether there is one online community or perhaps many. Previous studies have often assumed that there is a single type of experience associated with going online. Instead this essay argues that we need to distinguish different dimensions of Internet use. What this study suggests is that, while we may hope for a Virtual Democracy, with e-citizens becoming more politically engaged and informed, this activity may be confined to a minority. Some may choose to chat about Bill, the Bushes, or the budget, or, more realistically, Viagra, Monica, or Di; this does not necessarily click the mouse of other types of users. Only a few of the online community proved to be engaged in any form of political activity which can claim to be distinctively "new." Most online users are often using traditional journalistic outlets, like CNN or the *New York Times*, but from a more convenient source. Hence e-mails may gradually displace letters, Web pages may displace reference books, electronic newspapers may displace inky linotype. Communication flows through new channels, true. But will this have major political consequences for patterns of participation? In the midst of this process of change, prognostications would be foolhardy. We need systematic longitudinal panel studies examining changes in media use, and any subsequent impact in civic attitudes, to explore this process further. But there are persuasive grounds for skepticism about the more sweeping claims about the power of technology to change democracy as we know it. We all know that many tune-out from public affairs and go to MTV or the Home Shopping channel or the afternoon soaps. Given the fragmentation and choice of messages and activities available on the Net, users may never encounter politics in their Web bookmarks of choice. In this sense, although evolving into a mass medium in terms of numbers, the Net may never that status in terms of a shared political experience. My Internet—where I go, what I read, what I do—is not your Internet. Such a customized media environment is both empowering for users but also frustrating for analysts. In this sense, democracy.com looks more like anarchy than ABC News.

Endnotes

*   I am most grateful to Andrew Kohut and the Pew Research Center for the People and the Press for generous release of the survey data on online users. The main surveys are those of online users in 1995, 1996, and 1998, the May 1998 survey of the public's media consumption, and the November 1998 pre- and postelection surveys.

1. For details see *http://www.people-press.org.*

2. *The Statistical Abstract* of the United States estimated that in 1997 about one in seven adults logged onto the Net every month, rising to a fifth of all full-time workers and a third of all college graduates. See *http://www.census .gov/population/socdemo/computer*

3. "The Internet News Audience Goes Ordinary," The Pew Research Center January 16, 1999.

4. Eurobarometer 49 (Apr–May 1998). The survey asked *Do you have access to, or do you use . . . the Internet or the World Wide Web?* The survey estimated the following percentage with access to the Internet: EU-15 12 percent, Sweden 39 percent, Denmark 35 percent, Finland 31 percent, Netherlands 23 percent, UK 20 percent, Luxembourg 11 percent, Italy 9 percent, Belgium 9 percent, Germany 8 percent, Ireland 8 percent, Spain 8 percent, France 7 percent, Austria 7 percent, Portugal 6 percent, Greece 3 percent. For more details about the Information Society Project surveys see *http://www.ispo.cec.be/*

5. In Spring 1998 Mediamark Research estimated that sixty-two million adult Americans (31.9 percent) have any online Internet access at home or work while forty-four million (22.3 percent) used the Internet within the previous month. See *http://www.mediamark.com/*

6. Some evidence for this is provided in the May 1998 Pew survey where online users were asked *Have you ever gone online to follow-up or get more information on a news story you saw or heard in a newspaper or magazine or on TV?* In total 54 percent had done this, while 46 percent said they had not.

7. Unfortunately the evidence about public opinion on many of these items is not strictly comparable since it comes from different surveys. The comparisons which can be made can be found in "News Attracts Most Internet Users," The Pew Research Center for the People and the Press, December 16, 1996.

References

Bellamy, Christine and John A. Taylor. 1998. *Governing in the Information Age.* Buckingham: Open University.

Budge, Ian. 1996. *The New Challenge of Direct Democracy.* Oxford: Polity Press.

Davis, Richard, and Diana Owen. 1998. *New Media and American Politics.* New York: Oxford University Press.

Dertouzos, Michael. 1997. *What Will Be: How the New Information Marketplace Will Change our Lives.* San Francisco: Harper.

Douglas, Susan J. 1987. *Inventing American Broadcasting, 1899–1922.* Baltimore: Johns Hopkins University Press.

Flammang, Janet A. *Women's Political Voice: How Women are Transforming the Practice and Study of Politics.* Philadelphia: Temple University Press.

Grossman, Lawrence. 1995. *The Electronic Commonwealth.* New York: Penguin.

Harper, Christopher. 1998. *And That's the Way it Will Be.* New York: New York University Press.

Hill, Kevin A., and John E. Hughes. 1998. *Cyberpolitics: Citizen Activism in the Age of the Internet.* Lanham, MD: Rowan & Littlefield.

Just, Marion, Ann Crigler, and Montague Kern. 1998. *Information, Persuasion and Solidarity: Civic Uses of the Internet in Campaign '96.* Paper delivered at the Western Political Science Association Annual Meeting, Los Angeles.

Kimball, Penn. 1994. *Downsizing The News: Network Cutbacks in the Nation's Capital.* Washington, DC: Woodrow Wilson Center Press.

McChesney, Robert W. 1997. *Capitalism and the New Information Age.* New York: Monthly Review Press.

McLean, Iain. 1989. *Democracy and New Technology.* Cambridge: Polity Press.

McQuail, Denis. 1997. *Audience Analysis.* London: Sage.

Murdock, Graham, and Peter Golding. 1989. "Information Poverty and Political Inequality: Citizenship in the Age of Privatised Communications." *Journal of Communication.* 39: 180–193.

Negroponte, Nicholas. 1995. *Being Digital.* New York: Knopf.

Neuman, W. Russell. 1998. "The Global Impact of New Technologies." In Doris Graber, Denis McQuail, and Pippa Norris (eds.)*The Politics of News:The News of Politics.* Washington DC: CQ Press.

Norris, Pippa. 1998. "Blaming the Messenger? Television and Civic Malaise." Conference on Public Trust and Democratic Governance in the Trilateral Democracies, Bellagio, June.

Norris, Pippa, and David Jones. 1998. "Virtual Democracy." *The Harvard International Journal of Press/Politics* 3(2): 1-4.

Rash, Wayne, Jr. 1997. *Politics on the Nets: Wiring the Political Process.* New York: W. H. Freeman.

Rheingold, Howard. 1993. *The Virtual Community: Homesteading on the Electronic Frontier.* Reading, MA: Addison-Wesley.

Rubin, Alan. 1994. "Media Users and Effects." In Bryant Jennings and Dolf Zillman, *Media Effects.* Hillsdale, NJ: Lawrence Erlbaum.

Schwartz, Edward. 1996. *Netactivism: How Citizens Use the Internet.* Sebastapol, CA: Songline Studios.

Verba, Sidney, and Norman, Nie. 1972. *Participation in America: Political Democracy and Social Equality.* New York: Harper and Row.

Verba, Sidney, Norman Nie. and Jae-on Kim. 1978. *Participation and Political Equality: A Seven-Nation Comparison.* New York: Cambridge University Press.

Verba, Sidney, Kay Schlozman, and Henry E. Brady. *Voice and Equality.* Cambridge, MA: Harvard University Press.

Appendix A:
The Pew Research Center for the People and the Press
October 1998 Technology Online Re-Interview.
Factor Analysis Items and Coding for Table 2.
User Activities

GENERAL USERS:

Q41. E-MAIL

Do you ever send or receive e-mail or electronic mail? (IF YES, ASK: Is this everyday, 3 to 5 days per week, 1 or 2 days per week, once every few weeks, or less often?)

1. Everyday
2. 3–5 days week
3. 1–2 days week
4. Once every few weeks
5. Less often
6. Never
7. DK

Q58. NEWS

How frequently do you go online to get news? Is this every day, 3 to 5 days per week, 1 or 2 days per week, once every few weeks, or less often?)

1. Everyday
2. 3–5 days week
3. 1–2 days week
4. Once every few weeks
5. Less often
6. Never
7. DK

Q62. ONLINE ACTIVITIES

Please tell me how often, if ever, you engage in each of the following online activities. First, how often do you go online to (READ . . .

Q62A.   Communicate with other people through online forums, discussion lists,

Q62B.   Get financial information such as stock quotes or corporate information

Q62C.   Do research for school

Q62D.   Do research for work

Q62E.   Get news and information on current events, public issues or politics

Q62F.   Get travel information or services

Q62G.   Get information about hobbies, movies, restaurants or other

every day, 3–5 days per week, 1 or 2 days per week, once every few weeks, less often, or never?

NET POLITICAL ACTIVISTS:

Q69. POLITICAL DISCUSSIONS

Do you ever engage in online discussions about politics? (IF YES, ASK: Is this everyday, 3 to 5 days per week, 1 or 2 days per week, once every few weeks, or less often?)

    Q69A.   Communicate with other people through online forums, discussion lists,

    Q69B.   Get financial information such as stock quotes or corporate information

    Q69C.   Do research for school

    Q69D.   Do research for work

    Q69E.   Get news and information on current events, public issues or politics

    Q69F.   Get travel information or services

    Q69G.   Get information about hobbies, movies, restaurants or other

Q70. CONTACT OFFICIALS

Do you ever contact or e-mail any groups, organizations, or public officials about political issues or public policy questions? (IF YES, ASK: Is this every day, 3 to 5 days per week, 1 or 2 days per week, once every few weeks, or less often?)

Q78. ELECTION NEWS

Have you gone/ did you ever go online to get news and information about the 1998 elections? (IF YES, ASK: Is this every day, 3 to 5 days per week, 1 or 2 days per week, once every few weeks, or less often?)

REPLY TO PIPPA NORRIS'S "WHO SURFS"

<Anna Greenberg>

Norris poses the question, Does the Internet create political opportunities for the politically disenfranchised and marginalized ("the mobilization hypothesis") or merely bolster existing inequity in access to political resources and opportunity ("the reinforcement hypothesis")? After reviewing an array of sample survey evidence, she quite convincingly supports the latter hypothesis. Norris finds that online political activists demonstrate greater educational achievement and affluence than members of the mass public or general online users. Moreover, she shows that the people most likely to use the Internet for political purposes are already politically engaged and seek out political information from traditional news outlets, like the *Washington Post* site. In short, Norris's account shows that the Internet, at least as it is currently organized, remains a tool for the privileged, a source of conventional political activism, and a repository of standard political information.

These conclusions are entirely consistent with existing models of political participation, namely the socioeconomic status (SES) and resource models. The SES model holds that educational achievement and affluence elevate participation because high-status individuals have a strong sense of political efficacy and interest, ascribe to norms of civic duty, understand the political system and have access to fungible resources.[1] The resource model extends these insights by asserting that high socio-economic status embeds people in politically relevant social networks and exposes them to opportunities to acquire the civic skills necessary for efficacious political activity (e.g., public speaking).[2] In these models, Internet access and online political activity are endogenous. People with the resources to buy a computer or work in jobs with access to the Internet, with the skills to navigate the Internet and an interest in seeking political information online, are the same people who possess the politically relevant resources afforded by high socio-economic status.

So does the Internet hold any radical political possibilities? When the evidence is examined at the individual level, the answer is clearly not yet. But what if we change the unit of analysis from the individual to political groups or institutions? Institutions are important political actors that shape political events as they influence preferences, distribute resources and mobilize influence.[3] Social movement theory, for instance, points to the central role of institutions in the generation of collective action. This perspective notes that organizations, like the black church during the civil rights movement, are a source of constituents and pre-existing communication networks, as well as serve as locations of political consciousness raising.[4] As such, they are sites and vehicles of "strategic mobilization" of constituents and members.[5]

These insights suggest that perhaps the political promise of the Internet rests not so much on its effect on individuals, but rather on how groups are using it to facilitate political mobilization. There are at least two ways marginalized groups can exploit the political potential of the Internet. First, resource-poor groups can use the Internet to understand complicated, or find previously unavailable, information. Second, resource-poor groups can use the Internet to mobilize existing constituents and recruit new members.

There is a wide array of politically important information available on the Internet, such as public opinion data, government statistics, legislative histories, breaking news from the wires, and court decisions. Resource-poor groups, particularly socially isolated groups, can access this information for a relatively nominal sum—normally for the price of online service. For instance, small organizations that cannot afford $20-50,000 national sample surveys can find a wealth of publicly available data on the Internet. The Hotline (published by the *National Journal*) archives survey data on "key issues," like abortion, gun control, and the tobacco industry. The Roper Center, ICPSR, the Harris Organization, the Gallup Organization and the Pew Research Center for the People and the Press all archive a variety of media polls and academic surveys.[6] These data might help political groups think strategically about framing messages for different audiences, targeting resources demographically and regionally, and fundraising and making internal decisions.

Groups can use this information both *on- and offline*. For instance, a church group concerned about the denial of religious freedom in China can comb the local paper for a smattering of news or wait until the local public library archives enough material. Alternatively, on the National Council of Churches Web site, this church group can find analysis of legislation, model letters, press releases, and public statements, as well as a link to the legislative record through "Thomas," the congressional information site. This information could be used to create sample letters to members of Congress or to develop petitions to be distributed in church. The pastor could even deliver a sermon based on this information and encourage members to contact relevant officials or sign the petition. These activities take place off the Internet and, therefore, remain undetected by a random sample telephone survey.

Finally, groups can use the Internet to sustain organizations, mobilize membership internally and recruit new members through their Web sites and list-servers. As I noted earlier, communication networks are central to mobilizing and sustaining social movements. (During the elections in South Africa, for example, the African National Congress almost exclusively used Compuserve to communicate about campaign strategy and implementation with party leaders and advisors.) These networks provide important information concerning the status of the movement and relevant issues under debate. Sites often contain legislative action alerts with instructions for contacting members of Congress via the Internet, but also by snail mail and the telephone. They also publicize upcoming events, like rallies or marches, that members and visitors can attend or support in other ways. These sites frequently allow online visitors to join the organization, which systematically exposes them to political information over the Internet (e.g., on a list-server) and off the Internet (e.g., the organization's magazine or newsletter).

I do not want to overstate the mobilizing potential of the Internet. There are, as Norris points out, class biases in Internet access and usage that affect institutional capacity as well. Some groups are better able than others to exploit the resources available on the Internet. The question remains, what sorts of infrastructure do marginalized groups need to make the Internet a political resource?

It is also hard to imagine some aspects of political mobilization, like developing a sense of collective identity, occurring over the Internet. As William Galston points out in his chapter, face-to-face interaction creates important norms and social obligations that build and sustain communities. The same sorts of interactions underlie a sense of collective identity and linked fate, important ingredients of successful collective action.[7]

The anecdotes described above are not intended to refute Norris's findings, which are extremely persuasive. There is no question that class biases in Internet use serve to reinforce existing inequality in access to political resources and influence. It is also clear that the politically astute are not using the Internet to tap unfiltered or radical sources of political information. Rather this reply introduces the idea that mobilization may occur online in ways that cannot be measured by surveys of individual political behavior. The examples cited above simply point out ways that "mobilization" happens on the Internet when groups exploit its potential and put it to political use both on- and offline.

Endnotes

1. See Raymond E. Wolfinger and Steven J. Rosenstone. 1980. *Who Votes?* (New Haven: Yale University Press).

2. See Sidney Verba, Kay Lehman Schlozman, and Henry E. Brady. 1995. *Voice and Equality: Civic Voluntarism in American Politics.* (Cambridge, MA: Harvard University Press) and Norman H. Nie, Jane Junn, and Kenneth Stehlik-Barry. 1996. *Education and Democratic Citizenship in America.* (Chicago: University of Chicago Press).

3. See James G. March and Johan P. Olsen. 1984. "The New Institutionalism: Organizational Factors in Political Life." *American Political Science Review* (78: 7334–749).

4. See Doug McAdam. 1982. *Political Process and the Development of Black Insurgency, 1930–1970.* (Chicago: The University of Chicago Press).

5. Steven J. Rosenstone and John Mark Hansen. 1993. *Mobilization, Participation and Democracy in America.* (New York: Macmillan). Rosenstone and Hansen argue that we can account for the deterioration of electoral turnout by examining the decline of "strategic mobilization" by political parties.

6. Some of these archives do charge fees, but they pale in comparison to the cost of sponsoring a national sample survey.

7. See McAdam, *Political Process.* Also see the work of social psychologists, for example, John C. Turner. 1982. "Toward a Cognitive Definition of the Social Group." In *Social Identity and Intergroup Relations,* ed. Henri Tajfel (New York: Cambridge University Press).

CAMPAIGNING ON THE INTERNET IN THE ELECTIONS OF 1998

<Elaine Ciulla Kamarck>

The Internet Campaign Arrives

First there was the ground war. At the beginning of the Republic, politicians sought votes on the ground, plying prospective voters with food and liquor. Then there was the air war. By the mid-twentieth century Franklin Roosevelt's mastery of radio and John F. Kennedy's mastery of television brought politics to the air waves. And now, at the end of the twentieth century, we have the cyber war. Politicians have begun to campaign in the new medium of the Internet.

The 1998 midterm elections took place against the backdrop of the scandal surrounding President Clinton and his affair with an intern named Monica Lewinsky. And while that historical fact and the surprising victory of the President's party in that election will, no doubt, be the things mentioned most frequently in connection with that election, there will be another, less glamorous, footnote to the 1998

Elaine Ciulla Kamarck *is Director of the Visions of Governance for the Twenty-First Century project at Harvard University's John F. Kennedy School of Government. She also directs the Innovations in American Government program and lectures in public policy at the School. Previously, Dr. Kamarck served as Senior Policy Advisor to the Vice President of the United States, Al Gore. She joined the Clinton/Gore Administration in March of 1993 and, working directly with Vice President Gore, created the National Performance Review, a new White House policy council designed to reinvent government. Prior to joining the Administration, Dr. Kamarck was a senior fellow at the Progressive Policy Institute, the think-tank of the Democratic Leadership Council.*

midterms. 1998 will go down in history as the first election cycle in which a new medium—the Internet—played a major campaign role.

The Internet was used in the 1996 election cycle. But it appeared in those races as more of a novelty—made famous by Bob Dole's attempt to connect with young voters by giving out the Web address of his campaign—incorrectly. In 1996 there were so few campaign sites that surveys of Internet usage didn't even ask whether or not a voter had visited a candidate's Web site.[1] By 1998 however, the exponential growth of Internet usage in the public and the fact that the demographics of those users showed them to be more likely to vote than not, meant that many campaigns added the Internet to their repertoire of campaign tools—even though, as we shall see, many candidates were skeptical about its efficacy.[2]

The following study took place in the middle of the 1998 midterm elections. It was designed to be the first comprehensive look at the political use of the Internet in a national election cycle and to collect simple, basic data about how politicians were using this new medium. It was also designed to pose, but not necessarily answer, the questions that politicians and political scientists will ask for some time to come. From the last week in September through the first two weeks in October, a group consisting of Harvard University undergraduates, graduate students, and staff at the John F. Kennedy School of Government looked up every candidate for the United States House of Representatives, Senate, and governor who had qualified to appear on their state's ballot. (Write-in candidates were excluded.)*

The first task was to ascertain whether or not the candidate had a campaign Web site. Those who had only e-mail addresses, those who had only an official government Web site, and those whose Web sites came up as "under construction" and thus gave no information, were excluded. There were a total of 1296 major and minor party candidates running for Congress and for governor in 1998. Of these, 43 percent or 554 had a campaign Web site, as defined by the research team. Locating these sites was made easier by the emergence, in the fall of 1998, of political intermediaries such as *www.politics1.com*, a nonpartisan directory of links to all major and minor party campaigns, started and maintained by attorney and political afficionado Roy Gunzburger.

---

*Special thanks to Lynn Akin, my administative assistant, for coordinating all the students who helped with this project. Also, special thanks to John Cullinane for his support of the project.

Table 1. Candidates with Campaign Web Sites on the Internet

(late September and early October 1998)

	Total Number of Candidates	Number of Candidates with Campaign Web Sites	Percentage of Candidates with Campaign Web Sites
Major party candidates for U.S. Senate	68 29 incumbents 39 challengers	49	72%
Major party candidates for House of Representatives	780 409 incumbents 371 challengers	274	35%
Major party candidates for governor	73 25 incumbents 48 challengers	69	95%

While these sites provided us with most of our links, each researcher was instructed to search the major search engines for any candidate who was on a ballot and who did not appear in one of the campaign '98 directories.[3]

As Table 1 illustrates, nearly all major party statewide candidates in 1998 used the Internet as part of their political campaign. Internet usage in House of Representatives races, however, was significantly lower, due, in part, to the fact that so many House races are traditionally not competitive. (In 1998, for example, almost 100 House races were uncontested, and in many more races the opponent spent under $25,000.)

As Table 2 indicates there were no major differences between the two dominant political parties in terms of Internet usage. Democratic candidates used the Internet almost exactly as often as did Republican candidates—a finding that further puts to rest the perceived upper-class, Republican bias of Internet users.[4]

Table 2. Use of Campaign Web Sites by Major Political Parties

Total Democratic Sites	Total Republican Sites
193	199

Table 3 compares incumbents' and challengers' use of the Internet. In Senate and gubernatorial races, challengers were only slightly more likely to have an Internet campaign than were incumbents. However, incumbent senators and governors were slower to open up their Internet campaigns than were their challengers. In June of 1998, an initial, shorter version of this study found that 92 percent of the gubernatorial challengers were up and running on the Web, while only 20 percent of the incumbent Governors were on the Web. Similarly, 81 percent of Senate challengers were up and running on the Web at that point, but only 34 percent of incumbent U.S. Senators were on the Web.[5]

Table 3. Incumbent Versus Challenger Campaigns on the Internet			
(late September and early October 1998)			
	Total Number of Candidates	Total Number of Candidates with Campaign Web Sites	Percentage of Candidates with Campaign Web Sites
Incumbent U.S. senators running for re-election	29	20	70%
Major party candidates for U.S. Senate (challengers and contestants in open seats)	39	29	74%
Incumbent members of the U.S. House of Representatives running for re-election	409	80	19%
Major party candidates for U.S. House of Representatives (challengers and contestants in open seats)	371	194	52%
Incumbent governors running for re-election	25 (includes Independent ME)	21 (missing: OK, RI, SD, VT)	84%
Major party candidates for governor (challengers and contestants in open seats)	48	48	100%

The enthusiasm with which challengers embraced the Web is clearest, however, in the comparison, in Table 3, between incumbents and challengers in House races. Challengers were more than twice as likely as incumbents to conduct an Internet campaign. But Internet campaigning, like other campaigning, has a great deal to do with the competitiveness of a given race. Table 4 looks at Internet usage in competitive races only. In statewide competitive races Internet campaigning is ubiquitous. In competitive House races only, Internet campaigning is significantly greater than in all House races.

Finally, to round out a total picture of Internet campaigning in 1998 we looked at independent and minor party candidates for Congress and for governor to see how often they made use of the Internet.

Table 4. Use of Web Sites as a Campaign Tool in Competitive Races*		
(late September to early October 1998)		
	Percentage of Candidates on the Web in All Races	Percentage of Candidates on the Web in Competitive Races Only
U.S. Senate races	72%	100% (18 candidates in 9 competitive races)
U.S. House of Representatives races	35%	57%
Governor races	95%	96%

*Competitive races were ones designated as in play or an even bet in the October/November 1998 issue of *Campaigns and Elections* magazine.

Table 5 contradicts the popular perception, made famous by early Web enthusiasts, that the Internet is a place where, because of the low cost of communication, nontraditional political actors will thrive. Compared to major party candidates, minor party candidates made much less use of the Web as a campaign tool. (However, as we will see at the end of this article, the one instance in 1998 where the Internet seems to have been critical is in the campaign of a minor party candidate.)

Most of the minor-party candidates are part of the Reform Party (Ross Perot's Party), the Libertarian Party, or the Green Party. The sites tend to be very basic and very down-home. Some of the minor candidates' sites are thinly disguised advertisements for businesses. For instance, Kat Gallant *(www.kat-gallant.com)* is a Senate candidate on the Libertarian ticket in Arizona. She runs a beauty salon in which men can get their hair cut by a woman wearing only lingerie. Other than a bizarre and incomprehensible saga of her cross-country horseback ride, which ended when the West Virginia authorities took her horses away, there is little of a political nature on this site. Mostly it features Ms. Gallant and her hairdressers in skimpy clothes and sexy poses.

While it is obviously clear that third-party candidates can get access to cyberspace more easily than they can get access to traditional media such as newspapers and television, it may not be true that they will be more successful finding converts in cyberspace. Kevin A. Hill and John E. Hughes, using data from the Pew Research Center for the People and the Press, found that Internet activists were no more Republican or Democratic than the population at large and that, faced with third-party candidates, they were *more* likely to stick with the major parties than voters in the population at large.[6]

Without a doubt, 1998 was the year in which politics came to the Internet. But to what end? Does campaigning on the Internet make a difference between winning and losing? Does it change the relationship between the voters and the candidates? Does it strengthen or weaken intermediaries such as the press and political parties? Answering these questions will be difficult because so many things happen in a political campaign simultaneously and, as history teaches us, one campaign medium never completely replaces an older medium—it is simply

Table 5. Independent and Minor Party Candidates on the Internet			
(late September and early October 1998)			
	Total Number of Candidates	Total Number of Candidates with Campaign Web Sites	Percentage of Candidates with Campaign Web Sites
Candidates for U.S. Senate	72	24	33%
Candidates for U.S. House of Representatives	295	103	34%
Candidates for governor	78	35	44%

added on top of it. Therefore, before we attempt to answer the questions posed above, it pays to take a moment and review briefly the history of American political campaigning, and then to look at what candidates were actually doing in their Internet campaigns in 1998.

"Swilling the Planters with Bumbo"

In the colonial era very few political offices were open to election. And yet, for the few that were, prospective candidates were expected to personally meet every constituent and to offer them opportunities for food and drink—of the alcoholic variety. One contemporary referred to this as "swilling the planters with bumbo," a tradition that lives on in American electioneering in the form of shad plankings, oyster roasts, and other opportunities to combine electioneering with food and drink.

What this illustrates is that old, once dominant modes of electioneering take a long time to die, and some survive as quaint customs. Robert J. Dinkin makes this point in his history of American electioneering, *Campaigning in America: A History of Election Practices.* "Old ways often would be employed along with the new until the former were shown to be obsolete."[7] Fueling prospective voters with food and, especially, liquor, lasted a long, long time in spite of efforts to outlaw the practice. In 1777, James Madison attempted to imbue a bit of dignity to the process and refused to serve liquor to the voters. He lost.

In the early days of the Republic, "stump speaking" emerged as the most popular mode of campaigning because candidates would literally get on a stump to harangue the crowds at horse races, cockfights, or church meetings. In addition, the number of partisan newspapers increased dramatically as the first American political parties developed. Candidates let the partisan press engage in character assassination of their opponents while they remained comfortably above the fray.

By the Jacksonian era the electorate had expanded considerably— by 1825 most white men could vote—and this led to the need for a new, more energetic mode of electioneering. Politicians found themselves organizing huge extravaganzas such as parades, rallies, and barbecues and traveling long hours in an effort to reach the voters.

By midcentury political extravaganzas had become the hallmark of American political campaigns which were, by then, organized along a military model. Political parties created uniformed "marching parties," such as the Republican parties' "Wide Awakes," and the torchlight parade was born. (To this day, Chicago has a torchlight parade on the night before election.)

But by the end of the century the large-scale events and military-style marches decreased in frequency as a more sedate form of electioneering emerged. Voter registration laws, a product of the Progressive Era, had restricted the electorate, and a new, smaller, more highly educated group of voters were courted by politicians who often spoke to them in tent meetings, informing voters on the issues of the day. During this era candidates and parties started to market themselves with buttons, pins, and symbols, and campaigning began to resemble merchandising.

When the phonograph was invented toward the end of the nineteenth century, William Jennings Bryan became the first presidential aspirant to have his words recorded. He was also the first presidential candidate to appear in a brief campaign movie. But in this instance, at least, using new technology did not help win the election.

Radio was first used in the election of 1924 when Calvin Coolidge spoke over a hookup of 26 stations. Its campaign uses were immediately apparent, and by the election of 1928 both political parties were spending large amounts of money on radio. Al Smith, the Democratic nominee that year, was cursed with a scratchy radio voice in contrast to Franklin Roosevelt, whose voice was well suited to the new medium and who, four years later, used radio extensively. In addition to radio, the 1924 election saw the forerunner of the campaign commercial, as candidates made short movies about themselves to run in the movie theaters. Not surprisingly the first campaign consultants, Clem Whitaker and Leone Baxter, hung out their shingle in 1933 in the Bay Area of California and went into the business of helping campaigns conduct what we now think of as a public relations campaign.

By mid twentieth century candidates were using several generations of campaign techniques simultaneously. They would ride the rails and appear repeatedly at the back of the train to deliver the "stump" speech. (The name lives on in spite of the absence of the stump.) Large rallies were still held, as were parades in the big cities and barbecues and picnics in the South. The radio was used extensively, as were specially made movies about the candidates.

But by 1952 a new era was beginning—the television era. Dwight Eisenhower was probably the last nominee to ride the rails. By the 1960s candidates campaigned on airplanes, and previous generations of campaign events—large rallies, stump speeches, etc.—became set-tings for television extravaganzas. Television shortened candidates' statements even more than radio had (both of which were shorter than the hours and hours of speechmaking common a century before.) And the famous Kennedy-Nixon debate of 1960 introduced a new criterion into election campaigns—whether the candidate could communicate on the new and very personal medium of television.

By the 1996 presidential campaign television was clearly the dom-inant medium, but television had gone through its own revolution with the introduction of cable. The dominance of the three networks had ended, and campaigns which had mastered the art of controlling the "free" media to reinforce their paid media messages had to learn to buy and target media in a multichannel environment.

The 1996 election also saw the introduction of the Internet into the political campaigns. The first uses of the Internet to campaign were in the 1996 Republican primaries, in which Pat Buchanan in particular is reported to have used the Internet aggressively and well. Both 1996 con-ventions were on the Internet, as were both major political campaigns. Most reports credit the Republican National Committee and the Dole/Kemp campaign with the most sophisticated Web site—although, to state the obvious, the Internet was not a decisive factor in that race.

It is probably fair to say that in 1996 the Internet was still a novelty in American politics, interesting but not an integral part of anyone's campaign strategy. It may have been a factor in the close Senate race of Senator John Kerry (D-MA) in 1996, and it may have figured in the close gubernatorial race of Governor Christie Todd Whitman in 1997. In both instances the Internet campaign proved to be highly effective in the last-minute mobilization of volunteers.[8] But in general, the Internet didn't play a very big role in the 1996 election cycle. Bruce Bimber of the University of California–Santa Barbara studied Internet usage in the 1996 election cycle and found that the Internet was barely used at all as a medium through which to contact voters. Phone calls, letters, and personal contact were all preferred by candidate organizations and interest groups.[9]

As the 1998 midterm election cycle dawned, many candidates and professional campaign consultants were skeptical of this new medium. Jim Krog, who managed Florida Governor Lawton Chiles' successful gubernatorial campaigns, said, "If I were running a campaign I would have one [a Web site]. But I would not put a lot of money into it because I don't know what it's worth."[10] This uncertainty is understandable. Electioneering in America takes place on many levels. Because it is so difficult to know what goes into victory, candidates and campaigns will often invest in many technologies simultaneously. Thus in 1998 the Internet took its place alongside television, radio, direct mail, and phone banks as candidates, faced with uncertainty, and perhaps skeptical of investing too much in the new medium, sought to maximize their opportunities to get votes.

Yet along with the skeptics were those who wondered *when* not *if* the Internet would become an important political tool. In 1998, for the first time ever, candidates made the Internet an explicit part of their primary campaign strategy. Wendel Turner, a West Virginia lawyer, pinned his hopes of upsetting Congressman Bob Wise in the primary on his Internet site—only to end up with 6 percent of the vote. And Doug Ross, a candidate for the Democratic gubernatorial nomination in Michigan, whose Web site was one of the best reviewed for the earlier version of this study, had a well-articulated Internet strategy as part of his campaign. Nevertheless, he came in third in the Democratic primary. The political consultant Phil Noble confidently predicted that 1998 would be the year in which a candidate won or lost on the basis of his or her use of the Web. And, as we saw, challengers flocked to the Web in hopes that it would provide a secret weapon to break through the power of incumbency.

Thus by the time our research team began to look at the 1998 campaign on the Internet, the new medium had arrived with a mixture of skepticism and hopefulness. The next section shows what we found candidates were doing as part of their Internet campaigns.

How Candidates Are Using the Internet: Characteristics of the Internet Campaign

The Electronic Brochure

Most Internet campaigns looked like electronic brochures. The preponderance of biographical and other message oriented material on the candidates' sites indicates that in 1998, in many campaigns, the Internet was used primarily as one more mode of broadcast. As Table 6 indicates, almost all the candidates' Web sites offered both biographical information on the candidate and his or her family and information on the candidates' positions on the issues. Some sites contained copies of campaign speeches and many sites provided updated news about the campaign. The more sophisticated sites, such as that of successful Republican gubernatorial candidate Jeb Bush of Florida, featured up-to-date photos of the candidate taken with a digital camera at each campaign event and posted on the Web site that day. Senator Lauch Faircloth's site (R-NC) opened with a blast of patriotic music.

Some campaign Web sites were short and to the point. For instance, Dutch Hillenberg, Democratic candidate for the seventh Congressional District in Indiana, had a site consisting of just three pages.

Table 6. Analysis of Web Site Content		
What is Being Communicated on the Candidate's Web Page?		
	All Candidates	Minor Party Candidates Only
Information on issues only	42 (7%)	
Biographical information on the candidate only	52 (9%)	
All of the above	449 (81%)	
Under construction or couldn't be coded	11 (2%)	
Does the Web Site Contain Copies of Campaign Speeches?		
Yes	No*	
111 (20%)	443 (80%)	
*All "no" responses include the 11 Web sites that were under construction and thus could not be coded.		
Does the Web Site Provide Updated News About the Campaign Such as Press Releases, Reports, and/or Photos from Recent Events?		
Yes	No	
274 (49%)	280 (51%)	

The first was a standard home page; the second was a photo of the candidate with a gun, standing over a large animal; the third was a photo of the candidate on a shooting range holding some sort of very large automatic weapon. In very few words this site conveyed what this candidate was all about.

One of the potential campaign advantages to candidates who campaign on the Internet is the ability to get their message out "unmediated" by the press. This fact alone makes Internet campaigning very attractive, since there are very few candidates who ever feel they are getting a fair shake by the press. The bigger the campaign the more extensive the information on issues. Scott Harshbarger, Democratic candidate for governor in Massachusetts, was one of many candidates who offered a variety of lengthy issues papers on his site. But the extent to which actual voters read these pieces is unclear. According to one study the press itself is the basic consumer of Internet issues materials. Wayne Rash Jr., in his study *Politics on the Nets*, points out that in the 1996 election cycle at least ". . . a growing proportion of information found in the traditional media stems directly from the Net." He points out that with news media and television cutting back on costs, the Internet becomes a very easy way to keep up with the candidates.[11]

Nevertheless, the new medium of the Internet makes possible a degree of message targeting that was unknown several years ago. Senator Barbara Mikulski's (D-MD) site *(www.mikulski98.org)* allowed the viewer to click on a county in Maryland and find out what she has done for those who live there. For instance, if you click on Montgomery County, Maryland, home to many federal civil servants, you will find out that Senator Mikulski fought to keep the Uniformed Services University of the Health Sciences (a DOD facility located in the county) open and that she brought the Consumer Product Safety Commission to the county.

As the Mikulski example and others show, candidates strive to tailor their Web sites in the hope that they can talk directly to voters. There is some preliminary evidence that this feature of the Web is very appealing to average voters—appealing enough that the Web may come to be used by citizens in addition to the political press. In some research for the Markle Foundation, Marion Just, a professor at Wellesley College, found that voters in a focus group enjoyed the fact that they could compare candidates in an unmediated fashion. In the words of one participant ". . . the candidate gets to tell their side of the story."[12] Marty

Edlund researched the log files of 20 Web campaigns in 1998 and found "that the average user session, across 14 of the 20 campaigns where this information was available, was over eight and a half minutes." He went on to make the following comparison: "Now compare this to your average telephone script, which is 30 to 45 seconds, or your average TV commercial which is 30 seconds, and this is significantly longer, about 17 times as long." The conclusion of his study was that the Internet is "turning interested voters into informed voters and enabling these informed voters to participate more easily and become volunteers."[13]

The Lack of Negative Campaigning

Because candidates seem to use the Internet primarily as a communication medium, they are careful to put their best foot forward. All campaigns with resources conduct "opposition research." Most of it deals with the opponent's positions, votes etc. Sometimes it deals with their personal life. Nevertheless, smart campaigns use negative research and negative attacks with care since negative campaigns have been known to backfire. (Al Checchi, the millionaire California gubernatorial candidate, lost support rapidly in the polls after going negative against Jane Harman in the 1998 California Democratic gubernatorial primary.)

In 1998 most of the message oriented material on the Net was positive and upbeat. Table 7 reports the results of our search for negative information about opponents on the candidates' Web sites. Less than a quarter of all the Web sites featured negative information about the

Table 7. Negative Campaigning	
Does the Web Site Provide Negative or Critical Information About the Candidate's Opponent?	
Yes	No
124 (22%)	430 (78%)
Does the Web Site Criticize President Clinton for the Monica Lewinsky Affair?	
Yes	No
18 (3%)	536 (97%)

candidate's opponent. In addition we searched for references to President Clinton's troubles and found very few sites (3 percent of the total) that made any reference at all to the Lewinsky scandal.

Clearly, candidates in 1998 were cautious about putting negative information about their opponents on their Web sites. Those who did offer negative messages about their opponents tried to make them as entertaining as possible. For instance, the Jeb Bush site *(www.jeb.org)* offered a feature called "The Buddy MacKay Tax of the Day," which consisted of one month of daily press releases and articles about taxes attributed to MacKay. Gary Franks, the former Connecticut congressman who challenged incumbent Senator Chris Dodd, offered a feature called "The Top Ten Reasons Dodd Is a Hypocrite on Campaign Finance Reform" *(www.garyfranks.com)*.

The paucity of negative campaign information on the Internet leads one to wonder whether or not politeness is unique to the medium. On the other hand, as the Internet campaign matures, negative campaigning may become as important a part of the Internet campaign as it is of the television campaign.

Interactivity

One of the most important features of the Internet and the one that is most often cited by those who believe the Internet will fundamentally change politics is the ability of the citizen to interact with political candidates directly. Table 8 shows that the highly hyped interactive nature of the Internet is not yet a dominant feature of campaigns on the Internet.

We were very strict about coding a site as fully interactive. For instance, Senator Barbara Mikulski has a segment on her site called "Voices of Maryland" where she invites people to write in and tell about ". . . the impact of the Senator's policies on you and your family." Some of the comments—presumably the favorable ones—are published on the site, but there is no promise of a response from the campaign or from the candidate to the voter. Tom Volgy, Democratic candidate for Congress from Arizona's Fifth District also published a series of favorable e-mails that had come to his campaign from voters, but the site showed no evidence of two-way communication. Because the communication in these sites was essentially one way, they were coded as partially interactive, not fully interactive.

Table 8. Does the Web Site Make Use of the Interactive Capacity of This New Medium?		
The site is fully interactive.	The site is partially interactive (i.e., the visitor can send e-mail or answer a questionnaire).	The site is passive.*
2 (Tom Campbell, CA; Tom Ridge, PA)	401 (72%)	151 (27%)

*Includes the 11 Web sites that were under construction.

Many other candidates' sites fell into the partially interactive category as well. Peg Luksik, Constitutional Party candidate for governor of Pennsylvania, asked viewers to e-mail her the answers to two open-ended questions about her positions in the campaign but explicitly stated that not all responses would be acknowledged. Jean Leising, Republican candidate for Congress from Indiana's Ninth District, told voters on her home page that "Jean will occasionally share her personal thoughts"—not a very ringing endorsement for two-way communication. Other sites like those of Governor George Pataki of New York and Congressman Ron Packard of California allowed the visitor to check off answers on a traditional questionnaire.

For a site to be coded as fully interactive there had to be some ability to engage in a dialogue with the candidate or the campaign. For instance, Tom Campbell, congressman from the Fifteenth Congressional District in California, had a feature on his Web site called the Town Hall Meeting *(www.campbell.org)*. He invited voters to send him a message via the Town Hall Meeting to which he responded directly. Appendix A gives a sample of the dialogue that took place on one of the days during the campaign. Voters ask about campaign finance reform, about the budget, about cigarette taxes, about visa issues. The Congressman states that he tries to personally answer each message *every day*. (Of course there were only about ten questions a week.) Nevertheless the interaction is real, informal, and authoritative. There is none of the stilted prose that results when ten junior staffers answer the mail. It is a peep into the future of direct communication—one of the few instances where the full potential of the new medium seems to be on display—and it is fitting that this congressman represents the center of Silicon Valley.

Governor Tom Ridge of Pennsylvania invited visitors to "Talk with the Candidates" *(http://ridge1998.com/talk/home.cfm)*. They handled the greater volume that could be expected in a statewide race by scheduling online chat sessions with voters and asking the voters to sign a guest book in order to be scheduled to talk with the Governor and the Lieutenant Governor. In the last two weeks of the British elections in 1995, Prime Minister Blair invited both press and the public to an online press conference where they could discuss the issues.

Clearly the interactive potential of the Web is enormous. It is the feature of the Web that gives it superiority over television, the dominant campaign communications medium. Then why is there so little real interactivity on the Web? Control of the message is as much a campaign obsession as is money, and one explanation is that candidates fear losing control of the message. But entering into an online discussion with voters is no different than appearing on a radio call-in show or showing up at an open meeting—things which candidates regularly do—and where they are regularly subjected to difficult and sometimes embarrassing questions. In fact, online chats are probably a lot more controllable setting than live town meetings, since in all the interactive examples the campaign itself acts as the moderator, presumably filtering out objectionable questions and instances of "flaming" that could embarrass the candidate.

Participation

There are two ways that an interested citizen can participate in a political campaign. One is by making a political donation, the other is by volunteering. In both areas the 1998 Internet campaign seems to have helped enormously. Table 9 shows how the 1998 campaigns operated to solicit participation. Forty-two percent of the campaigns provided fundraising information and another 11 percent went so far as to allow you to make a contribution online with a credit card.

What is particularly surprising about the first part of Table 9 is that nearly half of all the Internet campaigns didn't bother to ask for money. Money, as has been said, is the mother's milk of politics. While many people give lip service to the moral superiority of many small political donations over a few large political donations, the fact of the matter is that small money is very expensive to raise. Direct mail works best for

Table 9. Participation	
Does the Web Site Have a Place Where It Solicits Campaign Donations?	
Yes, provides information on how to send a contribution through the mail.	232 (42%)
Yes, allows visitor to make a contribution through the mail or online with a credit card.	59 (11%)
No, does not solicit contributions.	263 (47%)
Does the Web Site Solicit Volunteers?	
Yes, allows the visitor to sign up for traditional volunteer activity.	278 (50%)
Yes, allows the visitor to sign up for traditional volunteer activity and allows the visitor to conduct volunteer activity on the Web (cyber-volunteering).	30 (5%)
No, does not solicit volunteers.	246 (44%)

those who are already well known and who are known for having intense positions on the issues, and as anyone who has ever looked into the cost of a mailing list can tell you, direct mail is very expensive up front. The Internet has the capacity to take the cost out of raising small donations. Having put a Web site up to begin with, it is somewhat surprising that so many candidates did not seek to raise money. Anything that came in would have been "free" in terms of the cost of raising the money.

Again, what is surprising about the second part of Table 9 is that so many Internet campaigns neglected to ask for volunteers. One of the most important functions of a political campaign is to recruit volunteers. Of course volunteering is not what it used to be in the days before media campaigns, but campaigns still have need for volunteers—especially on election day. Table 9 shows the types of volunteer activities being recruited for on the Web. Traditional volunteer activities include the sorts of things that campaigns recruited for in the days before the Internet. Pat Buchanan's 1996 primary campaign was probably the first one to recruit traditional volunteers in cyberspace. By the day of the

1996 New Hampshire primary he probably had more volunteers this way than anyone else.[14]

In 1997, Governor Christie Todd Whitman operated what was generally viewed as the best campaign Web site to date. Marty Edlund, a Harvard senior, studied the considerable volunteer activity that was generated over Whitman's Web site. "For thirty percent of the Internet and online volunteers this was their first campaign experience."[15] Most of the Internet volunteers came to volunteering of their own volition, as opposed to the other volunteers who had to be recruited by the campaign itself. The campaign thus succeeded in doing one of the things that campaigns find most difficult—bringing new people into political activity. Whitman won by only 26,000 votes. The high quality of the Web site and the recruitment efforts that went on in cyberspace may have played a significant role in her victory. Two years later, as Table 9 indicates, recruiting volunteers is a very common feature of politics on the Web.

The Whitman campaign also initiated one of the first instances of what we have chosen to call "cyber-volunteering." Cyber volunteer activities constitute a class of activities that can only be done on the Internet. The most popular cyber volunteer activity is a feature that allows a person to send an electronic postcard to a friend—often with a personalized message attached. Another form of cyber volunteering is a variation on the old "visibility" campaign. Evan Bayh, the Senate candidate in Indiana, allows you to put an "Evan Bayh for Senate" bumper sticker on your home page. And Lily Eskelsen, the Democratic candidate for Utah's Second Congressional District, offered a "Cyber Yard Sign" *(http://Lily4Congress.org/cyber.html)*. While most of the recruitment in 1998 was for traditional volunteer activities like working phone banks or doing mailings, cyber-volunteer activities will most likely grow in concert with the overall growth of the Web.

Connections

Most sites contained one or more link to other sites, as Table 10 illustrates. The most frequently used link was to a political party. Many of the minor party candidates had very short and simple Web sites; more extensive information was to be found on the Web site of their political party. Candidates also linked to ideologically similar interest groups and to governmental sites. For instance, Gil Aust, Republican congressional candidate for Alabama's Fifth Congressional district, provided visitors to his Web site with an entire page of "Cool Political Links" featuring

Table 10. Connections	
Does the Web Site Contain Links to Other Web Sites?	
No links to other sites.	273 (49%)
Yes, links to other sites. (Note: many link to more than one other site)	281 (51%)
Links to government sites.	89 (32% of total links)
Links to the incumbent's government site.	17 (6%)
Links to the Web site of a political party.	204 (73%)
Links to other sites (i.e. interest groups, think tanks, news media).	155 (55%)

Republican party Web sites, conservative Web sites, and links to conservative media such as the Rush Limbaugh show. (See Appendix.) Surprisingly, very few incumbents provided links to their own governmental sites—a reflection, perhaps, of the belief that this would constitute inappropriate use of government assets for campaign purposes.

Table 11. Voter Registration	
Does the Web Site Provide Voter Registration Information?*	
No voter registration information.	495 (89% of all sites)
Voter registration information.	34 (6% of all sites)
Provides a link to the state's voter registration office.	26 (5% of all sites)
Allows visitor to order an absentee ballot online.	16 (3% of all sites)
*Numbers exceed 100% because some sites give more than one form of voter registration information.	

Table 12. Does the Web Site Involve Multimedia Technology?	
Video (The visitor can view clips of television commercials or clips of the candidate speaking.)	47 (8% of all sites)
Audio (the visitor can hear the candidate or someone else talking in a radio ad or in some other venue.)	43 (8% of all sites)

Another major effort of most political campaigns is to make sure that their supporters vote. Thus it was again surprising that so few campaign Web sites offered information on how to register to vote. As Table 11 illustrates, the vast majority of sites gave out no voter registration information at all, and very few sites made it easy to get directly to the state voter registration office or to order an absentee ballot online.

Finally, very few Web sites linked their Internet campaign to their radio and television campaigns. Only 8 percent of all sites offered video and/or audio on their sites. Gray Davis, Democratic candidate for Governor of California, offered a full page of online videos consisting of television spots and a special 17-minute piece *(http://www.gray-davis .com/governor/video.html)*. Of course, the small number of sites with multimedia links is not quite so surprising when one considers that for many of the candidates in this sample, especially the minor party candidates and the congressional challengers, there were no radio or television commercials to link to.

Professionalism

Like any other aspect of a campaign, a campaign Web site needs to be kept up-to-date and in sync with the changing environment of the campaign if it is to be successful. Therefore we looked to see whether or not the campaign Web site was kept up to date. Table 13 shows the results of those findings. The results confirm what many of us found when looking at the sites. In a great many cases the sites were constructed and then forgotten.

It's difficult to tell who constructed the Web sites of 1998 since, as Table 14 indicates, the vast majority of sites listed no professional or individual as the Web creator. However, 1998 did see the rise of political Web professionals, and about 16 percent of the Web sites in 1998 were designed by Web professionals. (There may have been more

Table 13. Is the Web Page Kept Up to Date?	
Yes, information is within one week of the day on which the site was looked at	104 (19%)
Somewhat, information more than one week out of date	48 (9%)
No, information more than one month out of date	402 (73%)

designed by professionals, but we could only count what was up on the Web site itself.) In some instances the Web page was designed by an individual. In the case of Roy Barnes, the Democratic candidate for governor of Georgia, his 25-year-old son Harlan was the Web designer and the Webmaster.

Table 14. Who Created the Web Page?	
A professional consultant	86 (16%)
An individual	38 (7%)
No information available	430 (78%)

Conclusion: Does It Matter?

At the beginning of the 1998 election cycle, the political consultant Phil Noble confidently predicted that 1998 would be the year when the Internet "made" a political candidate in much the same way that television made John Kennedy in 1960. As we have seen, many candidates used the Internet in the 1998 election cycles, although few candidates took advantage of the full powers of the new medium. So was there an Internet candidate in 1998?

Jesse, formerly "The Body," currently "The Mind," Ventura is a colorful former professional wrestler who stunned the political establishment by winning the Minnesota governorship on a Reform Party ticket. On November 6, 1998 Phil Noble declared him the "JFK of the

Net"—i.e., the first candidate to successfully use the new medium. However, Phil Madsen, Webmaster for the successful Ventura for Governor campaign, had a more nuanced view of the influence of the Internet. At a conference following the election he said, "The Internet did not win the election for us, but we could not have won without the Internet."[16] In an example of just how hard it is to sort out the differing causal threads in a campaign, Madsen describes himself as a "Web site rookie" but a "skilled activist." In fact, the Ventura Web site was not one of the most elaborate of the Web sites in campaign 1998—for instance, it had no links to any other sites. Its purpose, in Madsen's words, was to "produce volunteers, money and votes."

But the Ventura campaign was, in fact, the first "virtual" campaign. Until the very end, this campaign did not have an office. When they finally got an office, it became mostly a warehouse for the piles of T-shirts and other campaign paraphernalia they were collecting to sell. For by that time this campaign was truly a "virtual" campaign—organizing everything from bus trips to finance over the Internet. Not only did they raise about a third of their total dollars over the Internet, they also used the Internet to solicit people who would guarantee bank loans to the campaign!

Listening to the story of Jesse Ventura's Internet campaign prompted Robert Arena, Jr., former director of Internet strategy for Dole/Kemp '96, to say, "If Phil had had any candidate but Jesse 'the Hulk' Ventura, everything he did right would have been wrong."[17] In other words, the Internet enabled an insurgent campaign to do what it otherwise would not have been able to do, but it took more than the Internet.

No one candidate illustrates this better than Doug Ross, unsuccessful candidate for the Democratic nomination for governor of Michigan. Ross was trying to use the Internet to find some sort of "competitive edge." His goal was to design an interactive process which would allow him to interact with about 50,000 Michigan primary voters. But difficulty getting people to leave them their e-mail addresses and resistance to uninvited e-mail—"spamming"—meant that they ended up engaging only about 5000 people, and Ross lost the Democratic nomination to Jack Kevorkian's flamboyant attorney.[18]

The contrast between the Ventura campaign and the Doug Ross campaign brings up an important point. The Ventura campaign used the Internet basically as a substitute for an infrastructure that did not exist for a third-party candidate. The Ross campaign attempted to use the Internet to build a network large enough to win a nomination against two other candidates—one with an established base in the labor movement and the other with statewide notoriety. In discussing this attempt, Ross pointed out one of the still great limitations of campaigning on the Internet. The voters are accustomed to politics coming "uninvited" through other mediums. Candidates knock on doors at dinner time. Candidates' phone banks call voters in the evening; they send voters junk mail. All of this activity is "uninvited," and, while often ignored, this activity does not risk turning off voters. And yet "uninvited" activity over the Internet takes on an entirely different meaning, and voters get angry at receiving spam. One candidate in 1998, Steve Langford, a gubernatorial candidate in Georgia, made news when after attempting to solicit voters over the Internet, he made so many voters angry that he had to publicly apologize and promise to stop using the Internet to solicit voters.[19]

The emerging "different" culture of the Internet may erode over time, but as of now the difference between Internet culture and the culture of other mediums seems to have a great deal to do with control and empowerment. As Kathleen deLaski of America Online pointed out, "This has been a pristine environment." In 1998 AOL found people hungry for do-it-yourself kits of all kinds—including in the political realm. The tag line for their efforts in the 1998 election cycle was "politics on your terms."[20]

"Politics on your terms" is a good way of describing the emerging Net campaign. When voters are drawn to a candidate, the Net becomes, in the hands of someone who understands old-fashioned political organizing, a powerful and inexpensive way to mobilize the voters, raise money from them, and keep them engaged in the campaign—with often surprising results. In addition to the Ventura campaign, the close Senate races of Barbara Boxer in California and Russ Feingold in Wisconsin seem to have had a great deal to do with skilled use of the Internet to mobilize volunteers.

But the Internet has yet to compete with television—the medium that goes out and "pulls" often reluctant citizens into contact with the candidates. (As Pippa Norris's essay in this volume illustrates, politics on the Internet is still about preaching to the converted—that is, reaching the already politically active—more than it is about reaching noninvolved voters.) It is possible that the Internet will become a place where candidates can come "uninvited" into the cyber homes of potential voters. It is possible that, once there, candidates will be able to engage in direct conversations with voters—conversations that change the role of traditional intermediaries such as the press and make the democratic process more deliberative. But, as Lawrence Grossman warns, "The only people more foolish than those who try to forecast the future of a new medium are those who listen to them."[21]

What we know is that 1998 established the Internet as a new feature of American politics. We can predict that, as the Internet becomes more and more a part of the lives of Americans, there will develop a set of political norms that define its use and a body of conventional wisdom which someone, seeking victory, will someday defy.

Endnotes

1. See Pippa Norris's essay in this volume, especially Table 5.

2. According to Andy Kohut, Director, Pew Research Center for the People and the Press, use of the Internet jumped from 10 percent of the population in 1996 to 15 percent in 1998. David King predicts that by the year 2000 primaries there will be 80 percent Internet penetration rates among voters. Comments made at "Politics on the Net: A Post-Mortem of the 1998 Elections," John F. Kennedy School of Government, December 3, 1998.

3. In addition to the difficulty of finding all the Web pages, another problem was that Web pages seemed to appear and disappear even during the campaign season. Thus we defined our universe as those Web pages that were up and running in the last week of September and the first two weeks of October 1998. During that time there were eleven Web pages "under construction" that probably became active later in October; these pages were included in our totals, making the total number of Web pages in our universe 554.

4. See the article by Frank Luntz, *Wired* magazine, December 1997.

5. See "Campaigning on the Internet in the Off Year Elections of 1998: A Snapshot in Time" by Elaine Ciulla Kamarck, prepared for the Bretton Woods Conference, July 20, 1998, John F. Kennedy School of Government, Harvard University.

6. Kevin A. Hill and John E. Hughes, *Cyberpolitics: Citizen Activism in the Age of the Internet,* (Lanham, MD: Rowman and Littlefield, 1998) p. 36.

7. Robert J. Dinkin, *Campaigning in America: A History of Election Practices* (New York: Greenwood Press, 1989), p. ix.

8. See Marty Edlund, *Net Effects: How the Internet Changes the Costs and Benefits of Campaign Volunteering,* March 1998, presented to the Department of Government, Harvard University.

9. "The Internet and Political Communication in the 1996 Election Season; Research Note" by Bruce Bimber, May 10, 1997. *(www.wsscf.ucsb.edu/survey1 /mobilize.htm.)*

10. Quoted in "Internet, Candidates, Click" by Tim Nickens, *St. Petersburg Times,* June 8, 1998.

11. Wayne Rash, Jr., *Politics on the Nets,* (New York: W. H. Freeman, 1997), p. 118.

12. Comments by Marion Just at "Politics on the Net: A Post-Mortem of the 1998 Elections," December 3, 1998, John F. Kennedy School of Government, Harvard University.

13. Comments by Marty Edlund at "Politics on the Net: A Post-Mortem of the 1998 Elections," December 3, 1998, John F. Kennedy School of Government, Harvard University.

14. Rash, op. cit., p. 37.

15. Marty Edlund, *Net Effects: How the Internet Changes the Costs and Benefits of Campaign Volunteering,* March 1998, presented to the Department of Government, Harvard University.

16. Comments made at "Politics on the Net: A Post-Mortem of the 1998 Elections," John F. Kennedy School of Government, Harvard University, December 3, 1998.

17. Ibid.

18. Ibid.

19. Political News from *Wired News,* August 6, 1998, *www.wired.com/news /news/politics/story/13815.html.*

20. Comments made by Kathleen deLaski at "Politics on the Net: A Post-Mortem of the 1998 Elections," John F. Kennedy School of Government, Harvard University, December 3, 1998.

21. Ibid.

CATCHING VOTERS IN THE WEB

\<David C. King\>

Elaine Kamarck documents how U.S. House, Senate, and gubernatorial candidates used the Internet in the 1998 campaign, and
her work will be regarded as the benchmark survey of the political Web in its infancy. While it is utter folly to predict which Internet
stocks on Wall Street will continue soaring past 1999, it is simpler to
imagine how political campaigns will use the new technology, since virtually all campaigns pursue the same ends—finding and motivating
people to vote. There are time-tested ways of getting voters to the polls,
and in a Darwinian way losing strategies (and candidates) are quickly
discarded. In political campaigns, the Web is a growth stock. Bet on it.

The keys to the future of the Web in campaigns are evident in
Kamarck's work. These include the importance of competition to innovation, the use of the Web to solicit campaign resources, the interactivity of the Web, and the Web's potential to knit together the internal
organization of campaign staffs.

Candidates in 1998 used the Web as an outlet for traditional campaign materials: press releases, nice candidate photos, and basic contact
information. This all fits nicely into any traditional campaign. Very few
sites maintain interactive chat rooms, but like any forum, chat rooms
empower loudmouths who have little better to do. One of the more dis-
tressing findings in Kamarck's work is that the overwhelming majority
of 1998 sites were rife with "old" and "static" information. Many were
electronic brochures that simply took the old political models of campaign publishing and put them on the Web.

David C. King *is Associate Professor at Harvard University's John F. Kennedy
School of Government, where he teaches about legislatures and interest groups. He
is the author of* Turf Wars: How Congressional Committees Claim Jurisdiction.

The Web coordinator of tomorrow's campaigns will be at the heart of any election strategy because the Web will soon be a device for collecting information about issues and specific individuals likely to support one's candidate, for "narrowcasting" about policies that concern voters most, and for helping campaign volunteers feel more a part of the campaign organization. These campaign innovations will emerge, naturally, through the magic of political competition.

In his classic 1968 *Candidates for Office,** John Kingdon found that winning candidates for Congress congratulated themselves for making good strategic moves in a campaign (overestimating their own importance) and losing candidates rationalized their losses as the results of factors outside their control. This makes winning candidates (incumbents in the election) more likely to follow strategies from the previous campaign, while challengers prove more likely to innovate and to take risks. It is through political competition that campaign innovations take hold, and these innovations are tested first by challengers.

Data on Internet innovations in political campaigns follow the Kingdon story closely. In her exhaustive survey, Kamarck tracked the Web presence (and absence) of 1,366 candidates (921 from the two major parties and 445 minor party and independent candidates). Among Democratic and Republican candidates, Web usage is twice as likely for challengers and contestants in open seats than it is for incumbents. Fifty-three percent of open-seat challengers and contestants had a Web site in 1998 while just 26 percent of incumbents adopted the new technology. Furthermore, the incumbents who used the Web were those most likely to be facing stiff competition, again demonstrating that competition spurs innovation in political markets.

In campaigns, politics is marketing, and politicians can learn a lot about Web marketing from General Motors and Nabisco. More important than displaying the product, marketers need to know (1) who the consumers are likely to be, (2) the preferences of their consumers, (3) where the consumers are, and (4) how to motivate the consumers to buy. How can the Web do all this for political campaigns? Here is a simple example using my friend (and noncandidate), David Hart.

---

*John W. Kingdon, *Candidates for Office; Beliefs and Strategies* (New York: Random House, 1968).

David Hart for Congress

Mike Capuano won the 1998 Democratic primary after Joe Kennedy (D-MA-8) retired. This being Massachusetts, Capuano captured the general election with only nominal Republican opposition, so the primary proved critical. Capuano (and his fellow challengers in the primary) had a Web site that almost perfectly matched Kamarck's description of the 1998 offerings. It was little more than an electronic brochure. Much of the information was out-of-date, and while it solicited volunteers, those solicitations were in no way targeted for specific kinds of voters.

Imagine that it is May 1998 and David Hart, a liberal Democrat in his late-thirties, decides to enter the crowded primary, jumping in as the eleventh candidate. With such a crowded field, we can expect that just 20 percent of the primary vote could win the Democratic nomination, but Hart faces four especially tough opponents: Ray Flynn (the former Boston mayor who has great grass-roots "get out the vote" skills), Marjorie Clapprood (who is well known as a radio personality), Chris Gabrielli (who has money to burn on TV and radio but no neighborhood operations), and Mike Capuano (the wildly successful Somerville mayor who is not known outside of his town).

Hart needs to identify and mobilize a niche of the Democratic Party that has not already been successfully targeted by his ten opponents. The Web can help.

Identifying Likely Voters

Anyone who has worked in a campaign remembers purging and "scoring" voter lists. It is a monotonous process, but it is crucial to identify quickly the subset of constituents who are likely to vote in the primaries. Nationwide, congressional primaries average just over 19 percent turnout, and candidates are careful not to "waste" time and money on the overwhelming majority of unlikely voters. Seeing who has voted in the past identifies likely voters, so every candidate in the Eighth District is working from virtually identical lists. With the Web, David Hart can do better.

Hart can begin by contacting the major Web search engines (Alta Vista, Yahoo, Lycos, Excite, Infoseek) and purchasing information about citizens within the Eighth District zip codes. Several months ago, these search engines began offering free e-mail, as a way of enticing users to yield their home addresses. (A year ago, identifying home addresses off Web traffic was very difficult. No longer.) Hart could purchase, for example, the names, addresses, and e-mail addresses of every "Web registered" Eighth District citizen who has recently searched for "Ray Flynn" or "Marjorie Clapprood" on the Web. For a small fee, a Web portal (or search engine) could identify registered users who visited virtually any political Web site in the world, including very narrowly defined interests. If, say, Hart wants to target environmentalist voters, he could identify Eight District Web users who searched for "The Sierra Club," "Ducks Unlimited," and so on.

Second, Hart should contract with *Townonline.com,* the online service of Community Newspapers—which has local papers in Watertown, Belmont, Cambridge, Brookline, and Boston. Online readers are encouraged to sign the site's "guest book." This allows *Townonline.com* to identify specific users—and their usage patterns—anytime they re-enter the site. Register once, and the user is automatically identified in subsequent visits. For a small fee, David Hart could buy the names, addresses, and e-mail addresses of every Townonline visitor who read any particular story. Does Hart want to do a targeted Belmont mailing about the incinerator controversy? Then simply identify who has been reading about the incinerator online. This may be a little disconcerting to people who care about their privacy, but *if* one is a registered user, one has almost no privacy. I registered to read the Associated Press Online through the *Los Angeles Times.* In theory, someone at the *LA Times* could identify every article I've read in the last 6 months and how I (and many others) surfed from one type of article to another. And through experiments on the Associated Press website, the AP can identify what kinds of headlines attract more readers and how readers link from one subject to another.

David Hart has a new book about the development of technology policy in midcentury. It is called *Forged Consensus*, and Hart could potentially pay *Amazon.com* for the names, addresses, and e-mail addresses of everyone in the Eighth District who bought his book online. (It would be a very small list.) Through *Amazon.com*, Hart could also conceivably purchase information about everyone buying "environmental" books in the Eighth District over the last six months. The Belmont book buyers might be a perfect audience to hear about Hart's concerns over the incinerator.

Recruiting Campaign Resources

Though Kamarck found the Web being used only sporadically for recruiting volunteers and soliciting funds, it could be an ideal tool. Campaign contributors know no boundaries, and the Web makes identifying potential issue-specific donors fairly easy. Again, with Alta Vista, one could do a *free* targeted search of all Web sites mentioning various words. For Hart, we might search for "Incinerator" AND "Environment" AND "Against." When I performed that search in July 1998, I found 203 separate Web sites mentioning those three words in combination. They are all potential Hart allies. Or, for a simple fundraising gambit, David Hart could send a mass mailing to every "David Hart" in the phone book nationwide. Using *Switchboard.com,* I found over 1,600 David Harts, with addresses and phone numbers, in under 20 seconds—and for free. *Four11.com* quickly identified 659 separate e-mail accounts registered to "David Hart" worldwide, and we could do a targeted e-mail to that list in less than 20 minutes. There are 37 David Harts in Massachusetts alone, many who would be thrilled to send $20 to their namesake for Congress.

It takes far less than a $20 contribution to catch a voter in the Web. Once a person contributes any small amount, say $5, that person makes a psychological commitment to seeing the candidate win. In most campaigns, $5 matters little, and a solid House campaign will cost David Hart more than $500,000. The importance of the small campaigns is in mobilizing voters and making them psychologically invest in the outcome.

Where do the Web viewers come from who might make small contributions? They are not likely to stumble across the site, and Web pollution is becoming more and more severe. Rather, David Hart has to send highly selective potential voters links to his Web site, using the identifying techniques discussed above. The more exclusive and "by invitation only" the site appears, the more likely Web-weary voters are to tune in.

Communicating within the Campaign

David Hart's campaign is ahead of its time; so in addition to a state-of-the-art narrowcasting Web site, he maintains a separate Web site for his own campaign volunteers and coordinators. This site may prove critical in coordinating events across the district and in quickly sharing strategic information.

For campaign workers on the bottom rung, working for a candidate can be solitary and alienating. Volunteers go door-to-door answering scattered questions from voters, though these volunteers may never have met the candidate and often use obsolete campaign materials. With a campaign Intranet, the huge gulf between door-knocking volunteers and the candidate can be bridged. Volunteers can be included in discussions and can share observations up the hierarchy much more quickly than in past campaigns.

That is David Hart's plan. His Web Intranet (password protected and with increased security the closer one gets to strategic documents) is updated daily with information about his campaign. Campaign schedules are modified almost hourly, so his staff can see when he'll arrive at schools, picnics, and the like. From his volunteers, he tracks the placement of signs in neighborhoods and quickly thanks volunteers for every door knock and campaign rally. It is not so much that David Hart forges a consensus within his campaign early and then sticks with it. Rather, he continually updates his strategy and personnel to gauge the consensus in his campaign and keep spirits high.

Benchmarks

David Hart did not run for Congress in 1998 and probably never will. Still, his could have been a model campaign. Some campaigns, notably Tom Campbell's race for the U.S. House in California and Jessie Ventura's gubernatorial run in Minnesota, used the Web's full potential. The Web itself is always changing, and its "full potential" will grow with each election cycle.

We owe Elaine Kamarck a debt for detailing the beginning of the political Web, noting not only the percentage of campaigns using the Web but, more importantly, ways in which the Web was used in 1998. The "electronic brochure" is the dominant image in her benchmark construct.

I am confident that this will all soon change, as campaigns follow the lead of retail marketers in identifying specific voters, narrowing their messages, and communicating within their campaign organizations. A similar study ten years hence will show a ubiquitous Web presence. More than that, the very structure of campaign organizations is likely to change. Today a typical organizational chart includes a manager, treasurer, press manager, and volunteer coordinator. Tomorrow a new position will be listed among the top team: Web coordinator. The Web will be that central to every campaign, and we will come to think of the computer—with its dynamic links to data and voters—as the new "political machine."

bureaucracy.org

THE VIRTUAL STATE

TOWARD A THEORY OF BUREAUCRACY
FOR THE TWENTY-FIRST CENTURY

\<Jane E. Fountain\>

There is little theory and no coherent research program within the discipline of political science that seeks to account for the potential or likely effects of major changes in information processing on the bureaucracy. This silence is curious given that during the past two decades, in popular writing and in political practice, many actors have been engaged in "breaking down," "abolishing," and "bashing" bureaucracy. Indeed, the stillness of political scientists on this matter has contributed to a verbal sleight of hand. Rather than use the term "bureaucracy" in its accurate meaning, political and media actors have shifted its definition to mean an organizational form productive of a set of inferior, outmoded processes and outputs. It is not even clear whether one should speak in terms of a post-bureaucratic government or of an evolutionary adaptation, or modernization, of bureaucracy.

This essay argues, first, that political science requires a theory of bureaucracy that accounts for far-reaching, fundamental advances in information processing and a sustained, coherent research program to develop such a theoretical perspective. Elements of such a research

Jane E. Fountain *is an Associate Professor of Public Policy at Harvard University's John F. Kennedy School of Government. Her current research focuses on information technology, organizational design and governance.*

program are outlined. It is difficult to argue against the importance and centrality of the bureaucratic form throughout twentieth-century American government. The structure and its constituent processes are largely responsible for the production of binding collective decisions and coordination of policy implementation. If changes in information technology have serious implications for bureaucracy, then theorists must account for such a modification in underlying assumptions regarding information processing.

Second, I submit that a useful starting point for a theory of information-based bureaucracy is provided within current bureaucratic and organizational theory. At minimum, an adequate theory must offer guidance to structure systematic research efforts. It should direct the attention of theorists to aspects of the terrain that are important. For the moment, I put aside the requirement for predictive power. Let us first decide on the variables of importance. Adequate theory also guides development of new policy tools, including organizational and program design, to foster improvements in government performance, accountability, and responsiveness.

It is impossible to sensibly discuss how information technology affects the bureaucratic paradigm without returning to the roots of that paradigm, the Weberian bureaucracy. This approach, although less exciting than intellectual excursions into cyberspace and sweeping speculation on the society of the future, provides an important starting point for the development of theory. Therefore, I begin this essay with an outline of the key elements of the Weberian bureaucracy and correlative, current, organizational phenomena. The second section draws the comparison between traditional bureaucracy and emergent forms by extending the scope of discussion to three levels of analysis. I then focus on the organizational processes that underpin and largely determine capacity and control: production, coordination, control, direction, and integration. The conclusions catalogue, at least partially, key streams of a research program to align bureaucratic perspectives with present information-processing capabilities.

Modern Officialdom:
Fundamental Properties of Weberian Bureaucracy

Although Weber described bureaucracy as an ideal type, he argued several times in his voluminous output that bureaucracy was the only form of organization able to cope with the complexity of modern enterprise.[1] His delineation of the chief elements of bureaucracy has been central to conceptual understanding of the form and of the role of the bureaucrat.[2] The extended quotation that follows establishes the definition of bureaucracy used in this analysis.

Characteristics of Modern Bureaucracy

Modern officialdom functions in the following manner:

I. There is the principle of *official jurisdictional areas,* which are generally ordered by rules, that is, by laws or administrative regulations. This means:

1. The regular activities required for the purposes of the bureaucratically governed structure are assigned as official duties.
2. The authority to give the commands required for the discharge of these duties is distributed in a stable way and is strictly delimited by rules. . . .
3. . . . Only persons who qualify under general rules are employed.

In the sphere of the state these three elements constitute a bureaucratic *agency,* in the sphere of the private economy they constitute a bureaucratic *enterprise.* Bureaucracy, thus understood, is fully developed in political . . . communities only in the modern state, and in the private economy only in the most advanced institutions of capitalism.

II. The principles of *office hierarchy* and of channels of appeal [or "levels of graded authority" in a different translation][3] . . . stipulate a clearly established system of super- and subordination in which there is a supervision of the lower offices by the higher ones. . . .

III. The management of the modern office is based upon written documents (the "files"), which are preserved in their original or draft form, and upon a staff of subaltern officials and scribes of all sorts. The body of officials working in an agency along with the respective apparatus of material implements and the files, make up a *bureau.* . . .

IV. Office management, at least all specialized office management—and such management is distinctly modern—usually presupposes thorough training in a field of specialization. . . .

V. When the office is fully developed, official activity demands the *full working capacity* of the official. . . . Formerly the normal state of affairs was the reverse: Official business was discharged as a secondary activity.

VI. The management of the office follows general rules, which are more or less stable, more or less exhaustive, and which can be learned. Knowledge of these rules represents a special technical expertise which the officials possess. It involves jurisprudence, administrative or business management.

The reduction of modern office management to rules is deeply embedded in its very nature.

Jurisdiction

Weber offers, in the first characteristic of bureaucracy, the kernels from which theorists have developed the powerful concepts of division of labor, functional differentiation and clear jurisdictional boundaries. One of the chief effects of advances in information technology on bureaucratic organization has been the ability to structure information using information systems rather than through strict delineation of role and organizational subunit. Professional and operational roles will continue. But they have become broader and more fluid. Recent major revisions to civil service position descriptions and classification system provide evidence for the current restructuring of roles within the federal bureaucracy. Similarly, jurisdictional boundaries have changed character. Although they have not disappeared, boundaries have become more permeable. This change is addressed later in the essay.

Hierarchy

Weber's second characteristic, hierarchy, forms the essence of bureaucracy for many theorists. Herbert Simon, a key figure in both bureaucratic theory and automated information processing, traces the dominance of hierarchy through a variety of natural as well as social systems.[4] Simon argues that hierarchy represents a structural form that encompasses and enables the decomposability of complex problems. The ability to factor complex problems and then to assign the results to specialists is the chief reason that complex organization, bureaucracy, supercedes other forms of organization. Simon offers as evidence of superiority not only greater efficiency of output, but the exceptional robustness of decomposable systems able to withstand and recover from interruptions and disruptions from a variety of sources.

Information technology, primarily in the form of shared databases and electronic communications, has promoted greater use of cross-functional groups and teams at both the operational and professional levels. The predominance of these problem-solving groups diminishes the centrality of hierarchy. The ability to place information and computing power at the operational levels of a hierarchy while making results rapidly transparent at upper levels underlies current capacity to devolve decision making to operational personnel. Thus, "empowerment," often viewed from the perspective of human relations, may be understood as a structural (and cultural) artifact of technological advancement.

Theorists as early as the 1950s predicted the demise of middle management as a direct result of mainframe computer use in complex organizations.[5] Their forecast was based on the clear obsolescence of middle management tasks in light of office automation. That their prediction took more than thirty years to come to fruition merely illuminates the difficulty of making deep structural modifications in complex organizations. The lag between technological and social change often is substantial. But a high proportion of positions lost through the downsizing of federal employees at the outset of the National Performance Review consisted of middle management.

In spite of some "flattening" and loosening of command and control systems, hierarchy remains central to most complex organizations. The important question for students of bureaucracy concerns the optimal, or appropriate, types of hierarchy in information-based organization. Reductions in levels within the chain of command in several bureaucracies signal the natural experiment currently underway. The rapid rise of scholarly interest in network forms, both internal to organizations as well as among them, has obscured the fact that networks continue to rest largely on a hierarchical base. Changes in hierarchy and its function in the bureaucracy have implications for the structure and practice of authority as well as for other properties, practices, and politics that flow from command and control systems of decision making.

The "Files" and the Staff

The third chief characteristic according to Weber, the "files," constituted an equally important departure from the idiosyncratic, personalized office. As bureaucracy became central to the modern state, for example, tax collectors could no longer individually define their operational methods. Written rules and the evolution of standard procedures, stored in the files, formed the basis for the rationalization of the state and the economy.

Digital files structured as shared databases place data and information throughout bureaucracy rather than in the hands of actors placed within specific functions and levels. A notable result has been the detachment of information from individuals holding a particular role. This fundamental structural shift has important implications for the meaning of the statement, "information is power." Much has been written concerning the assumed democratization expected to occur as a result of information sharing and transparency.

Bureaucratic Neutrality

Weber also articulated the role of the bureaucrat as neutral with respect to organizational direction, impersonal with respect to application of law and administrative regulations, and expert in the conduct of a particular, clearly defined office. Although several theorists have discounted the notion of bureaucratic neutrality,[6] the concept remains normatively powerful and a key feature of civil service professionalism. Chief contemporary changes in the bureaucrat's role have derived from the increasingly cross-functional and enlarged character of many positions in organizations where project teams form and disband according to agency requirements.

General Rules

Finally, Weber outlined the rationalization of bureaus and offices increasingly ordered by rules and procedures. Weber's then-radical perspective captured the transition from patriarchal, patrimonial, intensely political and personal systems of organization to the rational, impersonal, efficient, rule-based bureaucracy currently under siege. Information-based organization is equally, if not more strongly, rule-based and more highly rationalized. However, rules embedded within information systems become less visible and seemingly less constraining to bureaucratic discretion. Embedded rules will increasingly replace overt supervisory control. Indeed in many cases, so-called empowerment represents little more than a shift from overt to covert control through embedded rule systems and peer groups.[7]

Bureaucratic Transformation: Three Levels of Analysis

Theory must be sensitive to levels of analysis. Three levels are important for this analysis. Weberian properties focus implicitly on the bureaucratic structure as a whole, thereby missing intraorganizational (individual, group, subunit) and interorganizational phenomena. I flag some of the key implications of information processing advancement for the federal bureaucracy at each level. The main point is to extend the focus of Weberian analysis to capture effects that range from those operating primarily at the level of the individual to those that transcend the boundaries of the bureaucracy.

At the intraorganizational level, one finds effects on individuals, groups, and subunits. I note substantial change in the design of work, an area addressed partially through process redesign efforts initiated as part of the National Performance Review. Knowledge workers and knowledge work have replaced simple, repetitive, clerical tasks required in paper-based bureaucracy. Case workers, whose desktop computing capacity provides access to several databases and powerful analytic tools, perform work previously disaggregated into several positions. In some cases, automated tools allow relatively simple employees to make sophisticated evaluations. Task integration due to information technology has resulted in a collapse in the number of job categories and simplification of the position classification system in the federal bureaucracy.

The information revolution carries with it a host of human resource implications, such as the appropriate design of careers, reward systems, and performance measures in the bureaucracy. As command and control decision systems have modernized, a stream of secondary effects requires systematic attention. These include modifications to supervisory roles, transformation of hierarchical relations, and, at a deep cultural level, modernization of the nature of authority structures and systems.

At the organizational level, major advances in information technologies have led to several structural changes. The dominance of the manager, a direct outgrowth of bureaucratic development, formed a dominant focus of scholarly attention after the Second World War.[8] Technology has substituted machines for labor, leading to a sharp decrease in traditional middle management positions. An equally important, less-well-recognized, effect lies in the enormous number of new positions required to develop, maintain, and service the information-based organization and the information society. Growth of information technology-related positions is predicted to vastly outstrip labor market supply during the next decade.[9] Scholarly attention during the next decade may usefully be directed toward the growing dominance and influence of systems analysts within information-based bureaucracy.

Information technology diminishes, and in some cases eliminates, time and distance barriers leading to proliferation of work groups whose members are geographically distributed, to new agency arrangements, and new types of government services. One of the most important developments has been the growth of cross-functional arrangements. These arrangements exist both in human form, as cross-functional teams, and in automated form as process redesign, the consolidation and streamlining of tasks previously accomplished sequentially. In many cases "business" units (responsible for particular products or services) have been created in place of functional units.

Finally, interorganizational level change has been catalyzed as the external boundaries of agencies and other organizations have become more permeable. Agencies have increased partnerships with other agencies, with private and nonprofit entities, and with customers to gain efficiencies through improved problem solving and more effective design of production and operations. Although this phenomenon is best known through the efficiencies gained from contracting for business services, a comparable level of partnership activity characterizes many government activities.[10] Through the use of electronic data interchange, agencies have overcome costs of coordination to gain its efficiencies: reduced paperwork; increased speed and accuracy of transactions; improved control of inventories and suppliers; strengthened channel control; improved relationships with customers; resource and risk sharing; integration and synergy without ownership.[11]

Our inquiry thus far has classified some of the chief properties of information technologies that either presently affect or are likely to affect the bureaucracy. It has also outlined some of the chief modifications to bureaucracy in terms comparable to those used by Weber. I have done this because theory development requires more precise language than is typically found in discussions of technology and government. The invention of new terms provides excitement, but obscures theory.

Implications of Technology for Capacity and Control

One more lens is required through which to view the implications of the information revolution on the bureaucracy. Although bureaucratic theorists think in terms of structure and process, typical discourse in public administration and management uses a closely related but different terminology. It focuses on the activities of the bureaucracy and their achievement through agency capacity and control. Weber's concepts represent antecedents of capacity and control. Theoretical development, therefore, invites examination of technological change in light of these properties of the administrative state.

The National Performance Review has been criticized roundly by public administration scholars. Criticism by the public administration community reflects lack of theory adequate to guide analysis of technological change and bureaucratic behavior. Misled by rhetoric touting empowerment, critics have ignored fundamental technological change and its implications.

For example, as part of an extended critical essay on the National Performance Review, Gerald Garvey asks:

> How do you retain control when you eliminate bureaucracy, *whose essence is control achieved through the codification of knowledge, the inculcation of habits, and the structuring of hierarchical authority?* The answer may be you do not retain control. Or, if the existing system of controls is too deeply entrenched, you just talk about eliminating bureaucracy—citing anecdotal instead of systemic evidences of radical change—instead of really doing it.[12]

This critique follows from well-known principles of public administration. Administrative behavior must satisfy the dual requirements of capacity and control. Capacity indicates the ability of an administrative unit to achieve its objectives efficiently. Control refers to accountability due to "higher authority, most particularly to elected representatives in the legislative branch."[13]

Democratic accountability, at least since the Progressives, has relied upon hierarchical control, control by superiors of subordinates along a chain of command that stretches from the apex of the organization, the politically appointed agency head, and beyond to the members of Congress down to operational level employees. The National Performance Review, according to Garvey and most critics, "involves the substitution of bottom-up control, that is, control of officials in their day-to-day work by those officials' 'customers,' the citizens whom they serve."[14]

The scientific managers of the early and middle twentieth century developed governmental structures according to the Scientific Method of Frederick Taylor and the normative explanations of bureaucratic behavior developed by Max Weber.[15] The bureaucratic structure of modern organizations in the private and public sectors is a lineal descendent of Taylorism. It solved the problem of how to achieve capacity in complex problem-solving requiring coordination of a large number of subtasks and functions while retaining control over a disparate enterprise.

Political scientists typically explain the rise of the modern administrative state as a response to industrialization during the Industrial Revolution in the United States.[16] However, organizational forms developed by state and industry also were rendered possible by technological achievements that underlay the Industrial Revolution. The steam engine, telegraph, telephone, and early adding machines all made possible bureaucracy as well as the interorganizational forms underlying business and government using vertical integration and spatially dispersed headquarters and field organizations. Technological developments did not determine these forms in an inevitable fashion, but they made them possible and, in some cases, completely logical.

Information technology differs from other technologies in its capacity as a general-purpose manipulator of symbols used in all types of work. In the generality and breadth of its applications, it resembles the steam engine, and is having effects on a scale similar to that of the steam engine during the Industrial Revolution. *Information technology is different from other types of technology because it affects both production of goods and services (or capacity) as well as coordination and control.*[17]

One indicator of the tremendous applications of and demand for information technology is cost. The cost of information processing has dropped enormously during the past twenty years and is projected to continue to drop dramatically. As the economics of information technology continue to drive down its costs, its effects should continue to proliferate throughout government. Current estimates show cost performance ratios to be declining at a rate of 20–30 percent a year.[18]

I noted briefly the lag between advances in information technology and in bureaucracy. In spite of stunning examples of innovation in the federal government as well as in other sectors, empirical studies find few examples of fundamental organizational change to date either in the private or public sectors. I have argued in previous research that institutionalized norms and values, bureaucratic politics, and tightly coupled routines are highly resistant to change. Indeed, organizations often appear to change technology, rather than their practices, by using or *enacting technology* in suboptimal ways that allow the status quo to continue.[19] It is easy to discount the deep political and social adjustments that have to occur in order for organizations to leverage the potential afforded by information technologies.

Production

A key aspect of production, or capacity, in government affected by information technology is intellectual production or knowledge work. "The degree to which a person can be affected by [changes in information technology depends upon] how much of the work is based on information—that is, information on what product to make or what service to deliver and how to do it (the production task), as well as when to do it and in conjunction with whom (the coordination task)."[20] Government officials who develop loans and other financial instruments, provide counseling, write contracts, regulations, and legislation are involved in intellectual production. Other knowledge workers in the federal government include engineers, designers, budget analysts, lawyers, and so on. The knowledge worker adds value to information.

Clerical tasks, of which there are an enormous number in government, are affected by information technology. These tasks, often classified as "information work," include accounts receivable, billing, and payable. Thus, social security administration, tax administration, welfare disbursements, student loan programs, and a large number of other programs have been transformed by information technology—or have that potential easily at hand.

A major potential advance for government concerns the application of information technology to knowledge production in the form of workstations for those who assemble qualitative products, such as loans, letters of credit, or contracts, and for those who design "soft" products including legislation or new software. The application of information technology to knowledge work has been much slower than its application to physical production. Production processes involved in knowledge work—for example, professional expertise, research, creativity, and judgment—are less well understood and far less easily routinized. Experience with knowledge-based programs or expert systems demonstrates that rule-based systems work well as aids to clearly defined problems but tend to produce poor results outside well-bounded domains. Organizations, particularly in government, have been slower to exploit information technology in the area for this reason.

Coordination

Much of what federal agencies do falls under the category of coordination. Communication networks enabled by information technology are being built within subunits and agencies as well as among agencies and countries and comprise essential elements of much needed information infrastructure. The National Performance Review itself has been sustained and disseminated in part through a telecommunications network linking federal employees. ARPANET, and more currently the Internet, are among the largest networks connecting government employees and millions of other users. As an outcome of Information Technology Initiative 6 of the National Performance Review, the prototype of an Integrated Trade Data System (ITDS) has been built. The system will standardize and link trade-related data among more than sixty federal agencies and bureaus with responsibilities for trade policy and administration. Lack of consistent standards has inhibited the proliferation of communication networks both within and outside government. As standards are negotiated, the growth of electronic networks should increase dramatically.

Information technologies alter coordination through their effects on the relationship between information, distance, time, and memory. First, distance becomes far less relevant with regard to information flow. This has implications for partnerships and the location of work. Second, time becomes more fluid as federal organizations and their partners in different time zones shift work to gain efficiencies. Store-and-forward systems and common databases make time far less relevant. For example, the Social Security Administration shifts telephone calls dialed into its teleservice centers from one time zone to another in order to expand its service to the public beyond the typical federal workday.

Third, organizational memory, in the form of shared databases, collects data from and provides it to all authorized points in agencies as well as maintaining information in easily retrievable and malleable form over time. Organizational memory comprises an important aspect of coordination. Agency and interagency databases constitute a "memory" that can be accessed systematically and analyzed to benefit administration and future decisionmaking. For example, personnel databases may be used to identify skill mixes, possible succession plans, and candidates for positions. Shared databases containing retrievable, manageable information affect coordination through their potential to allow decisionmakers to better detect patterns.

These three aspects of coordination—time, distance, and memory—make it possible for agencies to establish and use teams whose members work in disparate locations, whose work is conducted without face-to-face meetings and whose production is shared throughout the team's existence. Telecommunications networks allow decision makers within the administrative apparatus to place nearly any information, any time, anywhere, and in nearly any format. This coordination capacity depends upon an infrastructure that is being put into place at different rates in different agencies. With this telecommunications infrastructure comes the ability to virtually link employees and work both within agencies and, increasingly, across agencies and entities.

Control

Two aspects of control are important to consider regarding public management. First, measurement of agency or program performance against a set of criteria is critical to control although sometimes devilishly difficult to implement in government. The second aspect of measurement involves timely, clear, and accurate feedback of measured results to decision makers, interpretation of those results, and subsequent decisions based on interpreted feedback.

Information technology cannot determine the appropriate performance measures for agencies. But information technology embeds routines in programs and procedures to make data collection easier, data collation automatic, and report generation in a variety of forms simple. Information technologies rationalize elements of tasks more powerfully than procedures manuals and first-line supervisors are capable of doing. Software applications make clear to federal employees those aspects of their tasks that are discretionary. And databases collect information so that control is far greater than was possible in a traditional bureaucracy because the actions of most employees are captured electronically and easily stored and analyzed in terms of quantity and some qualities of output. So information-based organizations codify knowledge and inculcate habits in a somewhat different but much more powerful fashion than is true in traditional bureaucracy. The control problem in government has never been easier to manage.

The marginal discretion granted to employees is meant in part to enhance "customer service," or empowerment or some other human relations objective. But greater discretion also is critical to prevent technologically constrained jobs from becoming completely uninteresting to employees. Given the capability to control employee behavior and outputs to such a great extent, added discretion at the margins achieves benefits without loss of discipline.

It is certain that a solid core of hierarchy and functional specialization will remain in information-based organizations. But the control apparatus that required multiple layers in the chain of command has been greatly simplified, with gains in accountability, through information technology. With information systems that render employee behavior largely transparent, hierarchical authority is relieved of the task of physically observing employees. In a transparent system shirking is obvious, as is greater output. Hierarchical authority takes on the more important task of direction setting in turbulent environments, keeping officials current with environmental changes, and ensuring the alignment of task, technology, human resources, and goals.

Control systems traditionally serve three functions. They help decision makers use resources more effectively by providing feedback, thereby making the production process more "visible." Second, control systems serve to put disparate units and divisions of the agency in line with agency goals. Third, control systems provide data for decision making at the strategic and operational levels.[21] Information technology has provided the potential for more than efficiency gains in existing processes and systems. It has created a set of new tools for collecting, managing, and using information. One of the challenges for gaining these new capacities lies in linking program managers, control staff, and information resource managers in agencies in order to put information into the most valuable locations.

Data storage is relatively inexpensive. To sustain innovation, the federal government should "reinvent" all information systems that stymie the efforts of users to manage information and that make information retrieval slow and complex. Those frictions are outmoded. Information-based control systems should be able to respond to changes in external conditions. Decision makers can use information-based control systems to decide where information should appear and in what form. For example, data collected at remote field locations is as easily available at headquarters as it is in its field locations and may be transferred with having to travel through several hierarchical layers. In other cases, the value of information generated at headquarters might be enhanced by making it available to operating managers in field locations. One of the important benefits of automated battlefield management systems for the U.S. Army, to note one example, is the ability to provide the same data to each battalion or brigade commander in a division nearly simultaneously thereby providing a consistent view of the battlefield to each decision maker.

Information technology renders the tension between centralization and decentralization obsolete. Data can be placed at either or both headquarters and field locations in forms useful to decision makers at several levels. So a critical management task becomes deciding which data are needed at various organizational locations, how timely those data should be, and in what form(s) they would be most useful to the decision makers who will use them.

In some cases, centralization of data collected from branch offices may be useful. Data are less useful that have been filtered through several hierarchical layers because "bad news" is routinely filtered out of aggregate numbers and because the data are often outdated by the time reports reach headquarters staff. Information systems allow for objective data reduction and near-real-time transmission. Alternatively, if field personnel lack the information to make effective operational decisions then agencies may benefit from decentralization of some data. When performance incentives are linked to control systems through shared information, the effect on performance is powerful and meaningful. Many managers perform suboptimally either because they are not fully aware of agency goals, lack the informational resources to make intelligent decisions, or lack motivation because their incentives fail to match their externally supplied objectives.[22]

Integration

Reengineering, a process redesign method used widely in the federal government, captures some of the coordination and integration capacities of information technology. But reengineering is limited by several constraints. First, integration of production processes depends largely on the telecommunications infrastructure available to make integration feasible. Second, some skill in work design, management of change, and leadership is necessary both to design the integration and, more importantly, to implement it.

Integration is actually a broader, more powerful concept than business process redesign, or reengineering. It can be classified into four levels. First, integration can occur within the operational processes of an agency. This is the typical application of reengineering in which teams are formed around one process linked by a local area network. Agencies have improved capacity greatly by breaking down barriers between functional areas and, more modestly, by reducing barriers between employee classifications. Increased ability to coordination provided by information technologies makes the traditional need for narrow task specialization far less important.

Second, agencies have a growing ability to integrate electronically production that lies across organizational boundaries. This capacity greatly speeds the flow of information and services across organizations. The ability to integrate processes in this way relies on electronic data interchange (EDI). Organizational boundaries in information-based organizations are highly permeable with respect to these interorganizational arrangements. Third, agencies can subcontract and outsource larger pieces of production processes to other state and local governments, private firms, and nonprofit organizations. Information technology enables these arrangements by greatly reducing coordination costs, by standardizing data elements across sites, and by making communication easier across organizational boundaries. Finally, information technology has made electronic markets possible.

Each of the levels of integration reduces coordination costs and increases the effectiveness of coordination by eliminating the need for buffers—"inventories" of supplies, information, and expertise—and by pooling expertise.[23] The capacity to provide resources where they are needed when they are needed removes time lags (or wait times) and further reduces the need for buffers.

These four types of integration require a threshold level of information technology infrastructure in communications capacity, data standardization, applications software, and human expertise.[24] Major increases in capacity, coordination, and control as a result of integration still reside largely in the future and await sufficient infrastructure.

The ability to integrate in various ways is changing and will continue to change the contours of government, the relationship between competition and collaboration among actors, and government-business relationships. To cite one example, the Internal Revenue Service has created the capacity to receive electronic filing of individual income tax returns prepared by tax preparation firms. The shift to electronic processing creates enormous efficiency gains within the IRS. Moreover, this integration creates opportunities for lending or borrowing approximately $70 billion, thereby driving a set of new opportunities among several actors in the financial services business. This example also highlights the importance of the federal government's role with regard to setting standards because of the potential impact of federal decisions on the competitive structure of most industries.

Direction and Transformation

In order to understand the effect of information technology on capacity and control, the executive functions of direction and transformation must be considered. Direction involves sensing environmental occurrences including changes that may affect a policy or program and public response to governmental action. It also involves interpretation of these data and of decision making that responds to feedback from the environment. The information technology systems involve strategic planning systems as well as systems to capture customer feedback.

The enormous potential of information technologies to both quantitatively and, more importantly, qualitatively improve and enlarge capacity should prompt agencies to rethink their missions. Many operational decisions are based on existing capacity. New capacities should prompt rethinking. Without direct competitive pressure, the federal government has an opportunity, but relatively little pressure some would say, to rethink its operations. However, I have argued that citizens expect transactions with their government to be roughly as efficient as those with private sector organization.[25]

Developments within information technology have spawned a progression in some organizations from automation to information to transformation. Automation occurred, and continues to occur, as production costs are reduced by automating work formerly carried out by people. Automation of traditional paper processing is proceeding in the federal government but needs to progress much further. Tracking tools, scanners, and bar codes have greatly improved knowledge of the status of processes and shipments in agencies as disparate as the Immigration and Naturalization Service, which processes applications for residency and citizenship, and the Defense Industrial Supply Center of the Defense Logistics Agency, which processes purchasing requests from the military services. Those workers who are not replaced by technology require new skill sets to work closely with information technologies. Their work has become more abstract, less tactile, more mathematical, less heuristic.

But the same technologies that potentially reduce production costs also, in most cases, provide the capacity to capture and systematically organize information as a by-product of the process. Zuboff coined the phrase "informate" to denote this capacity created by information technology and, until recently, largely ignored by automation efforts.[26] Informating processes not only implies capturing and generating useful information, but requires human resources and new internal processes to make use of this new information. Both operating-level personnel and managers must modify their skill sets in order to recognize useful patterns, exceptions to patterns, and information that may be useful to transmit to others.

Indeed, information generated by technologies used in government has spawned entire businesses. The Defense Department sells maps and other information collected by sensors, satellites, and related technologies. In other cases, information collected by the government, and paid for by taxpayers, is packaged and marketed by private firms. The amount of valuable information generated by the government will increase dramatically as information technologies are more fully exploited. The use of that information prompts a set of policy, procedural, and economic questions regarding markets for information.

The third, and most ambitious step, transformation, refers to organizations that have used information technologies to build internal and external infrastructures for communication, information transfer, and more, and that have taken advantage of integrative and coordinative capacities provided by those infrastructural elements. In many cases, new services have been developed, the boundaries of the organization have effectively changed, and work has been substantially redesigned. But this level and degree of change has been relatively rare so far in the private as well as public sectors. Technology is a necessary but far from sufficient condition for substantial structural change and redirection. Transformation occurs as a result of several years of knowledgeable, effective executive leadership and investments in technology and human resources.

The potential effects of information technology on capacity, coordination, control, direction, and transformation described above hint at the potential of information technology to substantially redistribute power, functional responsibilities, and control within and across federal agencies and between the public and private sectors. As coordination costs continue to decline dramatically and economies of scale change through technology, the effects on institutional design will be felt. The "metabolic rate" of administration is increasing in rapidity and quality.[27] Both greater rapidity in information processing and greater interdependence require new administrative systems to measure, reward, and motivate desired behaviors and new skills for both operational employees, public managers, and appointed and elected officials.

There appear to be two chief requirements for using information technology to increase capacity, coordination, and control in public administration. The first is difficult. Implementation and use of systems must be optimized to support a set of goals. Agencies often must espouse vague, conflicting goals for political survival. No amount of rationalization, either through performance measures or new technologies, has altered this fundamental political reality. Increased rationalization of information technology is at odds with this political fact. Second, a threshold is crossed when information infrastructure is put into place allowing for integration in data collection, management, communication, and retrieval. Both a technical infrastructure and a set of standards are required for a high level of coordination to be possible. The sheer scale of many federal operations, in addition to the balkanized culture that characterizes many agencies, creates considerable drag on infrastructure construction and interoperability.

Most agencies have constructed a ragtag assortment of incompatible systems. Capital investments have been made, but to suboptimal effect. Information resource managers traditionally have held operational, rather than strategic, roles. It is in the domain of information resources management, particularly strategic management of technology, that public managers require development.

Conclusions and Broader Implications

I have presented evidence to argue for the development of a theory of information-based bureaucracy. The line of evidence also supports the second argument presented here, namely, that a useful starting point for developing a body of principles already exists in bureaucratic theory. But a series of underlying assumptions, regarding the character of information processing, requires fundamental alteration in order to understand current efforts to modernize bureaucracy.

I have claimed that predictive theory is not important to develop at this juncture. First, such development would be premature. Second, this discussion has omitted critical intervening variables that strongly mediate any hypothetical direct effects of information technology on elements of bureaucracy. I have analyzed the role and importance of these intervening variables in previous research.[28] This essay simplifies causal analysis in order to identify and focus on key independent variables that have been neglected by students of government. I have showed several of the enabling features of information technology in relation to bureaucratic structure and practice, but have presented a simplified version of cause and effect.

The first part of this essay outlined the Weberian bureaucracy, the foundation of the modern state. Its chief properties—official jurisdictional areas, hierarchy, management by "files" and generalized rules—are affected in various and complex ways by the information revolution. It is insufficient, in fact it is inaccurate, to claim that bureaucracy is outmoded. Although greatly altered by changing information technology, each element of bureaucracy remains central.

The second section expanded the scope of the discussion to include intraorganizational and interorganizational features of bureaucracy. For many students of government, "the bureaucracy" is a phrase synonymous with the civil service. The bureaucrat of the Information Age will require a vastly different set of skills and expertise. The structure of careers and mobility within the Civil Service has already been altered as a second-order consequence of changes in information technology. Similarly, the incentive structure and behavior of key groups within the bureaucracy—task forces, interagency working groups, committees, and the like—have been irrevocably altered with implications for policy and politics.

Attention to the interorganizational level of analysis and the implications of technological change illuminates key phenomena. The level of contracting available to agencies is directly related to technical means available to coordinate across jurisdictions. Recent emphasis on partnership also represents a form of coordination not available without current information technologies in place. The "new" public management emphasizes the economics of organization but requires additional attention to the economics of information to account for explosive growth of partnerships and networks.

The third section focuses on capacity and control. This perspective provides a counterargument to critics of the National Performance Review. I have argued that absent an understanding of technological change and its effect on capacity and control, students of bureaucracy can make little sense of either the rhetoric or reality of human relations changes such as empowerment, increased employee discretion, and customer service. Rules embedded in hardware and software form a system of control unimaginable in paper based systems. Discretion in an embedded rule regime is highly constrained.

Information technology affects production, coordination, and control. The breadth and importance of these implications have yet to be fully appreciated. An emerging stream of research focused on the economics of information provides the most promising and powerful insights to date. But the perspective neglects key political variables. Political scientists must develop a political economy of information.

A theory of information-based bureaucracy should account for stability as well as change in the form of organization that undergirds the modern state. Just as bureaucratic theory, like all theory, accretes through successive refinements, a theory to account for vast changes in the information processing capacity of the bureaucracy will necessarily evolve during the next several decades. Features of information technology and bureaucracy outlined in this essay present the basis for a research program to bring bureaucratic theory into the next century.

Endnotes

1. Max Weber, *Economy and Society,* ed. Guenther Roth and Claus Wittich (Berkeley, CA: University of California Press, 1978).

2. Weber, *Economy and Society,* vol. 2., ch. 11, "Bureaucracy."

3. Hans Gerth and C. Wright Mills, eds., *From Max Weber: Essays in Sociology* (New York: Oxford University Press, 1946).

4. Herbert A. Simon, "The Architecture of Complexity," *Proceedings of the American Philosophical Society* 106 (December 1962): 467–82.

5. Harold J. Leavitt and Thomas L. Whisler, "Management in the 1980s," *Harvard Business Review* (November–December 1958): 41–48.

6. Among those theorists who at least partially reject the idea of bureaucratic neutrality see Chester Barnard, *The Functions of the Executive* (Cambridge, MA: Harvard University Press, 1948); James March and Herbert Simon, *Organizations* (New York: John Wiley, 1958); Anthony Downs, *Inside Bureaucracy* (Boston: Little, Brown, 1967); and Oliver E. Williamson, *The Economic Institutions of Capitalism* (New York: Free Press, 1985).

7. See the special issue, "Critical Perspectives on Organizational Control," *Administrative Science Quarterly* 43 (June 1998), especially John M. Jermier,

"Introduction: Critical Perspectives on Organizational Control," pp. 235–256; and Graham Sewell, "The Discipline of Teams: The Control of Team-based Industrial Work through Electronic and Peer Surveillance," pp. 397–428. See also Frederick M. Gordon, "Bureaucracy: Can We Do Better? We Can Do Worse," in James Heckscher and Anne Donnellon, eds., *The Post-Bureaucratic Organization,* (Thousand Oaks, CA: Sage, 1994).

8. See, for example, James Burnham, *The Managerial Revolution* (New York: John Day, 1941); William H. Whyte, Jr., *The Organization Man* (New York: Simon & Schuster, 1956).

9. United States Department of Commerce, Office of Technology Policy, Technology Administration, "America's New Deficit: The Shortage of Information Technology Workers," Fall 1997.

10. Jane E. Fountain, "Social Capital: Its Relationship to Innovation in Science and Technology," *Science and Public Policy,* vol. 25, no. 2, April 1998.

11. James I. Cash, Jr., et al., *Building the Information-Based Organization: Structure, Control, and Information Technologies* (Boston: Irwin, 1994).

12. Garvey, Gerald, "False Promises: The NPR in Historical Perspective," in Donald F. Kettl and John J. DiIulio, Jr., eds., *Inside the Reinvention Machine: Appraising Governmental Reform* (Washington, DC: Brookings Institution, 1995) p. 91. Emphasis added.

13. Garvey, p. 87.

14. Garvey, p. 88. I share concern regarding the customer service metaphor as a tool of government, but my critique differs from that of Garvey. See Jane E. Fountain, "Customer Service: An Institutional Perspective," paper presented at the annual meeting of the American Political Science Association, Boston, September 1998.

15. Frederick Winslow Taylor, *Principles of Scientific Management* (New York: W. W. Norton, 1967).

16. For an extended analysis, see Stephen Skowronek, *Building a New American State: The Expansion of National Administrative Capacities 1877–1920* (New York: Cambridge University Press, 1982).

17. I am indebted to Joanne Yates, Michael Scott Morton, and other students of information technology and organization at MIT for research and analysis, cited below, on the relationship between current information technology and earlier technologies. Michael S. Scott Morton, ed., *The Corporation of the 1990s: Information Technology and Organizational Transformation* (New York: Oxford University Press, 1991).

18. Joanne Yates and Robert I. Benjamin, "The Past and Present as a Window on the Future," in Michael S. Scott Morton, ed., *The Corporation of the 1990s.*

19. Jane E. Fountain, "Enacting Technology," Harvard University, John F. Kennedy School of Government, Faculty Research Working Paper Series, 1995.

20. Yates and Benjamin, "The Past and Present as a Window on the Future."

21. William J. Bruns and F. Warren McFarlan, "Information Technology Puts Power in Control Systems," *Harvard Business Review,* September–October 1987.

22. Bruns and McFarlan.

23. Michael Hammer and James Champy, *Reengineering the Corporation* (New York: Harper Business, 1993); Yates and Benjamin, 1991.

24. Regarding the convergence of intelligent transportation and the national information infrastructure, see, for example, Lewis Branscomb and James Keller, eds., *Converging Infrastructures* (Cambridge: MIT Press, 1996).

25. Jane E. Fountain et al., "Summary, Findings, and Recommendation," *Customer Service Excellence: Using Information Technologies to Improve Service Delivery in Government,* Harvard University, John F. Kennedy School of Government, Strategic Computing and Telecommunications in the Public Sector, 1993.

26. Shoshana Zuboff, *In the Age of the Smart Machine: The Future of Work and Power* (New York: Basic Books, 1984).

27. Yates and Benjamin, "The Past and Present as a Window on the Future," p. 18.

28. Fountain, "Enacting Technology."

REFLECTIONS ON "THE VIRTUAL STATE"

<Richard Darman>

A Few Reflections on the Extreme Hypothesis

Jane Fountain does not succumb to the temptation to project a radical new world. But several would-be leaders of an info-tech-led revolution do. So it seems appropriate to pause for a moment to consider the extreme hypothesis they entertain: that, one way or another, bureaucracy may wither away.

Suppose, for purposes of reflection, that Steve Forbes were President and most governmental functions were transferred to the private sector. Or, if that does not make you entirely comfortable, suppose Al Gore were President and all Americans were hooked up to the Internet, ready to participate in a seamless network as lifelong knowledge developers and knowledge workers in a glorious knowledge-based revolution. Or if that seems a bit too much like Revenge of the Nerds, suppose a populist political dimension were added—and a Ross Perot successfully persuaded the networked society to govern itself directly via continuous electronic polling in an endless national town meeting. Is it at all likely that, in any of these happy dreamworlds, bureaucracy would have disappeared? Or if bureaucracy were to disappear, would it likely be gone for long?

I think the answer that is clear to most of us is: no, of course not. In the Forbesian world, bureaucracy would be somewhat more private, but

Richard Darman *is Public Service Professor at Harvard University's John F. Kennedy School of Government, to which he returned after holding senior positions in the Bush Cabinet and Reagan Administration. He is the author of* Who's in Control? Polar Politics and the Sensible Center.

it still would be. In the Gorean world, bureaucracy might no longer reside in big ugly buildings. But it would reside instead in the protocols of an electronic world—the rules for categorizing, compartmentalizing, sifting, ordering hierarchies, providing security, and applying standard operating procedures. Such rules would be inescapably necessary to make a quarter-billion-person electronic network usable and efficient. And in the Perotian world of horizontal democracy, it wouldn't take too many cases in which a quarter-billion eager citizens decided simultaneously to "look under the hood" and "fix" something before hierarchy and a degree of specialization were reimposed.

Why then have techno-infatuated political futurists conjured up images of a nonbureaucratic world? The reasons are many: All recognize that current bureaucracy is unpopular, and nonbureaucratic images are therefore appealing. Some believe that the private sector is non-bureaucratic. Others believe a more user-friendly government is necessary to preserve and advance the role of government. Most wish to seem forward-looking. Some may be opportunistic. Others may be naïve. But it is important to note: None has in fact come close to demonstrating concretely that, in a large, complex society—however well-connected electronically—bureaucratic patterns can be radically reduced.

This is not to argue that the information technology revolution will have no significant effects on the character and performance of government. That would be foolish. The suggestion here is simply that notwithstanding significant effects of technological change, many of the characteristics of bureaucracy will persist. That is true for a compelling practical reason: bureaucratic patterns of specialization, hierarchy, coordination, rule-making, and standard operating procedures—with all their faults—are often necessary for efficient and coherent action, and sometimes necessary for the preservation of stability. Indeed, this may be even more true—not less—in a world of radically increased access to information, radically increased production of information, radically increased interdependence, and radically increased real-time interconnection.

A Few Reflections on Conventional Wisdom About Bureaucracy

Among many discussants of the vices of bureaucracy, there is conventional wisdom that would benefit from counterbalance before too much weight is given to the alleged antibureaucratic virtues of information technology. There is, for example, the notion that the private sector—having been quicker to adopt advances in information technology—is typically nonbureaucratic. This would be surprising news to millions of inhabitants of large and midsize corporations, as well as the many critics of "corpocracy." Or consider the following:

- The notion that "matrix" and "horizontal" organizations are either new or the product of advances in information technology. This would be surprising to those in the public and private sectors who made matrix organization fashionable in the fifties and sixties. It would also surprise those who have viewed the increase in horizontal organization as a function of motivational needs of modern workers (independent of the info revolution).

- The notion that the hierarchical organization charts of large bureaucracies correspond, in practice, to actual lines of authority and communication. This would be surprising to the many practitioners and analysts who have long appreciated that formal and informal *processes* are more important than—and very different from—formal organizational *structures*.

- The notion that entrepreneurship is confined to nonbureaucratic organizations. This would be surprising to the many generations of successful government entrepreneurs who (again, independent of the info revolution) have beaten the supposed system by going around formal lines of authority, and by practicing the fine art of coalition-building through networking.

To the extent that many of the alleged virtues of the information revolution—such as increased horizontal connection, networking, and entrepreneurship—have arisen within large bureaucracies prior to the current information revolution, the effects of that revolution may need to be discounted some. And in general, it seems relevant to consider whether and when changes that result from information technology go beyond matters of degree and pace, and become interesting changes in kind.

This is a separable matter from the question of the extent to which increased networking and entrepreneurship should, in fact, be seen as unmitigated virtues. In some cases requiring rapid response, increased networking—however rapid—might *reduce* responsiveness. In cases requiring stability and continuity, increased entrepreneurship—however creative—could prove undesirably destabilizing. So while increased networking and other features of the information revolution may generally be taken as virtues, care should be taken to distinguish cases where presumed virtues might become vices.

A Few Reflections on Theorizing

One senses that there is a problem with many of the facile generalizations that have accompanied the chatter about the information revolution. My suspicion is that it might be useful at this stage to try some rather detailed bottom-up examinations of a range of real and hypothetical cases—and only then to return to attempts at generalization. As a way of suggesting how difficult it may be to reach conclusions about effects of information technology on bureaucracy, let me offer three mini-cases:

- **Case 1: Info-tech and the border-patrol bureaucracy.** Imagine this: A combination of extensive ground cameras (including night vision cameras), ground sensors, wireless transmitters, and satellites makes continuous border surveillance foolproof and cost-effective. And, with telecommunications, the surveillance can be done by a small number of professionals, at a single remote location—say, in a Rocky Mountain resort rather than the desert of the southwest. Sounds a bit like info technology might make the ugly world of border patrol bureaucracy wither away. That is, of course, until one asks: what happens if the monitoring system reveals people illegally crossing the border? I think I need not go on with this example. . . . Let's try another.

- **Case 2: Info-tech and the State Department—part 1.** Recall the nineteenth century world in which ambassadors were several months removed from those who gave them instructions. Neither they nor messages could cross the ocean quickly. As a result, ambassadors had to be people of very high quality, worthy of trust, capable of adapting on the spot to unforeseen or changed circumstances, and broadly empowered to do so. There was no need for a bureaucracy to monitor events and update instructions—because there was nothing such a bureaucracy could communicate in time to be meaningful. The world of diplomacy was relatively non-bureaucratic. Now, fast forward: add the ability to communicate quickly. What happens? Bureaucracy goes up, not down. The fudge factory is born. It seems that not all information technology breakthroughs can be counted on to reduce bureaucracy. . . .

• **Case 3: Info-tech and the State Department—part 2.** Imagine
there is a world in which: (a) The State Department's intelligence
functions are no longer needed because satellite-based information
gathering is comprehensive and continuous; private news and
investigative organizations report routinely, comprehensively, and
continuously on foreign culture, economics, politics, weather, etc.;
and all this reporting is available in near-real time electronically. (b)
State's travel support services are no longer needed because private
transportation and travel have expanded so much that private
global organizations (from American Express to Medjet Assistance)
are widely available to provide all necessary travel support efficiently and professionally. (c) State's (largely second-rate) negotiating capabilities are no longer needed because first-class private
negotiators can be hired for particular projects and transported
immediately to foreign sites when and as needed. In short, imagine
a world in which technology and private enterprise suggest that the
State Department should shrink to little more than a central pass-
port office. That is pretty much the world we live in—except that
the State Department remains a bloated, bureaucratic fudge factory.

For those who are inclined to think that the leap is easy or obvious
from technological advance to bureaucratic transformation, I would
respectfully suggest that these simple cases (among many) suggest otherwise. My guess is that the effect of technological advance on bureaucracy may be one of rather modest evolutionary change. For a while,
the theories of bureaucracy that explain a lack of rapid change may be
more relevant than new theory for a new era. The Fudge Factory may
be a useful indicator. When the politico-bureaucratic world is ready to
get rid of it, then it may be time to project (and explain) changes in
bureaucracy that rise beyond the ordinary, and justify use of adjectives
like "revolutionary."

SOME CAUTIONARY NOTES ON
THE "VIRTUAL STATE"

\<Sheila Burke\>

Jane Fountain does an excellent job helping us envision the traditional characteristics of bureaucracy, and how they are potentially enhanced or inhibited by the presence and implementation of information technology. In identifying the levels of change driven by IT, she provides us with the opportunity to consider what the optimum outcome might be. She wisely suggests, however, that those who presume these dramatic changes discount the deep social changes that must occur in order for organizations to leverage the potential afforded by information technology. Using a variety of interesting examples of innovations, Jane demonstrates "the impressive modernization efforts that are taking place," but again acknowledges that these innovations in and of themselves hardly constitute transformation of bureaucracies.

I would associate myself with these conclusions. Furthermore, I would posit with little or no hesitation that bureaucracy is very much here to stay, and IT is only one of many factors, albeit an important one, to potentially alter structure and responsibilities. Let me be clear that I make these observations from the standpoint of a practitioner, not an academic. The comments that follow are therefore based on experience rather than on a review of the literature or a study of the theory. I begin where Jane left off—with broad implications and questions for us to consider. She is correct in saying that, regardless of its size, the federal government will need to be managed with systems that

---

Sheila Burke *is Executive Dean of Harvard University's John F. Kennedy School of Government. Prior to joining the Kennedy School, she served as Chief of Staff to former Senate Majority Leader Bob Dole from 1986–1996.*

are different from those in current use. To understand how these systems might change and their potential impact on the bureaucracy, I believe we need to further explore what the public sector hopes to achieve through the use of these new systems. If asked, many within the bureaucracy, and among its elite leadership, would view this discussion largely as a question of how to use a new set of tools to do old jobs. For example, I believe that members of Congress have neither altered their views of what jobs must be done or their views of bureaucracy that serves them.

Do members theoretically want a smaller government? Yes. Do they want a better, more efficiently organized government? Yes. Do they want a less costly government? Yes. Do they want to bring government closer to the people? Yes. Do they want to integrate and coordinate more programs? Yes. Can we do all these things by improving and expanding in the use of IT? Unclear. To what extent will it result in transforming the bureaucracy? Unclear.

This commentary will examine the four key roles for bureaucracy as noted in Jane's paper and briefly note the extent IT changes bureaucracy's capacity to perform these functions.

Production

Examples given: loan officers, contract lawyers, regulation writers, budget analysts, Social Security clerks.

Expectations:

- Compile accurate information, process checks (payments), draft and negotiate contracts, publish regulations on time.
- Access input from external sources.
- Analyze complex data from multiple sources.

Increased and easy access to information will be much enhanced by the use of IT. Fewer people may be needed to perform the aforementioned functions. They may, however, need to be trained on these systems and there will still need to be a live person on the phone when the constituent calls. IT, however, may enable the individual answering the call to be better informed and more able to solve the constituent's problem. Will automation replace these individuals? Not likely. Many of the services they provide are at the heart of constituent service. Changes will come slowly. Think of the battles that resulted in the consolidation of the Department of Agriculture field offices and the Social Security district offices.

Coordination

Examples given: Telecommunications network, the Integrated Trade Data System, Social Security service calls, the creation of interagency databases.

Expectations:

- Coordination makes it possible for agencies to establish and use teams.
- Infrastructure makes it possible to work within and across agencies, and makes it less costly to do so.

The politics of jurisdiction will pose the greatest challenge to achieving these goals. IT could make the sharing of information possible, assuming all agencies and divisions it affects are similarly capable of assembling the data and utilizing it. A bureaucracy's need to perform these functions will not change. But, as has been the case since time began, information is power. An agency may be reluctant to share information if sharing results in others assuming its responsibilities and spending its money. Politics may also prevent the sharing of information, e.g., the historical reluctance to allow access to tax return data by other federal agencies.

Control

Examples given: Enables measurement of agency performance against a set of criteria. Enables timely feedback of results of work of agency decision makers.

Expectations:

- Better control of agencies and changes in their behavior if information-based performance reviews are implemented.
- More accurate and timely information upon which to base changes in policies or programs.

There are ample recent examples of how the power of access to information drives performance reviews and policy decisions. The most obvious example is the recent IRS restructuring. There was a great deal of emphasis placed on the timelines and accuracy of the work of the IRS. The report prepared by the Portman/Kerry Commission cites numerous areas where IT could improve, and in some cases dramatically alter, the way the Service does its work. At the end of the day, however, what drove IRS reform was the power of the anecdote, i.e., the human tales of abuse, not the data. Could data help avoid these problems? Not clear, but certainly IT will provide a better set of tools to evaluate what is happening and whether the bureaucracy is responding to the directions it was given. New uses of IT may also, as in the cases noted earlier, reduce the number of people needed to accomplish a task and improve the timeliness and accuracy of the information to which they have access. Employees' skills may change and their ability to work with their colleagues throughout the country should be enhanced. Technology, alas, will not replace the IRS agent. Better data and systems will not solve all the problems.

Integration

Examples given: IRS capacity to receive electronic filing.

This might include the use of Social Security numbers to track delinquent parents for child support payments.

Expectations:

- Improve capacity by breaking down barriers.
- Reduce need for narrow task specialization.
- Make organizational boundaries highly permeable.
- Reduce coordination costs and increase effectiveness.

Once again, as was the case with coordination, the best of intentions may be overwhelmed by the political considerations.

Case 1. Great effort has been made to get control of the welfare bureaucracy, while many still want to target resources to those most in need. Efforts to integrate data allowing one-stop shopping by recipients of cash assistance, food stamps and Medicaid benefits has been the goal for some number of years.

Case 2. Recent efforts at welfare reform have created the need for good data gathered from many sources, allowing a determination of whether the desired results have been achieved.

In the first case, jurisdictional battles between the committees with authorizing authority (Ways and Means, Finance, Labor, Agriculture, and Commerce) and among the external constituencies for these programs have prevented consolidation and are hampering integration. All the technology in the world will not solve the political problems. However, on a positive note, the recent child-health initiative is calling upon states to think of smarter ways to run their low-income programs, which may be dramatically affected by new methods of processing information. In the second case, many have argued that insufficient resources have been committed to developing, collecting and analyzing the necessary data to allow evaluation. Technology may help to solve the problem, although the cost of the personnel necessary may actually increase rather than decrease.

Again, in both cases the bureaucracy remains in place but, as a result of IT, there may be fewer bureaucracies, and they may be better able to do their jobs.

Cautionary Final Notes/Questions

- The speed with which any one agency or program can implement new IT strategies will vary enormously. *Example*: Social Security vs. IRS.

- The availability of IT tools does not insure competence. *Example*: Department of Labor has on file the prior citations for violations of the child labor laws but cannot, when applying new penalties, identify those companies previously cited and therefore subject to enhanced penalties.

- The availability of tools, even accompanied by incentives, does not ensure their use. *Example*: For years the federal government prodded, pleaded, incentivized and finally penalized states for refusing to implement Medicaid management information systems—yet many states stuck to paper processing.

- The desire to change and implement new systems will be dramatically affected by the willingness of an agency to spend sufficient amounts of money to achieve the intended outcomes. *Example*: The current controversy over the ability of the Health Care Financing Administration to implement the new Medicare law.

- In a world of more, and electronically available, personal data (tax returns, Social Security history, medical records) how do we make information available and keep it confidential?
- While there may be a reduction in the number of personnel necessary (i.e., a smaller bureaucracy), those remaining need new skills and are likely to be more expensive.

Finally, while this story relates more to the issues surrounding the impact of IT on the business of politics, it has some bearing on this discussion relating to the bureaucracy as well. Senator Russell Long was famous for sharing either his or his Uncle Earl's populist views of the business of politics. He made the following observation one day in the midst of a Finance Committee meeting: "Never write when you can call; never call when you can personally visit; never talk when you can whisper; and never whisper when you can wink."

No matter how good it gets, information technology will never replace the wink.

INFORMATION AGE GOVERNANCE

JUST THE START OF SOMETHING BIG?

\<Jerry Mechling[1]\>

Human societies are made up of incredibly diverse interactions within and among units such as families, tribes, villages, companies, churches, symphony orchestras, colleges, car manufacturers, nation states, and international organizations.

These interactions require governance, i.e., an authoritative means of coordination and conflict resolution. For situations where we can't or won't cooperate voluntarily, we need a mutually respected authority to resolve things. While we often dislike the specific applications of such authority, we recognize that some sort of socially authorized governance is essential for a safe and civilized life.[2]

Over the eons, as societies grew more extensive and complex, so did governance. In this context, governance includes the influence of culture and organizational management, as well as constitutionally authorized government units such as courts, legislatures, police departments, school departments, and tax agencies.

Over the past fifty years, many societies have been moving into what has been called the Information Age.[3] Enabled largely by the growth of scientific and technical knowledge, information can now be codified for easier access and communication over computer networks.[4] Human interactions—especially those associated with the production

Jerry Mechling *is Director of the Program on Strategic Computing and Telecommunications in the Public Sector at Harvard University's John F. Kennedy School of Government. He is the author most recently of* Information Technology and Government Procurement: Priorities for Reform.

and distribution of goods and services—can now utilize these networks to overcome barriers of time and distance. Fewer face-to-face meetings are required. As organizations increasingly coordinate their work—especially their knowledge work—over networks, information technologies and information workers have emerged as a key economic resource.[5]

Given such trends, what influence will the Information Age exert on governance in general and bureaucratic government in particular? The answers that follow are based heavily on case studies and surveys of practitioners involved in government information technology projects.[6] The analysis will explore how societies (1) shape and legitimize the values and rules needed to establish priorities and resolve conflicts (politics and policy-making) and then (2) implement and enforce such values and rules (largely via governmental bureaucracies).

We will find that governance changes, so far, have involved the mostly incremental efforts of government agencies to produce and distribute services over computer networks. Nevertheless, because networked information flows are so powerful and different from the bureaucratic flows that preceded them, what we find to date is unlikely to be the final story, but merely a suggestion of the much larger changes yet to come. These changes will respond to a relatively recent shift in the dominant governance challenge. The earliest challenge was to assemble the powers needed to protect public safety and order. Next, governance needed to protect against abuses of governmental power, largely through the invention and elaboration of democratic controls. Now—and for the foreseeable future—the dominant challenge will be to adapt to changing societal conditions while continuing to protect safety and avoid abuses of power.

Shaping and Legitimizing Values: Gently Exploring "Digital Democracy"

A healthy society needs good governance to resolve the conflicts that arise as individuals interact. In a society with few interactions and homogeneous values, relatively little authoritative governance would be required. But such a society could hardly be called healthy. The interactions and complex division of labor that create conflict are also needed to create economic wealth and military strength, and to generate the diversity of perspectives needed to respond to new threats or opportunities.[7]

The Information Age creates new challenges for governance by encouraging a more complex division of labor and interactions. Geographic proximity is becoming much less powerful in shaping our identity and sense of community.[8]

The movement of production and other communications to computer networks could thus significantly restructure our politics and governance. For most people, participation in the political community is a somewhat remote concern, at least relative to more immediate concerns of personal well-being, family, and job. But networks make it more convenient to participate in conversations that were formerly remote. This will lead to new patterns of political communication and participation. At least conceptually, there may be less reliance on representatives and a greater reliance on direct decision-making by the community.[9] There may also be a need to legitimize the role of communities organized around nongeographic boundaries.[10] As but one example, the Internet Council for Assigned Names and Numbers (ICANN) was recently formed as a nonprofit corporation whose board represents global stakeholders but not nation-states; while the authority of ICANN will certainly be tested, it represents an interesting experiment in non-geographically-based governance. ICANN was designed in hopes that it could respond more quickly (and therefore effectively) than could a typically slow-acting multinational organization.[11]

While the theories of digital democracy are bold, real-world applications have lagged behind considerably.[12] Public hearings in some jurisdictions are beginning to take testimony via videoconferencing, rule-making groups are seeking comments over the Web, and agencies are opening up e-mail links to constituents.[13] We also see the Internet used in lobbying and political campaigns.[14] Of a more aggressive nature, a few jurisdictions are experimenting with voting over the Internet, as Brazil did in a recent election, and as Florida and other jurisdictions are now planning for the future.[15]

Such activities may eventually grow to become pervasive and powerful. So far, however, work on the political and legislative side of governance (the "inputs") has been small relative to work by executive agencies (who produce the primary service and regulation "outputs"). Given people's inherent conservatism when it comes to political and constitutional structures—the devil you know is better than the one you don't—this should not be surprising.

New Ways to Implement and Enforce Values:
The Creation of Networked Government

What has happened with IT-related changes on the output side of governance? Are computers being used in government service delivery much as they have been in the private sector? Well, not exactly. But we do see investments that are essentially following along the same path.[16]

In general, governments have started by using computer networks to expand service customization and delivery channels, then moved to bigger innovations often referred to as "reengineering." Finally, in some cases, they have turned to the more controversial steps of outsourcing specific functions or entire services. In the long run, this path may or may not be optimal in terms of equity. The path may also be modified in unpredictable but large ways, as electronic money grows more powerful. Much is yet to be determined.

Networked Service Delivery: Taking the Easy Next Steps

Government services have long been based on face-to-face interactions between citizens and government bureaucrats. Such interactions have fostered equal treatment of all citizens and, when kept simple enough, have allowed for manageable record keeping. The result, however, has been that most services offer little customization. Nonstandard problems often create nightmares for customers who are forced to travel to different facilities to get a building permit, resolve a tax dispute, or attend a public school class. Face to face, paper-based services are often burdensome to citizens and government workers alike.[17]

In recent years, these inefficiencies have become less tolerable. More citizens have jobs, and more families have two careers demanding attention.[18] The opportunity costs of interrupting life in order to wait in line at a government office have increased. Many citizens have come to expect the convenience of services delivered over networks. Once people learn that they can resolve a billing problem with VISA from anywhere in the world and at any time of the day or night, they want to solve similar problems in similar ways with local, state, or federal tax collectors.[19]

Fortunately, computers often offer easy ways to improve service accessibility, customization, and integration. Given the growing pervasiveness of interconnected networks, governments may be able to provide major new benefits for service recipients through minor changes in organizational procedures. One of the most heavily used government Web sites, for example, merely allows citizens to download tax forms from the Web; as the April 15th deadline approaches, however, many citizens find this to be of great value, especially on nights and weekends.[20]

Using computers for relatively simple service extensions has been a major theme of winners of the Innovations in American Government Program.[21] Some examples:

1. *Accessible Service Delivery—the Ramsey County Electronic Benefit Transfer Program.* In Ramsey County, Minnesota, which includes the city of St. Paul, welfare payments used to be distributed as in most other jurisdictions—via paper checks through the U.S. mail. Because few welfare recipients had bank accounts, direct deposits were impossible.

Though Ramsey's method was typical, it was far from ideal. Recipients had to cash their checks either at the county's depository bank or at a check-cashing service. Under Minnesota law, the bank had to cash the check for free; however, it offered only one site for service. As a result, recipients crowded the bank's lobby on the monthly distribution day, creating long lines for all bank customers. While the check-cashing services offered more locations and hours, they charged as much as 10 percent to cash the check—a stiff fee, especially for welfare recipients. In either case, recipients had to cash the entire benefit at one time. Many checks were lost, and fraud and theft were significant problems.

The county was pushed to the brink when the last bank large enough to serve as a depository announced it would stop doing so because of the long lines and disruption. At an impasse, the county looked for a new means to distribute welfare. Working with local banks and a computer firm, the county arranged for clients to use magnetically encoded plastic cards to withdraw welfare benefits from the same bank-owned automated teller machines (ATMs) that serve the general public.

The conversion to network-delivered service took a great deal of planning and negotiating with stakeholders, along with careful pilot projects. The care paid off, and the Electronic Benefit Transfer program became a well-documented success. The new distribution method leverages economies of scope and scale inherent in the ATM network. Welfare benefits are now accessible from hundreds of locations on a 24-hour basis. Says Margaret Philben, who manages the project, "The system is easier, faster, safer, more convenient, and more reliable than the check method. Clients say they can manage the money better because they don't have to draw all of it out at one time. But most often they say they like the system because it's less embarrassing. They're using the same cash machines you or I would use to get our money."[22]

2. *Customized Service Delivery—the L.A. Automated Traffic Surveillance and Control Program.* Like many government services, traffic regulation by traditional traffic lights is not customized to particular situations. While the lights make travel faster and safer, they operate under simple rules: a specified amount of time for red, green, and yellow. They only pay attention to time, not to the traffic needs of the moment.

But traffic lights within the Automated Traffic Surveillance and Control (ATSAC) system of Los Angeles, California, work differently. Within the ATSAC system, detectors embedded in the street work with remote-controlled video cameras to measure traffic flow. The system draws conclusions for site-specific guidance to individual traffic lights. Lights no longer work independently, but rather as participants in a system that optimizes flow based on real-time traffic. Since the Summer Olympics of 1984, when the system was implemented on a pilot basis, ATSAC has cut commuter travel time by 50,000 hours *per day*. It has also reduced the number of vehicle stops at red lights by eight million per day, lowered fuel consumption within ATSAC areas by 13 percent, and cut auto emissions by 26 percent. It has proved especially effective for traffic caused by special events, accidents, and roadway construction.

ATSAC initially met with skepticism because computer-controlled signaling had not gone well earlier, in the 1960s. Since then, however, computer and telecommunications technologies and programming have improved dramatically. Computer-based traffic control, as evidenced by ATSAC, is now decidedly more effective and efficient.

3. *Integrated Service Delivery—the Info/California Program.* For some services, such as complex medical procedures or certain types of family counseling, face-to-face interactions may always be preferred. Still, face-to-face raises barriers of time and distance, especially when multiple agencies are involved. For instance, many welfare families also need other services, but these require extra trips for eligibility determination and service delivery. Even a simple address change involves giving the same information to many different agencies.

The Info/California program, sponsored by the California Health and Welfare Agency Data Center, addressed this problem by offering a "one-stop" solution. Using kiosks like those seen in airports, Info/Cal communicated with citizens via a combination of text, pictures, sound, and full-motion video. With kiosks linked to the Health and Welfare Data Network, citizens could access government in shopping malls and supermarkets, and at hours when government offices were normally closed. The services supplied were not only those of the Health and Welfare Department, but those of any federal, state, or local agency that wanted to use the kiosk infrastructure. Simply by touching the screen, users could find out how to recycle old batteries, report child abuse, re-register cars, look for vacant jobs, or order a copy of a birth certificate; using a credit card, they could pay whatever charges might be required.

Through pilot projects, Info/Cal learned that 40 percent of its usage fell outside normal office hours and 30 percent relied on a language other than English. Roughly 50 percent of its users reported that the kiosks had saved them a trip to one or more government agencies.[23]

Info/Cal's central idea was to offer service on a "virtual one-stop" basis. For the citizen, a kiosk visit required only one stop, but behind the scenes the computer network shuttled the conversation back and forth to whatever governmental programs the citizen requested. As an implementation matter, agencies could minimize change in their own operations while cooperating with other agencies via the Info/Cal network. While Info/Cal offered less than fully integrated service—citizens might have to key in the same address more than once to deal with different agencies—it provided a quick and easy way to expand convenience. The kiosk, while inherently more expensive than Web-based PCs, also provided early experience in how to shift face-to-face services to networks.

Welfare via ATMs, computer-controlled traffic lights, and kiosk-delivered services—all are stories of how to make services better via networks. The incremental innovations pursued by such projects are important. Further, because networks can typically turn a staff-assisted transaction into one that can be handled by the citizen on a self-service basis, they are likely to increase efficiency more dramatically in the future. Note that none of these innovations, however, have either promised or achieved radical cost cutting. The benefits have been captured primarily as service accessibility, customization, and integration—and possibly as reduced stress on service employees—not as tax cuts.

Reengineered Service and Self-Service:
Controversial and Slow Progress

In the private sector, many technology-based changes have focused on reengineering. Reengineering doesn't seek incremental improvement—say, 10 percent—but something much larger—say, 1000 percent. The goals are radical, so the entire process is quite different from the process used for normal productivity improvements.

Reengineering has been often discussed in both the private and the public sectors.[24] But when public sector projects—including the Innovations winners—are examined closely, very few are found to involve radical change or cost cutting. What is called reengineering in the public sector is generally a more gradual change than what is called for by the pure theory of reengineering.

Let's look at two Innovations winners that have significantly—if not radically—changed how public sector work gets done:

1. *Executing Handoffs Quickly and Remotely—the St. Louis Police Reporting Project.* Service production involves many handoffs of work from one specialized worker to another. The best division of labor requires balancing the benefits of specialization against the costs of the resultant handoffs. Computer networks open up new possibilities in two primary ways. First, they make it easier for individual workers to search for the information they need without asking for advice or handing off a job to other workers. Second, networks make many of the handoffs faster and easier, thus offering new possibilities for specialization.

The Computer Assisted Report Entry (CARE) project of the St. Louis police department took advantage of remote hand-offs to keep officers focused on street work. Under the old system, officers transcribed their own field reports. This was surprisingly costly work, consuming up to 20 percent of an officer's time. The paper-based reports typically took a week to then assemble and distribute for use throughout the department.

Using telephones and a computer network, however, the officers now simply call in their reports to computer-assisted clerical workers. The time per report has been cut from between 20 and 45 minutes to between three and nine minutes (the specialized transcribers being faster report writers than the nonspecialized officers). Further, with the reporting computerized, reports are immediately available for distribution and analysis. As a side benefit, the system is used for reports called in by citizens as well. On some nonemergency calls—for example, reporting stolen or vandalized property—the system eliminates the need to dispatch an officer altogether. The new process frees up time for officers, gives them better information, and increases patrol effectiveness.

"Civilianization" in police and fire departments—using civilian rather than uniformed personnel for work—is not a new idea. St. Louis, however, is not simply targeting a few officers doing clerical duties in the station house, but all those field officers who were spending one hour in five on clerical work. Another difference, and a key in St. Louis, was skill in project planning and implementation. The project benefited from strong top management leadership and careful steps to gain worker support. While the project changed patrol life considerably, it was a change the officers supported. Productivity was captured as expanded policing, not as a reduction in the force.

2. *Eliminating Handoffs—the Arizona QuickCourt.* While computer networks sometimes improve productivity by making specialists accessible, they can also improve information access so citizens don't need so much help from specialists. Thus, in many organizations (but not yet much among the Innovations winners) we see the development of "case worker" roles where one worker handles nearly all the work for a given client. We also see efforts to make information so easy to use that clients handle transactions by themselves.

The Arizona QuickCourt is an example of using technology for self-service, thus freeing government personnel to concentrate on more difficult problems. Arizona found that its courts were not informing citizens adequately about the judicial system or making themselves accessible to litigants who sought to represent themselves in court. Financially unable to add staff to meet these needs, Arizona instead used a grant from the State Justice Institute to develop software. The software captured the input and advice of judges, court clerks, attorneys, computer experts, and private citizens. The QuickCourt software, like Info/California, uses multimedia kiosks, in this case to help clients produce standard legal forms such as eviction notices and divorce documents. By mid-1994, 80 percent of the people who had used the system for some 23,500 transactions said they had found it easy to use and would recommend it to others. It was no small feat to design a system so that court documents could be filled out by average citizens, whether

English- or Spanish-speaking. But QuickCourt has done this, again turning the productivity gains into better service rather than lower taxes.

Outsourcing: Much Smoke, Some Fire

Coordinating work through bureaucratic hierarchies economizes on information processing. But hierarchies operate many activities at less than optimal scale. They also shield employees from market pressures for efficiency. Thus, if a given project (say, developing a new software system) would be equally costly from either an internal unit or an external unit, then the production component of the cost would typically be higher for the internal approach. By the same logic, the coordination component (finding the right supplier, negotiating and monitoring contracts, etc.) would cost more for the external approach. Over time, as coordination costs fall more or less proportionately for both internal and external approaches, the external or market-based suppliers will grow relatively more attractive since they will enjoy the bigger cost reductions. Market-based suppliers should also benefit as competition forces them to pay closer attention to customer needs and to innovation.[25]

This argument suggests that the Information Age will encourage outsourcing in both the private and public sectors. While government support for outsourcing has often been more rhetorical than real, U.S. governments today spend roughly 30–35 percent of their operational budgets—or $20–25K per worker—to purchase services from the private sector.[26] Outsourcing has become less tactical (designed to cut costs or apparent payroll) and more strategic (allowing government to focus on its core competency—"steering"—while giving other organizations the less critical work—"rowing").[27] At the local level, for example, we see Mayor Steven Goldsmith of Indianapolis fostering competition through outsourcing while also letting his own agencies compete for the work.[28] At the state level, particularly in the technology arena, we see the Service Arizona project outsourcing entire programs (e.g., motor vehicle registration)[29] and the State of Connecticut outsourcing its data centers and information management functions (to create high-tech private sector jobs as well as to gain efficiency).[30] At the national level we see U.S. efforts to adopt procurement procedures more like those of commercial enterprises, and U.K. efforts to outsource all data processing within Inland Revenue, its national tax collection agency.[31]

As the Information Age reduces coordination costs, look for continued government outsourcing. Although outsourcing will often be mistake-ridden and controversial, it should—to the extent that it enhances competition—lead to better and more innovative services. It will also force a greater fraction of organizational life into the private sector, with potentially more stressful work lives for those pushed from public sector to private sector styles of management.

Social Equity and Cohesion: Serious Anxiety, But Not Much Government Action

Many leaders believe that the Information Age will soon produce strong economic growth, but with growing inequality and divisiveness as well.[32] Clearly, in contrast to the first two-thirds of the twentieth century, recent decades have expanded the gap between rich and poor. This trend may continue, since many jobs in the knowledge economy require expensive educational investments as a prerequisite. It is no longer as easy as it used to be to start at the bottom of the ladder and climb upward, since the transition from back work to brain work has become too difficult.[33]

Inequality is a problem of ethics as well as politics, efficiency, and social stability. To protect the information "have-nots" in an era of digital services, some governments are working towards a new definition of universal access.[34] Others argue that government should do more to foster open standards and to directly subsidize computer-based services, especially for education and health.[35] Typical proposals call for free access to electronic services through libraries, schools, and hospitals.[36] Other proposals seek stronger intervention to protect those who would be harmed from the downside risks of globalization.[37]

On the opposite side of most equity issues, many supporters of free markets argue that the government should not intervene strongly, at least yet. They believe that government is not capable of sensible regulation or investment, and society's best hope is to allow competitive markets to produce low unit costs; after all, unsubsidized television has penetrated to more households than subsidized telephones.[38] In the grand scheme, income inequality results when some group is able to restrict access to a critical factor of production such as land or capital. In the Information Age, however, codified knowledge is a critical factor of production and may become so easily replicated as to flow rather freely and equally throughout the world. Knowledge of job openings and who is available to fill them may also become more efficiently net-worked, and serve in the long run to increase rather than decrease equity.[39]

So far, the debates about equity have been energetic. They have not, however, had much impact on governmental action. Governments feel themselves as too poor to invest much.[40] Further, given how easy it is for jobs to be moved from high-tax to low-tax jurisdictions in cyberspace, protecting equity through income transfers is not likely to soon become widespread or effective.

Electronic Money—A Force for New Pricing and Tax Policies?

Eons ago, the development of coins and paper money facilitated trade. It is clearly easier for a shoemaker to use cash to buy a loaf of bread than to use a pair of shoes to barter with the baker. Money and pricing systems thus support complexity in the organization of economic activity. In the Information Age, new payment methods based on com-puter networks—electronic money—may exert a new influence on how activities are priced and organized. Electronic money will make micro pricing and payments efficient (charges and payments of less than a penny, for example). In addition, it should provide better secu-rity against fraudulent trading (via stronger encryption to authenticate messages and identities) and also offer opportunities for anonymity (as happens today with cash).[41]

Electronic money may make it possible for governments to effi-ciently administer prices for new services and/or for services that are now given away for free. Examples would include prices for the research and analysis of census data, for motor vehicle titles and owner histories, for surveyor reports, for property tax data, for name and address change services, etc.

Governmental use of fees is, of course, controversial. The core argument is about who should pay for services—the service users or the general public. To the extent that the general public gains the ben-efits of use, as for most regulatory services, then broadly based taxes clearly will continue to make the most sense. To the extent, however, that the consumers capture the benefits, as for services such as camp-site reservations, then fees make sense, as they do in the private sector. If there is a *mix* of beneficiaries, as when auto records are used both to ensure highway safety (a public benefit) and also to improve car com-pany profits through marketing, then perhaps the groups should pay proportionate to their benefits. The pricing system could serve to allocate such joint costs.[42]

Pricing systems could also be constructed for transactions internal to the government. It is clear that government agencies don't share information easily with each other despite repeated exhortations to do so. Requests to freely provide data to outside agencies—even simple data such as names and addresses—are typically received as unfunded mandates. However, once electronic money options are more fully implemented, it should become much easier to keep track of the producers and users of any piece of data. This would permit transaction prices even for something as small as looking up a single name and address. With this kind of pricing, public organizations might be given better incentives to "share" the data they have collected and cleaned. In general, electronic money might create sizable information markets within and among government agencies and the public.

While electronic money might lead to an increase in marketlike activity, it might also lead to black-market or fraudulent activity (where transactions are invisible to the government or payments are made to the wrong parties). Cheap computing leads to powerful encryption and the ability of any two parties to keep secrets from the rest of society.[43] These secrets could include deposits and withdrawals at offshore banks. Electronic cash could make such invisible trades easier, much as babysitter clubs, neighborhood-based service coupons, and cash payments to service providers today support economic activities that are rarely taxed. Invisible trades could conceivably grow into a meaningful threat to the tax base, especially for taxes based on the (easily moved) location of an income-generating activity instead of the (not so easily moved) residency of the receiver. While large corporations may not be prime candidates for hiding transactions, individuals and small operations will be tempted. Note also that fraud in electronic government payment systems—such as the Earned Income Credit system or Medicare and Medicaid payments—is also a threat. Electronic fraud has already grown to huge and yet largely invisible proportions.[44]

Changes in Governance: Just the Start of Something Big?

Governments are building huge and interconnected computer networks, but there is a long way to go before these become ubiquitously available to all workers and citizens. The momentum is clearly established, however, and nothing is likely to stop it. Putting services on these net-works so they can be "virtually integrated"—i.e., found and accessed by a few clicks of the mouse or, in a few years, by a few spoken words[45]—will continue until nearly all services offer network access as an option. That alone will significantly change how people interact with government.

More fundamental reengineering will take longer. Nevertheless, given ongoing pressures to do so, and ongoing support for leading-edge practice through efforts such as the National Partnership for Rein-venting Government, governments will continue to pursue technology-related productivity improvements and other innovations. Outsourcing will continue to expand. In addition, more governments will begin to work with the private sector to reform entire industries and economic infrastructures, much as Singapore has been doing for the past several decades.[46] Multinational and nongovernmental groups such as the ICANN will be formed to govern different elements of cyberspace. Over the next ten to fifteen years, the expansion of net-work-based communications should exert a strong influence on how communities are formed and governed. Table 1 summarizes some of the predicted directions for governance and some milestones that may be reached by approximately 2010.

So far, the impacts of the Information Age on governance have been rather modest. We've been nibbling at digital democracy, little more. While Net-enabled communication has undoubtedly begun to exert an influence on social values and politics, individuals and institu-tions have been slow to risk fundamental change. Politics and gover-nance are about resolving conflicts, and efficiency is not the paramount virtue. Nevertheless, proposals are being pursued to establish new gov-ernance forms for cyberspace, and these may grow extremely impor-tant as the proportion of human interactions conducted over computer networks increases.

The impacts of the Information Age on traditional governmental bureaucracies have been, in contrast, much clearer and more immedi-ate. Public organizations are rapidly becoming networked and are using these networks to offer services. This will ultimately lead to effi-ciency improvements, much as has happened in the private sector.[48] Government bureaucracies will gradually become flatter, faster, and more customer-friendly. Services will become better integrated and customized, with rich self-service options. Prices rather than taxes will

Table 1. Impacts of the Information Age on Governance[47]	
Future Directions	Possible 2010 Milestones
1. Shaping and legitimizing values: *non-geographic communities* (the Internet) and *digital democracy* (new participation options)	• 15 hours per capita per week online, with greater involvement in and identification with nongeographic communities; • 15% of all purchasing online, with some online voting
2. Enforcing values: *heavily networked and outsourced government* • reengineered processes, customization sourced • rich self-service options • user charges, transfer pricing • collaborations on services, security, tax policies	• 95% penetration of Net to all government workers • 50% of government work out- • 30% unit cost reduction of half of government services • 20% of transactions on a self-service basis • 20% of government revenues via user charges • government-wide indexing and search engine standardization, security redundancies, and antifraud strategies
3. Core principle: *adapting to new conditions and needs*	• consensus needed on the imperative for R&D (not just DoD-based), with aggressive diffusion of best practice

be used more extensively to raise revenues and coordinate production and consumption.

As we proceed more deeply into the Information Age, the new core problem and principle for governance—at both organizational and societal levels—will be to learn how to adapt to new conditions and needs. To govern successfully, we must figure out how to protect public safety and prevent abuses of power while we simultaneously work better to promote governmental flexibility and learning. We have made some progress on this problem, but our status as we enter the twenty-first century might best be described as "just at the start of something big."

Endnotes

1. The research reported in this paper was supported by grants from the John F. Kennedy School's Visions of Governance in the 21st Century project, and from the Ford Foundation through the Kennedy School's Innovations in American Government program. The author thanks those who gave comments or otherwise assisted in drafting this paper including: Scot Barg, Teresa Cader, Jack Donahue, Sandra Hackman, Fred Hayes, Norm Jacknis, Bob Knisely, Mark Moore, Richard Sobel, Kimberly Spragg, Zach Tumin, Jim Van Wert, Jim Vollman, and Irene Yarmak.

2. See Esther Dyson, George Gilder, George Keyworth, and Alvin Toffler, "Cyberspace and the American Dream: A Magna Carta for the Knowledge Age," available from *http://www.pff.org/position.html*; Internet; accessed January 1999. Also see James R. Beniger, *The Control Revolution: Technological and Economic Origins of the Information Society* (Cambridge, MA: Harvard University Press, 1986); Nicholas Negroponte, *Being Digital* (New York: Knopf, 1995); Esther Dyson, *Release 2.0: A Design for Living in the Digital Age* (New York: Broadway Books, 1997); and, Bill Gates, Nathan Myhrvold and Peter Rinearson, *The Road Ahead* (New York: Viking, 1995).

3. See Daniel Bell, *The Coming of Post-Industrial Society: A Venture in Social Forecasting* (New York: Basic Books, 1976); Alvin Toffler, *The Third Wave,* (New York: Bantam Books, 1981); Alvin and Heidi Toffler, *Creating a New Civilization: The Politics of the Third Wave* (Atlanta: Turner Publishing, Inc., 1995).

4. For a discussion of the social benefits derived from better comunications and information infrastructure see National Information Infrastructure Steering Committee, National Research Council, *The Unpredictable Certainty: Information Infrastructure through 2000,* Lewis M. Branscomb, Computer Science and Telecommunications Board, Steering Committee Chair, National Academy Press, October 1996. Full text available from *http://www.nap.edu/readingroom/books/unpredictable/*; Internet; accessed January 1999. Also see Don Tapscott, *The Digital Economy: Promise and Peril in the Age of Networked Intelligence* (New York: McGraw-Hill, 1996).

5. An early analysis of the economic contribution of information workers to GNP is found in Marc Uri Porat, *The Information Economy*, Washington, DC, U.S. Office of Telecommunications, 1977. Also see Beniger (1986); Computer Science and Telecommunications Board, National Research Council, *Information Technology in the Service Society: A Twenty-First Century Lever,* 1994; and Ellen M. Knapp, "Unique Challenges: Computing and Telecommunications in a Knowledge Economy," in *Defining a Decade,* Proceedings of the CSTB's 10th Anniversary Symposium, May 16, 1996, Washington, DC, Computer Science and Telecommunications Board

Commission on Physical Sciences, Mathematics, and Applications, National Research Council, Chapter 9.

6. Two Harvard programs focusing on these issues at the John F. Kennedy School of Government are the Innovations in American Government Program, *http://www.ksg.harvard.edu/innovations*, and the Strategic Computing and Telecommunications in the Public Sector Program, *http://www .ksg.harvard.edu/stratcom*. The Innovations Program gives cash awards to highly innovative and replicable local, state, and federal government programs, and facilitates program dissemination by honorees throughout all levels of government. The Strategic Computing Program is similarly engaged in identifying and disseminating best practice. Recent research engagements include a study of factors obstructing intergovernmental efforts; the need for IT leadership and government; the feasibility of government reengineering and customer service excellence initiatives; and, requirements for successful IT procurement and IT investment reforms.

7. For the importance of diversity and even irritation in responding to adaptive challenges, see Ronald A. Heifetz, *Leadership Without Easy Answers,* (Cambridge, MA: Harvard University Press, 1994).

8. An exploration of future governments and their possible specialization by function is in Bruce E. Tonn and David Feldman, "Non-spatial Government," *Futures,* Jan–Feb 1995, vol. 27, no. 1, p. 11. Tonn and Feldman view IT as possible catalysts for government specialization by function: a nonspatial government populated by individuals with a strong affinity for one another, but who do not necessarily share common spatial boundaries; another government that is spatial and responsible for infrastructure; and others with responsibility for enforcement and coordination. See also, *The Cultural Meaning of Urban Space,* Robert Rotenberg and Gary McDonogh, eds., (Westport, CT: Bergin & Garvey, 1993); Gerald E. Frug, "Geography of Community," *Stanford Law Review* 48 (1996):1047.

9. Limited experiments in proving the ability of direct decision making to deal with complex problems have been conducted in the U.S. A report of one such effort, "Telecommunications and the Future of Democracy," Preliminary Report on the First U.S. Citizens' Panel, can be found at *http://www.amherst.edu/~loka/alerts/loka.4.3.htm;* Internet; accessed January 1999. The Danish Technology Board Web site provides information on similar processes, and documents the effects on Danish policy: *http://www.ing.dk/tekraad/metod/pps/pps.htm;* Internet; accessed January 1999.

10. Toffler, 1990.

11. The ICANN Web site may be found at *http://www.icann.org;* Internet; accessed January 1999. See also Tamar Frankel, "Statement of Tamar

Frankel, Professor of Law, Boston University, Joint Hearing on the Internet's Domain Name System," Congressional Testimony, October 7, 1998, Federal Document Clearing House, Inc.; Carl S. Kaplan, "A Kind of Constitutional Convention for the Internet," *New York Times, http://www.nytimes.com*, October 23,1998, Internet, accessed January 1999.

12. How information technologies are transforming citizen experience of the democratic process—and potentially the democratic process itself—is explored in Lawrence K. Grossman's, *The Electronic Republic: Reshaping Democracy in the Information Age* (New York: Penguin, 1996). (Also see transcript, "The Electronic Republic," from Research Roundtable Series, Shorenstein Center for the Press, Politics, and Public Policy, John F. Kennedy School of Government, Harvard University, *http://www.ksg.harvard.edu/~presspol/pubs/tran/gross.htm*, Internet, accessed January 1999.) More on the impact of technology on governance is found in, "The Death of Distance," *The Economist*, Sept. 30, 1995, p. S5.

13. Kennedy School teaching case by Pamela Varley with Ted Lascher, advisor, "Blip on the Screen or Wave of the Future? 'Electronic Democracy' in Santa Monica," Cambridge, MA, John F. Kennedy School of Government, Harvard University, C16-91-1031.0. Explores "participatory democracy" experiment in Southern California involved establishing a network of computer terminals to allow citizens to discuss public affairs online, both with each other and with elected officials. The case reviews the two years of the system's operation, including a description of the PEN system's apparent effect in influencing a new city policy on homelessness. The relatively small number of users, however, as well as the indifference of some elected officials to the system, raises questions both about the extent of the impact of such a system and whether technological innovation dramatically changes assumptions about the role of representative democracy.

14. See Grossman (1996) and "The Death of Distance" (1995) for influence of the Internet on the political process. Also see Wayne Rash, Jr., *Politics on the Nets: Wiring the Political Process* (W. H. Freeman & Co.: 1997); Graeme Browning and Daniel J. Weitzner's *Electronic Democracy: Using the Internet to Influence American Politics* (Pemberton Press: 1996); W. Russell Neuman, Lee McKnight and Richard Jay Solomon, *The Gordian Knot: Political Gridlock on the Information Highway* (Boston: MIT Press, 1996); Steven E. Miller, *Civilizing Cyberspace: Policy, Power, and the Information Superhighway* (Perseus Press: 1995); *Cyberdemocracy, Technology, Cities and Civic Networks*, Roza Tsagarousianou, Damian Tambini and Cathy Bryan, eds., (New York: Routledge Kegan Paul, 1998): Ziauddin Sardar (Contributor) in *Cyberfutures: Culture and Politics on the Information Superhighway*, Jerome R. Ravetz ed., (New York, New York University Press, 1996); and,

Kevin A. Hill and John E. Hughes, *Cyberpolitics: Citizen Activism in the Age of the Internet,* (People, Passions, and Power), (New York: Rowman and Littlefield, 1998).

15. Rebecca Fairley Raney, "Voting on the Web: Not Around the Corner, but on the Horizon," *New York Times,* September 17, 1998, G8; Marc Strassman "An Internet E-Ballot for Democracy; Feasible and Cost-Effective, Electronic Voting Could Empower Citizens," *Los Angeles Times,* January 31, 1999, p. 17; David Swafford "Is Electronic Voting a Panacea?," *LatinFinance,* no. 84, p. 84, ISSN: 1048-535X.

16. U.S. population, 265.3 million, according to 1996 census data. For more on annual IT expenditures see 1998 survey released by Federal Sources, Inc. U.S. government (all segments) workforce, 19.8 million, according to U.S. Bureau of Labor Statistics.

17. Jane Fountain, Linda Kaboolian, Steven Kelman, and Jerry Mechling, *Customer Service Excellence: Using Information Technologies to Improve Service Delivery in Government,* Cambridge, MA, Strategic Computing and Telecommunications in the Public Sector Program, John F. Kennedy School of Government, Harvard University, June 1994. See also, National Partnership for Reinventing Government reports on customer service, including *Putting Customers First '97: Standards for Serving the American People,* *http://www.npr.gov/cgi-bin/print_hit_bold.pl/custserv/csreport.html ?customer+service,* Internet, accessed January 1999.

18. According to Donald J. Hernandez, chief of the Marriage and Family Statistics Branch of the U.S. Bureau of the Census, "between 1940 and 1989, the percentage of young children living in dual-earner families (that is, two-parent families with both parents in the labor force) increased sevenfold, from 5% to 38%. During the same period, the proportion of children living with a lone parent who worked increased fivefold, from 2% to 13%." "Changing Demographics: Past and Future Demands for Early Childhood Programs," *The Future of Children,* vol. 5, no. 3, Winter 1995.

19. Professor Jane Fountain found in a survey of toll-free telephone center operators from the public and private sectors that "callers to private sector over-the-telephone operations are generally more pleasant than those who use public sector over-the-telephone lines." A number of reasons were cited, including the generally more difficult nature of the calls (Jane Fountain, "The Use of 800 Numbers in Government," Cambridge, MA, Strategic Computing and Telecommunications in the Public Sector Program, John F. Kennedy School of Government, Harvard University, 1993).

20. Steven E. Brier, "Library/Tax-Filing Web Sites—It May Still Be Certain, But at Least It's Easier," *New York Times,* January 21, 1999, G8.

21. All examples that follow are taken from Innovations in American Government Program award-winning applications and third-round evaluator site visit reports.

22. Kennedy School teaching case by Esther Scott with Jerry Mechling, advisor, "Electronic Benefits System in Ramsey County, Minnesota," Cambridge, MA: John F. Kennedy School of Government, Harvard University, C16-91-1038.0. See also, Strategic Computing Program teaching case, "Electronic Benefits Transfer: From Local Innovation to National Standard," by Scot N. Barg with Kennedy School professors Jerry Mechling and Steven Kelman, advisors. Cases explore how Ramsey County (St. Paul), MN, developed a way for welfare recipients to receive their benefits via a radically different benefits delivery system—the use of an ATM (automatic teller machine) card which allows welfare recipients to draw down their account at a variety of locations, at their own convenience—and how electronic benefits transfer systems have been deployed nationally.

23. Kennedy School teaching case by Harvey Simon with Jerry Mechling, advisor, "Introducing Computer-Based Remote Services in California: Over-the-Counter Government," Cambridge, MA: John F. Kennedy School of Government, Harvard University, C16-91-1256.0. Case involves the development of the vision and mission driving implementation of California's Health and Welfare Agency interactive "kiosk" system allowing citizens to transact business with the state government without going to a government office.

24. Influential process design literature includes: Thomas H. Davenport, *Process Innovation Reengineering Work Through Information Technology*, Boston, MA, Harvard Business School Press, 1993; Michael Hammer and James Champy, *Reengineering the Corporation: A Manifesto for Business Revolution* (New York: HarperBusiness, 1993); and Michael Hammer, "Reengineering Work: Don't Automate, Obliterate," *Harvard Business Review*, July–August 1990, vol. 68, no. 4, p. 104.

25. Lynda M. Applegate, F. Warren McFarlan, James L. McKenney, *Corporate Information Systems Management: The Issues Facing Senior Executives.* (New York: Richard Irwin, 1996). Also see *The Rise of Managerial Computing: the Best of the Center for Information Systems Research, Sloan School of Management,* Massachusetts Institute of Technology, John F. Rockart and Christine V. Bullen, eds., (Homewood, IL: Dow Jones-Irwin, 1986). Also see Thomas W. Malone and John F. Rockart, "Computers, Netwoks, and the Corporation" *Scientific American,* 1991, 265 (3 (Sept.)), 128–136.

26. The Bureau of Economic Analysis' *1998 Survey of Current Business* suggests that U.S. governments spent about $1.405 trillion in 1996 (National Product and Income Table 1.1), and a related report (Bureau of the Census,

Federal Expenditures by State for Fiscal Year 1996) suggested that roughly 38 percent of federal government expenditures went to the procurement of goods and services from the private sector. Assuming that the state and local percentage is roughly the same as the federal percentage, and using 19.5 million as the number of government workers overall, we generated $28,000 as the annual procurement expenditure per government worker. These numbers have been adjusted downward to produce the ranges quoted in the text.

27. David Osborne and Ted Gaebler (contributor), *Reinventing Government; How the Entrepreneurial Spirit is Transforming the Public Sector* (New York: Plume Books, 1993).

28. Stephen Goldsmith, "Can Business Really Do Business with Government?" *Harvard Business Review,* May 1, 1997.

29. Peter Fabris, "Just IS for all," *CIO,* April 1, 1998; David Baum, "Arizona Motor Vehicles Division: $26 million investment will save $50 million a year," *InfoWorld,* September 19, 1994, p. 88.

30. Mark Leibovich, "Va. Unit of EDS Tentatively Wins Big Conn. Contract," *Washington Post,* December 31, 1998, p. E03.

31. John Grigsby, "Outsourcing: Taxing Spectre of Big Brother Public Sector Policy under Labour Is Changing," *The Daily Telegraph* (London), May 28, 1997; Michael Dempsey, "Suppliers are cautious: outsourced services— despite the lucrative contracts available, some IT companies are wary about taking on too much government work as the switch to outsourcing continues," *The Financial Times* (London), November 5, 1998, Survey Edition 1, p. 19. Inland Revenue's home page, *http://www.inlandrevenue.gov .uk/home.htm;* Internet, accessed January 1999.

32. Canadian government officials have explored information age futures through the use of scenario planning, similar to that used by Royal Dutch Shell. Four primary outcomes emerged from their effort, including (a) an economy both rich and socially cohesive, (b) one rich but not socially cohesive, (c) one neither rich nor socially cohesive, and (d) one socially cohesive but not rich. (Review of Canadian demography and its implications for economic and social policy in Steven A. Rosell, et. al., *Changing Maps: Governing In a World of Rapid Change,* (Ottawa: Carleton University Press, 1995).

Surveys of the perceptions of leaders in government have also been conducted by Harvard's Strategic Computing and Telecommunications in the Public Sector Program, where respondents described their organizations as "lagging far behind the private sector in using IT for fundamental improvements in organizational strategies or operations." (Jerry Mech-Jerry and Thomas M. Fletcher, *Information Technology and Government:*

The Need for New Leadership, John F. Kennedy School of Government, Strategic Computing and Telecommunications in the Public Sector, 1996, p. 33.)

33. Robert B. Reich, *The Work of Nations : Preparing Ourselves for 21st-Century Capitalism* (New York: Knopf, 1991).

34. Gary Chapman "High-Tech Heroes Who Work for the Public Good," *Los Angeles Times,* Monday October 26, 1998.

35. Gary Chapman "Time to Cast Aside Political Apathy in Favor of Creating a New Vision for America," *Los Angeles Times,* August 19, 1996; Internet, *http://www.utexas.edu/lbj/21cp/Convention.html,* accessed January 1999.

36. For similar proposals, see the initiatives of Vice President Gore's National Partnership for Reinventing Government, *http://www.npr.gov,* and particularly its *Access America* program and report *(http://gits.gov/htm /access.htm),* operated through Government Information Technology Services (GITS), *http://gits.gov.*

37. Patrick J. Buchanan *The Great Betrayal: How American Sovereignty and Social Justice Are Being Sacrificed to the Gods of the Global Economy* (New York: Little, Brown, 1998).

38. Neuman, McKnight, and Solomon (1996) make the argument for a historic pattern of innovations "freezing" into Gordian knots under the pressure of social, political, and business forces brought about by new technologies. The emergence of each new technology brought about a clash of economic superpowers struggling to control access, standards, and proprietary technology in a given emerging industry.

39. Note that the One-Stop Career Centers of the Department of Labor have created a dramatic shift towards self-service that seems to promote equity as well. In the early 1990s, 95 percent or more of the transactions in government employment centers were staff mediated. By 1998, however, nearly 80 percent of the transactions occurred through the Internet or in computer-based resource rooms. Because of the Internet base for service delivery, libraries and even church social rooms have become nearly full service career centers. Electronic government service delivery has the potential of equalizing access to key information that had once been available primarily to those of high status with valuable and inherently exclusionary networks of personal connections.

40. *Unpredictable Certainty: Information Infrastructure through 2000* (1996).

41. Stephen J. Kobrin "Electronic Cash and the End of National Markets," *Foreign Policy,* June 1, 1997, vol. 107.

42. Jerry Mechling and Victoria Sweeney, *Finding and Funding Good IT Initiatives in Government,* Sacramento: Government Technology Press; K.

McCarthy, J. K. Neels, C. P. Rydell, J. P. Stucker, and A. H. Pascal, "Exploring Benefit-Based Finance for Local Government Services: Must User Charges Harm the Disadvantaged," Santa Monica, CA: *RAND Corporation,* 1984.

43. For more information on encryption, see Electronic Privacy Information Center, *http://www.epic.org,* Internet, accessed January 1999; Electronic Frontier Foundation, *http://www.eff.org,* Internet, accessed January 1999; Internet Free Expression Alliance, *http://www.ifea.net,* Internet, accessed January 1999; Global Internet Liberty Campaign, *http://www.gilc.org,* Internet, accessed January 1999; Harvard's Information Infrastructure Project, *www.ksg.harvard.edu/iip,* Internet, accessed January 1999; and, Harvard's Berkman Center for Law and Society, *http://cyber.law.harvard.edu/,* Internet, accessed January 1999.

44. This enormous social problem is well documented in Kennedy School Professor Malcolm K. Sparrow's *License to Steal: Why Fraud Plagues America's Health Care System,* with introduction by Lawton Chiles, (Boulder, CO: Westview Press, 1996).

45. Bob Weinstein "Now You Can Be on Speaking Terms with Your Computer," *Boston Globe,* November 5, 1998, F2.

46. See Harvard Business School teaching case series on Singapore's efforts, including, "Singapore TradeNet: A Tale of One City" (1995) by Benn Konsynski and John King, and "Singapore TradeNet: The Tale Continues" (1995) by Lynda M. Applegate, Boon-Siong Neo, and John King.

47. While the numbers in Table 1 could all be estimated via sampling from field observations and other data, the figures used in this paper were based on intuitive judgments (guesstimates, not estimates). Getting better numbers could make an interesting and useful measurement project, however.

48. According to Eric Brynjolfsson and Shinkyu Yang, the pendulum is currently swinging from the skeptics such as Robert Solow—"You can see the computer age everywhere but in the productivity statistics" (in Erik Brynjolfsson, "The Productivity Paradox of Information Technology," *Communications of the ACM,* Dec. 1993, vol. 36, no. 12, p. 66)—to the views expressed in a number of *Fortune* magazine articles regarding the "technology payoff" (including, Stratford Sherman's "How to Bolster the Bottom Line: Information Technology Special Report," *Fortune,* Autumn 1993, vol. 128, no. 7, p. 14). The truth, it appears, probably lies somewhere in between. For an in-depth examination of literature on the "productivity paradox" see Brynjolfsson and Yang, "Information Technology and Productivity: A Review of the Literature," *Advances in Computers* (San Diego: Academic Press) 43, pp. 179–214, 1996, and available on-line at *http://ccs.mit .edu/erik/itp;* Internet, accessed January 1999.

THE START OF SOMETHING BIG?

PREDICTIONS

\<John D. Donahue\>

erry Mechling has offered a panoramic, provocative overview of how the information revolution might change the trajectory of government's evolution. I'll respond in the same spirit of provoking debate, and will condense my comments into five broad predictions and a concluding anecdote.

1. **For those governmental functions that are essentially similar to business functions, the information revolution will have essentially similar effects on cost, access, and innovation—but with a lag.**

Where government activities are closely analogous to business activities—that is, where the work concerns delivering services, processing information, orchestrating transactions, and so on—the information revolution will have significant and mostly positive implications for the public sector. Costs will fall, productivity will increase, process reinvention will accelerate. The "virtual one-stop" service centers linking multiple agencies through shopping-mall kiosks and the IRS's exemplary Web site will, in this sense, indeed turn out to be harbingers of "something big."

John D. Donahue *is Associate Professor of Public Policy at Harvard University's John F. Kennedy School of Government. His most recent book,* Disunited States, *explores the shift toward the states in the American government's center of gravity.*

But government will continue to lag business in the adoption of IT advances, for two general reasons. First, constraints on financial and human resources will retard innovation. Second, insulation from competitive pressures will tend to keep government behind the frontier of best practices.

2. **Among the information revolution's most important impacts on government will be expanding opportunities for outsourcing.**

The range of public functions suitable for delegation to private suppliers is generally constricted by the difficulty of specifying expectations, monitoring compliance with contractual terms, and measuring contractors' performance. Improvements in information technology will ease contractual monitoring and evaluation, and thus raise the proportion of public functions where it is feasible to exploit the cost advantages of competitive private supply.

3. **Wherever the information revolution improves potential *public* performance, it will also tend to ease privatization.**

The same characteristics that make a public function subject to major improvements from advanced information technology—relatively clearcut goals; a well-defined clientele; insulation from other agendas—also render it a promising candidate for privatization. For governmental functions that are well-defined and charged with limited political voltage, the potential for privatization will generally outpace the potential for bureaucratic productivity improvements.

4. **The information revolution will tend to increase the productivity gap between public and private organizations.**

Both because public organizations will generally lag private organizations in the exploitation of new information technologies, and because functions with high potential for public-sector productivity gains will be outsourced with disproportionate frequency, the average level of productivity in public agencies will increasingly diverge from the average level of productivity in private businesses. The information revolution, in other words, will subject the public sector to a more chronic and virulent form of Baumol's "cost disease." Unless the reasons for this gap become understood and accepted, it could further depress public esteem for government.

5. **For those governmental functions that are essentially *dis*similar to business functions, the information revolution will have real but modest effects.**

Where functions are *not* well-defined, goals are multiple and interdependent, and accountability has to do with *means* as well as *ends*, new information technologies offer far less potential for improvement. Other sessions will cover electoral and legislative politics, but my prediction is that the information revolution will have effects in these areas no larger (but possibly more benign) than has the advent of television. Public deliberation and collective choice are not *entirely* immune to technological advance, but the scope for transformative innovation is narrower in this realm than it is for service delivery or transactions processing.

Business is characterized by "intensive"accountability—concrete, unambiguous, enforceable obligations to customers, creditors, and owners. Government is characterized by "extensive"accountability—a larger number of claimants with less definitive claims. The instruments of intensive accountability (retail channels, financial accounting, capital markets) are more subject to technological improvement than the instruments of extensive accountability (elections, interest groups, mass media, litigation.) Politics will remain a largely artisanal realm.

In a Wilsonian world of clean divides between public choice and public administration, there would be a bright line separating artisanal politics and wired, heavily outsourced implementation. But implementation is often infused with politically charged choice. Executive functions frequently require policy judgment or political compromise. So the boundary will remain shifting and ill-defined.

An anecdote on wired versus artisanal public policy

Early in 1993 I became enchanted with the notion of an online policy development process for the Labor Department. Enlisting outside experts, I set up a modified LotusNotes system with a site for each active policy initiative. The initiative's manager "owned"the site, laid out key issues and alternatives, reported weekly on progress and new developments, and granted access (editing access, or read-only) to the appropriate staffers. Selected senior officials had full access to all the sites.

At first it worked wonderfully. The asynchronous process let many more people weigh in with their special perspectives and privileged information than would have been possible with low-tech meetings. Top officials could bring themselves up to speed on an issue late at night, or whenever an outside meeting or a journalist's call required. They could pass on new information, raise questions, or revise priorities at any time, without assembling the full circle of staffers working on the issue. It was fun.

But before long the open, eager back-and-forth that the system at first made possible gave way to more guarded and cautious communication. People took to scrolling through the sites hunting for threats to their agendas, zapping in electronic vetoes, and (moving on to the next site) shirked the hard work of synthesis and compromise. And creative policy deliberation, it turned out, was all but impossible without occasionally writing something that seemed on the screen to be impolitic, insensitive, ill-informed, or simply foolish. The online colloquy *felt* more like paper than like conversation, and gradually reverted to the comparatively cramped and infertile style of paper exchanges. And I came to concede that real policy work required the primitive but high-bandwidth solution of a bunch of people sitting around a table. Within six months or so we abandoned the electronic system. Maybe the technology of online policy development has advanced enough since then to overcome the defects I discovered, or maybe it will in the near future. But I doubt it.

g⊥obal.gov

POWER AND INTERDEPENDENCE IN
THE INFORMATION AGE*

<Robert O. Keohane and Joseph S. Nye, Jr.>

Throughout the twentieth century, modernists have been proclaiming that technological change would dramatically transform world politics. In 1910 Norman Angell declared wars to be irrational as a result of economic interdependence, and he looked forward to the day when they would therefore be obsolete. Modernists in the 1970s saw telecommunications and jet travel as creating a "global village," and believed that the territorial state, which has been dominant in world politics for the four centuries since feudal times ended, was being eclipsed by nonterritorial actors such as multinational corporations, transnational social movements, and international organizations. Likewise, prophets such as Peter Drucker, the Tofflers, and Esther Dyson claim that the contemporary information revolution is bringing an end to the hierarchical bureaucratic organization, or is creating the

---

* A version of this paper appeared in the September/October 1998 issue of *Foreign Affairs.*

Robert O. Keohane *is the James B. Duke Professor of Political Science at Duke University. He is the author most recently of* Internationalization and Domestic Politics.

Joseph S. Nye, Jr., *is Dean of Harvard University's John F. Kennedy School of Government and author of the first article in this book.*

"disintermediation of government," leading to a new electronic feudal-ism with overlapping communities and jurisdictions laying claim to multiple layers of citizens' identities and loyalties.

The modernists of past generations were partly right. Angell's understanding of the impact of war on interdependence was insightful: World War I wrought unprecedented destruction, not only on the bat-tlefield but by wrecking the sociopolitical systems and networks of eco-nomic interdependence that had thrived during the relatively peaceful years since 1815. As the modernists of the 1970s predicted, multina-tional corporations, non-governmental organizations, and global financial markets have indeed become immensely more significant during the last quarter-century. But the state has been more resilient than modernists have expected. Not only do states continue to com-mand the loyalties of a vast majority of the world's people; their con-trol over material resources in most wealthy countries of the OECD, where markets are so important, has stayed at a third to half of GDP.

The modernists of 1910 and the 1970s were right about the direc-tion of change but simplistic about its consequences. Like some con-temporary commentators on the information revolution, they moved too directly from technology to political consequences, without suffi-ciently considering the continuity of belief systems, the persistence of institutions, or the strategic options available to leaders of states. They failed to analyze how holders of power could wield that power to shape or distort patterns of societal interdependence.

Twenty years ago in our book *Power and Interdependence*, we ana-lyzed the politics of such transnational issues as trade, monetary rela-tions, and oceans policy. We commented then that

> modernists point correctly to the fundamental changes now taking place, but they often assume without sufficient analysis that advances in tech-nology and increases in social and economic transactions will lead to a new world in which states, and their control of force, will no longer be important. Traditionalists are adept at showing flaws in the modernist vision by pointing out how military interdependence continues, but find it very difficult accurately to interpret today's multidimensional eco-nomic, social, and ecological interdependence."

This is still true for the information age.

Interdependence is not new. What is new is the virtual erasing of the costs of distance as a result of the information revolution—sometimes called globalization. No longer is it sufficient to analyze flows of raw materials, goods, and capital across borders, or to understand how states construct territorial boundaries on the high seas. Cyberspace is itself a "place": everywhere and nowhere. Traditionally, political activity has focused first at the local level, only extending to national and international spheres as the activity being regulated escaped jurisdictional boundaries. The contemporary information revolution, however, is inherently global, since "cyberplace" is divided on a nongeographical basis. The addresses "edu," "org," and "com" are not geographical.

Prophets of a new cyberworld, however, like modernists before them, often overlook the extent to which the new world overlaps and depends upon the traditional world in which power depends upon geographically based institutions. In 1998, 100 million people used the Internet. Even if this number reaches one billion in 2005, as some experts predict, a large portion of the world's people will not participate. Moreover, globalization is far from universal. Three quarters of the world's population does not own a telephone, much less a modem and a computer. Rules will be necessary to govern cyberspace—not only protecting lawful users from criminals but ensuring intellectual property rights. Rules require authority, whether in the form of public government or private or community governance. Classic issues of politics—who governs, on what terms? who benefits?—are as relevant to cyberspace as to traditional physical space.

Information is power, as Francis Bacon wrote 400 years ago. Undoubtedly, the information revolution has profound political implications. It therefore makes sense to seek to analyze some of these implications, using tools developed in studying the politics of interdependence. As traditionalist realists maintain, much will be the same: states will play important roles; vulnerability will lead to bargaining weakness and lack of vulnerability to power; actors will seek to manipulate cyberspace, as they manipulate flows across borders, to enhance their power. Yet as modernists insist, the information revolution is not "déjà vu all over again": cyberspace is truly global; it is harder to stop or even monitor the flow of information-carrying electrons than to do so for raw materials or goods; and dramatic reductions in the cost of information transmission make other resources relatively scarce.

In 1977 we raised the following question: "What are the major features of world politics when interdependence, particularly economic interdependence, is extensive?" One aspect of our analysis took the interstate system as given and asked how interstate power relations would be affected by economic interdependence, especially by vulnerabilities produced by such interdependence. The second dimension of our work went further, asking about the character of politics in domains where conventional realist assumptions about international relations no longer applied. These thoughts led us to imagine a politics we called *complex interdependence* with three conditions: (1) a minor role of military force; (2) absence of hierarchy among issues; (3) multiple channels of contact among societies.

Conditions approximating complex interdependence were emerging even in the mid-1970s, among wealthy democratic states. They affected both interstate relations and the emerging domain of transnational relations, where nonstate actors played a major role. Yet there remained great variation among regions and across issues. Force was of minor significance in the relations between the U.S. and Canada; or among the states of the European Union. But force remained of crucial significance in the U.S.-Soviet relationship or—as it still does—among many states in the Middle East, Africa, or Asia.

In this essay we apply the same analytic lens to the contemporary information revolution. We begin by analyzing different types of information, and how the information revolution has altered patterns of complex interdependence. We then turn to the impact of the information revolution on power among states. Finally, we explore some more novel implications of the information revolution for world politics. In particular, we argue that by drastically reducing the costs of transmitting information, the information revolution creates a new politics of credibility in which transparency will increasingly be a power asset.

The Information Revolution and Complex Interdependence

By "information revolution," we refer to the rapid technological advances in computers, communications and software that have led to dramatic decreases in the cost of processing and transmitting information. For our purposes, the distinguishing mark of the information revolution is the enormous reduction in the cost of transmitting information. For all practical purposes, the actual transmission costs have become negligible; hence the amount of information that can be transmitted is effectively infinite—as the proliferation of "spam" (junk mail) on the Internet suggests. Furthermore, neither costs nor the time taken to transmit messages are significantly related to distance. An Internet message to a colleague a few miles away may be routed through thousands of miles of computer networks, but neither the sender nor the recipient knows or cares.

However, the information revolution has not transformed world politics to a new politics of complete complex interdependence. One reason is that information does not flow in a vacuum, but in political space that is already occupied. States have for the last four centuries established the political structure within which information flows across borders and other transactions take place.

The information revolution itself can only be understood within the context of the globalization of the world economy, which itself was deliberately fostered by United States policy, and by international institutions, for half a century after the end of World War II. In the late 1940s the United States sought to create an open international economy to forestall another depression and contain communism. The resulting international institutions, formed on the basis of multilateral principles, fostered an environment that put a premium on markets and information. American-led market-based approaches have shaped developments in the technologies of transportation and communications. In turn, the information technologies and institutions have made it increasingly costly for states to turn away from the patterns of interdependence that had been created.

The information revolution occurred not merely within a pre-existing political context, but within one characterized by continuing military tensions and conflicts. Although the end of the Cold War removed one set of military-related tensions, it left some in place (as in the Middle East), and created situations of state-breaking and state-making in which violence was used ruthlessly to attain political ends—notably in Africa, the Caucasus, Central Asia, and southeastern Europe. Even in East Asia, the scene until recently of rapid economic growth, political-military rivalries persist. At the same time, the military presence of the United States plays a clearly stabilizing role in East Asia, Central Europe, and—tenuously—in Bosnia. Contrary to some early predictions after the end of the Cold War, NATO remains popular in Western and Central Europe. Markets thrive only with secure property rights, which depend on a political framework, which in turn requires military security. To ignore the role of military security in an era of economic and information growth is like forgetting the importance of oxygen to our breathing.

Outside the democratic zone of peace, the world of states is not a world of complex interdependence: in many areas, realist assumptions about the role of military force and the dominance of security issues remain valid. However, the third feature of complex interdependence—multiple channels of contact among societies—has changed dramatically. We see an order of magnitude shift as a result of the "information revolution." Now anyone with a computer is a desktop publisher and anyone with a modem can communicate with distant parts of the globe at trivial costs. Barriers to entry into the world "information market" have been dramatically lowered.

Earlier transnational flows were heavily controlled by large bureaucratic organizations like multinational corporations or the Catholic Church, with the resources to establish communication infrastructure. Such organizations remain important, but the vast cheapening of information transmission has now opened the field to loosely structured network organizations, and even individuals. These nongovernmental organizations and networks are particularly effective in penetrating states without regard to borders and using domestic constituencies to set the agendas of national leaders. By vastly increasing the number of channels of contact among societies, the information revolution is changing the extent to which some aspects of world politics are approximating our notion of complex interdependence.

However, information is not like goods or pollution, for which quantities flowing across borders are meaningful. The quantity of information available in cyberspace means little by itself. To focus only on the quantity of information, and on attention, would be to overlook the issue of information quality, and distinctions among types of information. Information does not just exist; it is *created*. We therefore need to pay attention, as economists do, to incentives to create information. When we do so, we discover three different types of information that are sources of power in world politics.

1. *Free information* is information that actors are willing to create and send without financial compensation from the recipient. The sender gets advantages from the receiver believing the information, hence has incentives to produce it. Motives may vary. Scientific information falls into the category of a public good, but persuasive messages, such as those in which politicians specialize, are more self-serving. Marketing, broadcasting, and propaganda are all examples of free information.

The reduction in average costs of production and transmission has reduced barriers to entry and greatly increased the flows of free information. The explosion in the quantity of free information is perhaps the most dramatic effect of the information revolution.

2. *Commercial information* is information that actors are willing to create and send at a price. Actors neither gain nor lose by others believing in the information, apart from the compensation they receive. For such information to be available on the Internet, issues of property rights must be resolved, so that producers of information can be compensated for it by users. Creating commercial information before one's competitors can—if there is an effective system to protect intellectual property rights—generates first-mover advantages and enormous profits, as the history of Microsoft demonstrates. In contrast to free information, where low average costs have had a strong impact on increasing flows, much of the profit from commercial information comes from the advantage of being first and the ability to withhold information unless recipients pay for it. The rapid growth of electronic commerce and the increase in global competition will be other important effects of the information revolution.

3. *Strategic information* is information that confers great advantage on actors only if their competitors do not possess it. Strategic information provides asymmetrical knowledge of a competitor's strategy so that the outcome of a game is altered. There is nothing new about strategic information: it is as old as espionage. One of the enormous advantages possessed by the United States in World War II was that the U.S. had broken the Japanese codes, but the Japanese were not aware of this fact. In many cases, the quantity of strategic information may not be particularly important. For example, the strategic information available to the United States about the weapons programs of North Korea, Pakistan, or Iraq depends more on having reliable satellites or spies than on the vast flows of the Internet. Critical messages may be brief and delivered by dedicated communications systems.

In a nutshell, creators of free information benefit from others' believing in the information they possess. Creators of commercial information benefit if compensated. But with respect to strategic information, information-creators benefit most if their possession of the information is not known to others.

The information revolution alters patterns of complex interdependence by exponentially increasing the number of channels of communication in world politics—among individuals in networks, not just among individuals within bureaucracies. But it appears within the context of an existing political structure, and its effects on the flows of different types of information are highly variable. Free information will flow faster in the absence of regulation. Strategic information will be protected as much as possible, for example, by encryption technologies. The flow of commercial information will depend on whether effective rules that protect property rights in cyberspace are established—by governments, business, or non-governmental organizations. Politics will affect the direction of the information revolution as much as vice versa.

Information and Power among States

Knowledge is power—but what is power? A basic distinction is between behavioral power—the ability to obtain outcomes you want—and resource power, or the possession of the resources that are usually associated with the ability to get the outcomes you want. Behavioral power, in turn, can be divided into hard and soft power. Hard power is the ability to get others to do what they otherwise would not do by using threat of punishment or promise of reward. Whether by economic carrots or military sticks, the ability to coax or coerce has long been the central element of power. As we pointed out two decades ago, asymmetrical interdependence is an important source of hard power. The ability of the less vulnerable to manipulate or escape the constraints of an interdependent relationship at low cost is an important source of power. For example, in 1971 the United States halted the convertibility of dollars into gold and increased its influence over the international monetary system. In 1973, Arab states temporarily gained power from an oil embargo.

Soft power, on the other hand, is the ability to get desired outcomes because others want what you want rather than do what you make them do. It is the ability to achieve desired outcomes through attraction rather than coercion. It works by convincing others to follow or getting them to agree to norms and institutions that produce the desired behavior. Soft power can rest on the appeal of one's ideas or culture or the ability to set the agenda through standards and institutions that shape the preferences of others. It is the ability to frame issues. It depends largely on the persuasiveness of the free information that an actor seeks to transmit. If a state can make its power legitimate in the perception of others and establish international institutions that encourage others to define their interests in compatible ways, it may not need to expend as many of its costly traditional economic or military resources.

Hard and soft power are related, but they are not the same. Samuel P. Huntington is correct when he says that material success makes a culture and ideology attractive, and decreases in economic and military success lead to self-doubt and crises of identity. He is wrong, however, when he argues that soft power is power only when it rests on a foundation of hard power. The soft power of the Vatican did not wane because the size of the papal states diminished. Canada, Sweden, and the Netherlands tend to have more influence than some other states with equivalent economic or military capability. The Soviet Union had considerable soft power in Europe after World War II but squandered it with the invasions of Hungary and Czechoslovakia even at a time when Soviet economic and military power were still continuing to grow. Soft power varies over time and different domains. America's popular culture, with its libertarian and egalitarian currents, dominates film, television, and electronic communications in the world today. However, not all aspects of that culture are attractive to all others, for example conservative Moslems. In that domain, American soft power is limited. Nonetheless, the spread of information and American popular culture has generally increased global awareness of and openness to American ideas and values. To some extent this reflects deliberate policies, but more often soft power is an inadvertent by-product.

The information revolution is also affecting power measured in terms of resources rather than behavior. In the eighteenth century European balance of power, territory, population, and agriculture provided the basis for infantry, which was a crucial power resource, and France was a principal beneficiary. In the nineteenth century, industrial capacity provided the crucial resources that enabled Britain and, later, Germany to gain dominance. By the mid-twentieth century, science and particularly nuclear physics, contributed crucial power resources to the United States and the Soviet Union. In the next century, information technology broadly defined is likely to be the most crucial power resource.

The new conventional wisdom is that the information revolution has a decentralizing and leveling effect. As it reduces costs, economies of scale, and barriers of entry to markets, it should reduce the power of large states and enhance the power of small states and nonstate actors. In practice, however, international relations are more complex than the technological determinism of the new conventional wisdom suggests. Some aspects of the information revolution help the small, but some help the already large and powerful. There are several reasons why.

First, important barriers to entry and economies of scale remain in some aspects of power that are related to information. For example, soft power is strongly affected by the cultural content of what is broadcast or appears in movies and television programs. Large established entertainment industries often enjoy considerable economies of scale in content production and distribution. The dominant American market share in films and television programs in world markets is a case in point.

Second, even where it is now cheap to disseminate existing information, the collection and production of new information often requires major costly investments. In many competitive situations, it is the newness of information at the margin that counts more than the average cost of all information. Intelligence collection is a good example. States like America, Britain, and France have capabilities for collection and production which dwarf those of other nations. In some commercial situations, a fast follower can do better than a first mover, but in terms of power among states, it is usually better to be a successful first mover than a fast follower.

Third, first movers are often the creators of the standards and architecture of information systems. The path-dependent development of such systems reflects the advantage of the first mover. The use of the English language and the pattern of top-level domain names on the Internet is a case in point. Partly because of the transformation of the American economy in the 1980s (which was missed or misunderstood by the prophets of decline) and partly because of large investments driven by the Cold War military competition, the United States was often the first mover and still enjoys a lead in the application of a wide variety of information technologies.

Fourth, military power remains important in some critical domains of international relations. Information technology has some effects on the use of force that benefit the small and some that favor the already powerful. The off-the-shelf commercial availability of what used to be costly military technologies benefits small states and non-state actors, and increases the vulnerability of large states. Information systems add lucrative targets for terrorist (including state-sponsored) groups. Other trends, however, strengthen the already powerful. Many military analysts refer to a "revolution in military affairs" that has been produced by the application of information technology. Space-based sensors, direct broadcasting, high speed computers, and complex software provide the ability to gather, sort, process, transfer, and disseminate information about highly complex events that occur in wide geographic areas. This dominant battlespace awareness combined with precision force provides a powerful advantage. As the Gulf War showed, traditional assessments of balances of weapons platforms such as tanks or planes become irrelevant unless they include the ability to integrate information with those weapons. Many of the relevant technologies are available in commercial markets, and weaker states can be expected to have many of them. The key, however, will not be the possession of fancy hardware or advanced systems, but the ability to integrate a system of systems. In this dimension, the United States is likely to keep its lead, and in terms of information warfare, a small edge makes all the difference. For instance, a recent Australian assessment of the future balance of power in East Asia finds that the revolution in military affairs will not diminish and may, in some instances even increase the American lead.

Contrary to the expectations of some theorists, the information revolution has not greatly decentralized or equalized power among states. If anything, thus far it has had the opposite effect. But what about reducing the role of governments and the power of all states? Here the changes are more likely to be along the lines the modernists predicted. But to understand these changes, we need first to explore how the information revolution, by minimizing the costs of transmitting information, has increased the relative significance of the scarce resource of attention, and the implications of this shift for what we call the politics of credibility.

The Paradox of Plenty and the Politics of Credibility

To understand the effect of free information on power, one must first understand the "paradox of plenty." A plenitude of information leads to a poverty of attention. Attention becomes the scarce resource, and those who can distinguish valuable signals from white noise gain power. Editors, filters, and cue-givers become more in demand, and this is a source of power. There will be an imperfect market for evaluators. Brand names and the ability to bestow an international "Good Housekeeping" seal of approval will become more important.

But power does not necessarily flow to those who can withhold information. Under some circumstances private information can cripple the credibility of those who have it. For instance, economists point out that sellers of used cars have more knowledge about their defects than potential buyers. Moreover, owners of bad cars are more likely to sell than owners of good ones. These facts lead potential buyers to discount the price they are willing to pay in order to adjust for unknown defects. Hence the result of the superior information of sellers is not to improve the average price they receive, but instead to make them unable to sell good used cars for their real value. Unlike asymmetrical interdependence in trade, where power goes to those who can afford to hold back or break trade ties, information power flows to those who can edit and credibly validate information to sort out what is both correct and important.

Hence among editors and cue-givers, credibility is the crucial resource, and asymmetrical credibility is a key source of power. Reputation has always mattered in world politics, and it becomes even more important because of the "paradox of plenty." The low cost of transmitting data means that the ability to transmit it is much less important as a power resource than it used to be, but the ability to filter information is more so. Political struggles focus less on control over the ability to transmit information than over the creation and destruction of credibility.

Three types of state action illustrate the value of credibility. Much of the traditional conduct of foreign policy occurs through the exchange of promises, which can only be valuable insofar as they are credible. Hence, governments that can credibly assure potential partners that they will not act opportunistically will gain advantages over competitors whose promises are less credible. Second, to borrow from capital markets at competitive interest rates increasingly requires credible information about one's own financial situation. Finally, the exercise of soft power implies credibility, in order to be persuasive.

One implication of the abundance of free information sources, and the role of credibility, is that soft power is likely to become less a function simply of material resources than in the past. When ability to produce and disseminate information is the scarce resource, limiting factors include the control of printing presses, radio stations, and newsprint. Hard power—for instance, using force to take over the radio station— can generate soft power. In the case of worldwide television, wealth can also lead to soft power. For instance, CNN was based in Atlanta rather than Amman or Cairo because of America's leading position in the industry and technology. When Iraq invaded Kuwait in 1990, the fact that CNN was basically an American company helped to frame the issue, worldwide, as aggression (analogous to Hitler's actions in the 1930s) rather than as a justified attempt to reverse colonial humiliation (analogous to India's capture of Goa).

This close connection between hard and soft power is likely to be somewhat weakened under conditions of complex interdependence in an information age. Propaganda as a form of free information is not new. Hitler and Stalin used it effectively in the 1930s. Milosevic's control of television was crucial to his power in Serbia. In Moscow in 1993, a battle for power was fought at a TV station. In Rwanda, Hutu-controlled radio stations contributed to genocide. The power of broadcasting persists, but will be increasingly supplemented by the Internet with its multiple channels of communication, controlled by multiple actors that cannot use force to control one another. The issue is not only which actors own television networks, radio stations or Web sites—once a plethora of such sources exist—but who pays attention to which fountains of information and misinformation.

Soft power today can also be the legacy of yesterday's hard and soft power. Britain's resources over a half-century ago enabled it to construct the BBC, and the nature of British society and politics made the BBC what is has become: a relatively reliable and unbiased source of information worldwide. The BBC was an important soft-power resource for Britain in Eastern Europe during the Cold War, as a result of the credibility it had established earlier. Now it has more competitors, but to the extent that it maintains credibility in an era of white noise, its value as a power resource may actually increase.

Broadcasting is a type of free information that has long had an impact on public opinion. By focusing on some conflicts and human rights problems, broadcasters have pressed politicians to respond to some foreign conflicts rather than others, e.g., Somalia rather than Southern Sudan. Not surprisingly, governments have sought to influence, manipulate, or control television and radio stations, and have been able to do so with considerable success, since a relatively small number of physically located broadcasting sites were used to reach many people with the same message. However, the shift from broadcasting to narrowcasting has major political implications. Cable and the Internet enable senders to segment and target audiences. Even more important for politics is the interactive role of the Internet; it not only focuses attention, but facilitates coordination of action across borders. Interactivity at low cost allows for the development of new virtual communities: people who imagine themselves as part of a single group regardless of how far apart they are physically from one another.

These technologies create new opportunities for nongovernmental actors (NGOs). Advocacy networks find their potential impact vastly expanded by the information revolution, since the fax machine and the Internet enable them to send messages from the most obscure corners of the world, from the rain forests of Brazil or the villages of Chiapas or sweatshops in Southeast Asia. The movement that produced the recent Landmine Treaty was a coalition of network organizations working with middle-power governments like Canada and some individual politicians like Senator Leahy and celebrities like Princess Diana to capture attention, set the agenda, and put pressure on political leaders. The role of NGOs was also important as a channel of communication across delegations in the global warming discussions at Kyoto. Environmental groups and industry competed in Kyoto for the attention of the media from major countries, basing their arguments in part on the findings of nongovernmental scientists. Many observers have heralded a new era for NGOs as a result of the information revolution; and there seems little doubt that substantial opportunities exist for a flowering of issue advocacy networks and virtual communities.

Yet the credibility of these networks is fragile. Greenpeace, for instance, imposed large costs on Royal Dutch Shell by criticizing Shell's planned disposal of its Brentspar drilling rig in the North Sea, but Greenpeace itself lost credibility and membership when it later had to admit the inaccuracy of some of its factual claims. The findings of atmospheric scientists about climate change have gained credibility, not just from the prestige of science but from the procedures developed in the Intergovernmental Panel on Climate Change (IPCC) for extensive and careful peer-review of scientific papers, and intergovernmental vetting of executive summaries. The IPCC is an example of an intergovernmental information-legitimating institution, whose major function is to give coherence and credibility to masses of scientific information about climate change.

As the IPCC example shows, the importance of credibility is giving increasing importance to transnational networks of like-minded experts. By framing issues where knowledge is important, such professional communities become important actors in forming coalitions and in bargaining processes. By creating knowledge, they can provide the basis for effective cooperation. But to be effective, the procedures by which this information is produced have to appear unbiased. It is increasingly recognized that scientific information is in part socially constructed. To be credible, the information has to be produced through a process that is dominated by professional norms and that appears transparent and procedurally fair. Even if their information is credible, professional communities will not resolve contentious issues that involve major distributional costs. But they will become more significant actors in the politics of decision.

The politics of soft power do not depend only on the "information shapers," who seek to persuade others to adopt their practices and values. They also depend on the characteristics of their targets: the "information takers," or the targets of free information flows. Of course, the shapers and takers are often the same people, organizations, or countries, in different capacities. Information shapers, as we have seen, require credibility. The takers, on the other hand, will be differentially receptive depending on the character, and internal legitimacy, of their own institutions. Self-confident information takers with internal legitimacy can absorb flows of free information more readily, with less disturbance, than can institutions (governmental or nongovernmental) lacking such legitimacy and self-confidence.

Not all democracies are leaders in the information revolution; but, as far as countries are concerned, most information shapers are democracies. This is not accidental. Their societies are familiar with free exchange of information and their institutions of governance are not threatened by it. They can shape information because they can also take it. Authoritarian states, typically among the laggards, have more trouble. At this point, governments such as China's can control the access of their citizens to the Internet by controlling Internet service providers and by monitoring the relatively small number of users. It is possible, but costly, to route around such restrictions, and control does not have to be complete to be effective for political purposes. Singapore has thus far combined its political controls with an increasing role for the Internet. But as societies like Singapore reach levels of development where a broader range of knowledge workers want fewer restrictions on access to the Net, Singapore runs the risk of losing its scarcest resource for competing in the information economy. Thus Singapore today is wrestling with the dilemma of reshaping its educational system to encourage the individual creativity that the information economy will demand, and at the same time maintain existing social controls over the flow of information. Closed systems become more costly.

Another reason that closed systems become more costly is that it is risky for foreigners to invest funds in a country where the key decisions are made in an opaque fashion. Transparency is becoming a key asset for countries seeking investments. The ability to keep information from leaving, which once seemed so valuable to authoritarian states, undermines the credibility and transparency necessary to attract investment on globally competitive terms. This point is illustrated by the Asian financial crisis. Governments that are not transparent are not credible since the information they offer is seen as biased and selective. Moreover, as economic development progresses and middle class societies develop, repressive measures become more expensive not merely at home, but also in terms of international reputation. Both Taiwan and South Korea discovered in the late 1980s that repression of rising demands for democracy and free expression would be expensive in terms of their reputation and soft power. By beginning to democratize then, they have strengthened their capacity—as compared with, for instance, Indonesia—to cope with economic crisis.

Whatever the future effects of interactivity and virtual communities, one political effect of increased flows of free information through multiple channels is already clear: states have lost much of their control over information about their own societies. States that seek to develop (with the exception of some energy suppliers) need foreign capital and the technology and organization that go with it. Geographical communities still matter most, but governments that want to see rapid development will find that they will have to give up some of the barriers to information flows that protected officials from outside scrutiny. No longer will governments that want high levels of development be able to afford the comfort of keeping their financial and political situations inside a national black box. The motto of the global information society might become: "If you can't take it, you can't shape it."

From a business standpoint, the information revolution has vastly increased the marketability and value of commercial information, by reducing costs of transmission and the transaction costs of charging information users. Politically, however, the most important shift concerns free information. The ability to disseminate free information increases the potential for persuasion in world politics—as long as credibility can be attained and maintained. NGOs and other states can more readily influence the beliefs of people within other jurisdictions. If one actor can persuade others to adopt similar values and policies, whether it possesses hard power and strategic information may become relatively less important. Soft power and free information can, if sufficiently persuasive, change perceptions of self-interest, and therefore how hard power and strategic information are used.

If governments or NGOs are to take advantage of the information revolution, they will have to establish reputations for credibility in the world of white noise that constitutes the information revolution.

Conclusion

We are at such an early stage of the information revolution that any conclusions must be tentative. Nevertheless current evidence supports three main arguments. First, the new conventional wisdom is wrong in its predictions of an equalizing effect of the information and communications revolutions on the distribution of power among states. In part, this is because economies of scale and barriers to entry persist in regard to commercial and strategic information; and in part because with respect to free information, the larger states will often be well-placed in the competition for credibility. Second, cheap flows of information have created an order-of-magnitude change in channels of contact across state borders. Non-governmental actors operating transnationally have much greater opportunities to organize and to propagate their views. States are more easily penetrated and less like black boxes. Political leaders will find it more difficult to maintain a coherent ordering of foreign policy issues. Third, the information revolution is changing political processes in a way in which soft power becomes more important in relation to hard power than it was in the past. Credibility becomes a key power resource both for governments and NGOs, giving more open, transparent organizations an advantage with respect to free information. Although the coherence of government policies may diminish in more pluralistic and penetrated states, those same countries may be better placed in terms of credibility and soft power. In short, geographically based states will continue to structure politics in an information age, but the processes of world politics within that structure are undergoing profound change.

INDEX

215

VISIONS OF GOVERNANCE FOR THE TWENTY-FIRST CENTURY

The Imperative for Change

Momentous social and economic forces are reshaping democratic governance around the world. Current political rhetoric insists that the era of big government is over—but what will take its place?

The answer is not at all obvious. While some national governments are getting smaller, they are not necessarily getting less powerful. Information technology, which has allowed industry to do more with less, is opening up the same opportunities for governments, while bringing with it new threats to their traditional roles and functions. The increasing number and authority of supranational organizations is countered by trends toward devolution in the United States and Europe. Nonprofit and even for-profit entities are taking on tasks once thought of as the sole province of government. Markets are being created and used to produce public as well as private goods.

All of this is taking place amidst a loss of confidence on the part of citizens with their governments. This unhappiness transcends partisanship and economic well-being. It is as if, on some level, the public knows that its government is simply out of step with the times.

Dean Joseph Nye believes it is a critical part of the Kennedy School's mission to address the precipitous decline in confidence in public institutions, by identifying and illuminating some of the most important trends affecting governments, and by creating a public conversation with citizens and policy makers about appropriate responses to changing realities and expectations of government. This imperative is not an artifact of the millennium. In fact, were public trust in government high, change could be incremental. What is needed now, however, are new ways of thinking about governance.

Growing Mistrust in Government

The first year of the Visions Project focused on generating a critical mass of intellectual activity among a core group of Harvard faculty around the issue of trust in government, which resulted in the publication in October 1997 of *Why People Don't Trust Government.* The book was the culmination of over a year of inquiry into the scope and performance of government (actual and perceived) and the possible causes of citizens' dissatisfaction with the government.

The Project is continuing this investigation of declining trust in government with both a study of anomalies in the evidence, such as high levels of confidence in the military, and an international comparative study of public trust in government (*Critical Citizens,* forthcoming in the spring of 1999).

New Ways of Thinking about Governance

The Project is focusing its attentions on several new areas of inquiry:

- New paradigms for national security policy. The Universities Study Group on Grand Terrorism will recommend a comprehensive program of responses by the U.S. government to the danger of large-scale, catastrophic terrorism.

- The future direction of social policy. Is it possible to bring the productive and innovative power of markets to traditional questions of social welfare? "Who's Responsible? Renegotiating the Social Contract" will evaluate the central question of alternatives to traditional government activism in various areas of social policy.

- How governments can manage and measure their performance to better serve their citizens. A series of Executive Session and Practitioner Forums on Performance Management will seek to engage and invest political decision makers in a management movement which offers the possibility of a new kind of democratic accountability.

- How information technologies are changing the realities and expectations of governments. The explosive growth of information as a resource and of computer networks as a medium is at once evident everywhere and yet very little understood. The Visions Project has begun a continuing effort to understand the many changes being wrought by information technologies in order to focus attention on maximizing their benefits and minimizing their costs to society.

The Visions Project will weave these themes together in a book which will raise significant questions that are central to democratic governments. Will a more effective capacity to fight global crime and global terrorism be compatible with our deeply held beliefs that we should protect the privacy of our citizens from internal spying? Can a system which attempts to meet a variety of social needs through market mechanisms and via non-governmental organizations really guarantee equality of treatment? Can innovative governmental organizations also be accountable to elected officials and to the public?

These are momentous questions, and they illustrate why large-scale social and governmental change does not happen overnight. Our challenge is to find the value in change, and that will require new visions of governance for the 21st century.

Project Staff

Joseph S. Nye, Jr., *Dean*
Elaine C. Kamarck, *Executive Director*
Kristin A. Schneeman, *Project Director*

Visions of Governance for the Twenty-First Century
John F. Kennedy School of Government
Harvard University
79 John F. Kennedy Street
Cambridge, MA 02138
(617) 496-6844 phone
(617) 496-1722 fax
http://www.ksg.harvard.edu/visions